HÉLÈNE SMIT

THE DEPTH FACILITATOR'S HANDBOOK

Transforming Group Dynamics

ISBN 978-0-9922356-1-1
First published in 2009 by Moonshine Media
www.moonshinemedia.co.za
New edition published in 2014 by The Depth Leadership Trust

Copyright © 2014 in published edition: Hélène Smit
Copyright © 2014 in text: Hélène Smit
Copyright © 2014 in cover design: Pluto Panoussis

Publishing Manager: Dominique le Roux
Editor: Roxanne Reid
Proofreader: Tamaryn Jupp
Cover Designer: Pluto Panoussis

All rights reserved. No part of this publication may be reproduced, stored in a retrieval system, or transmitted, in any form or by any means, electronic, mechanical, photocopying, recording or otherwise, without the prior written permission of the copyright owners.

Hélène Smit can be contacted at The Depth Leadership Trust
www.depthleadership.co.za
helene@feather.co.za

To the people and spirit of the town of Prince Albert,
for bringing me home

ACKNOWLEDGEMENTS

There are many people who have supported and influenced me over the years that it took to develop the ideas in this book. It is hard to keep this short, but in particular, I would like to thank:

Dominique, for making it happen; Roxanne and Tamaryn, for the long hours of editing;

Pluto, for the cover and unleashing the writer in me;

My clients and students, who have allowed me to work with them and learn enough to write this book;

Suzie, for the unfailing loyalty and support of my work and life;

Nancy and Cornelio, for helping me to create a home;

My "surrogate" family, Imke, Rudi, Emma and Oscar, for all the love and support and, especially Jacob, for those welcoming hugs;

Rod Anderson, Ruth Eastwood, Arthur Colman, Pilar Montero, Arnold Mindell and Marc Feitelberg, for teaching me about myself and how the psyche works;

Abby, for being my dear friend and work partner, who understands how it feels at the end of the day;

Ingrid and Adele, Elspeth, Katherine, Sandy, and Sue Fourie for the many, many conversations and support;

Suzy Lake, for her passionate support of my role as facilitator;

Bruce, for letting me practise on him;

Raffael, for clearing my heart;

My father, James, for his generous and uncomplicated practical support;

My son, Sylvan, for enriching my life with his wisdom, wit and helpfulness;

My daughter, Sophia, for delighting me with her love and for having the dreams for all of us.

CONTENTS

SECTION 1: FOUNDATION THEORIES

CHAPTER 1: INTRODUCTION TO FACILITATION — 19

Introduction	20
What is facilitation?	21
The complexity of group processes	22
Surface processes	23
Depth processes	24
"Surface" and "depth" facilitation	24
Learning facilitation skills	26
Personal Exercises	27

CHAPTER 2: UNDERLYING PHILOSOPHIES — 29

Introduction	30
Theories of human behaviour	30
Organisational Psychology	31
The different schools of Clinical Psychology	31
The Behavioural School of Psychology	31
The Cognitive School of Psychology	32
The Humanistic Perspective	32
The Developmental School of Psychology	32
Depth Psychology	33
The importance of the unconscious	33
The difficulty of working with the unconscious in organisations	33
Systems thinking	34
Process and content	37
Deep democracy	37
Typologies, frameworks & developmental stages	39
Conclusion	39
Personal Exercises	40

CHAPTER 3: DEPTH PSYCHOLOGY – THE INDIVIDUAL — 41

Introduction	42
The logic of the individual	42
The architecture of the individual psyche	43
The origins of Depth Psychology	43
Archetypes	45
Instincts	45
The creation of the individual unconscious	46
Intra-psychic conflict	48
Anxiety	49
Sources of anxiety and how individuals respond	49
Mindell's concept of the edge	50
Edge behaviour	53
The role of defence mechanisms	58
Projection	59
Projective identification	61
Transference and counter-transference	63
Complexes	63
Repetition compulsion	63
Conclusion	64
Personal exercises	65

CHAPTER 4: DEPTH PSYCHOLOGY – THE GROUP — 67

Introduction	68
The Architecture of the Group Psyche	68
The Notion of the Group Psyche	68
What is a group?	70
Types of groups	70
Functions fulfilled by groups	71
The group context	71
The group history	72
Group complexes	72
The group field	73
Psychological systems in a group	73
The group identity	76
Group power	76
Group sizes	77
Group energy	77

The group task and intention	78
Group behaviour	79
Archetypes and instincts	80
Role types	81
Role differentiation	83
Individual role valency	83
Role casting	84
Role suction	84
Role identification	85
Scapegoating	85
The ghost role	87
Roles and positions	87
Role dances	88
Group processes	90
Defensive processes	90
Group anxiety	90
Group defence mechanisms	91
Group developmental processes	95
Power dynamics in groups	99
Some definitions	99
The impact of power and difference in groups	100
Types of rank	100
The psychological impact of rank	101
The dynamics of rank differences	101
Rank and responsibility	102
Rank awareness	103
Creating rank awareness	103
Minorities and majorities	103
Rank inversion	104
Formal versus informal rank	104
The role of rank in projective processes	104
Rank and group constitution	105
Conclusion	105
Personal exercises	106

SECTION 2: YOU AS FACILITATOR

CHAPTER 5: MANAGING YOUR OWN PSYCHOLOGY — 111

Introduction	112
The demands on a facilitator	112
The importance of self-awareness	112
An attitude of neutrality	114
Inner work	115
Inner work exercise	115
Getting hooked	117
Inner work in front of a group	118
Ongoing inner work	118
Managing Transference	119
Managing Counter-transference	120
Managing positive projections	120
Managing negative projections	121
Managing the demands of individual members	122
The inner critic	122
Barriers to awareness	123
Paying attention to depth processes	123
Protecting yourself	123
Attacks on the facilitator	124
Popularity as a facilitator	124
Leadership and facilitation	125
The facilitator's need for connection	125
Rest and recovery	125
Conclusion	126
Personal exercises	127

CHAPTER 6: THE ETHICS AND METASKILLS OF A FACILITATOR — 129

Introduction	130
The ethics of facilitation	130
An ethical attitude	130
Ethical guidelines	131
Metaskills	132
Compassion	132
Playfulness	133
Detachment	133

Fluidity	134
Intelligence	134
Discipline	134
Courage	135
Humility	135
Patience	135
Ruthlessness	136
Imagination	136
Collective consciousness	136
Harnessing energy	136
Curiosity	137
Renewal	137
Reverence	138
Conclusion	138
Personal exercises	139

CHAPTER 7: YOUR ROLE AND TASKS AS A FACILITATOR 141

Introduction	142
Facilitation roles	142
Clarifying the facilitation role	143
Roles, tasks and skills	143
Managing Structure	144
Facilitator's role	144
Facilitator's tasks	144
Facilitator's skills/knowledge	144
Managing People	145
Facilitator's role	145
Facilitator's tasks	145
Facilitator's skills/knowledge	145
Managing Content	146
Facilitator's role	146
Facilitator's tasks	146
Facilitator's skills/knowledge	146
Managing Process	147
Facilitator's role	147
Facilitator's tasks	147
Facilitator's skills/knowledge	148
Skills and knowledge development	148
Personal exercises	149

CHAPTER 8: ESSENTIAL FACILITATION SKILLS — 151

- Introduction — 152
- Presentation skills — 152
  - Credibility — 152
  - Mobility — 152
  - Confidence projection — 153
  - Voice projection — 153
  - Mannerisms and bridging sounds — 154
  - Eye contact — 154
- Awareness and observation skills — 154
  - Observation guidelines — 155
  - Other awareness prompts — 156
- Listening skills — 156
  - Reflective listening — 156
  - Reflective listening guidelines — 157
- Language skills — 158
  - General language guidelines — 158
- Feedback skills — 159
  - The function and value of feedback — 159
  - Basic guidelines for giving feedback — 159
  - Guidelines for receiving feedback as a facilitator — 161
  - Defensive behaviour as a result of negative feedback — 161
- Stimulation skills — 162
  - Open questions — 162
  - Closed questions — 162
  - Verbal techniques for stimulating discussion — 163
- Support skills — 164
  - Verbal techniques for supporting participants — 164
- Control skills — 165
  - Verbal techniques for controlling the discussion — 165
- Conclusion — 166
- Personal Exercises — 167

SECTION 3: FACILITATION PRACTICE

CHAPTER 9: DEPTH FACILITATION GUIDELINES — 171

Introduction	172
Making the unconscious conscious	172
Approaches to depth work in organisations	173
When is depth facilitation needed?	173
Benefits of a depth facilitation intervention	174
Costs of a depth facilitation intervention	175
The implications of depth facilitation for leadership	175
The implications for business processes	176
Situations where depth facilitation will not work	176
Caution required	177
The importance of contracting for depth work	178
The importance of Depth Psychology education	179
Helpful psychological mechanisms	179
Phase entrainment	179
The transcendent function in groups	180
Conclusion	180
Personal exercises	181

CHAPTER 10: MANAGING STRUCTURE — 183

Managing structure overview	184
Facilitator's role	184
Facilitator's tasks and related skills	184
Facilitator's guidelines, tools and techniques	185
1. Analysing client requirements	185
2. Contracting with the client	186
3. Designing a group session	187
4. Organising a session	188
5. Clarifying session objectives and structure	188
6. Clarifying session roles	189
7. Gaining group agreement for objectives, structure and roles	189
8. Providing information and education about depth facilitation	190
9. Ensuring task completion	190
10. Setting and maintaining boundaries and limits	190
11. Ensuring that group agreements are adhered to	191
12. Managing housekeeping	192
Conclusion	193
Personal exercises	194

CHAPTER 11: MANAGING PEOPLE — 195

Managing people overview — 196
    Facilitator's role — 196
    Facilitator's tasks and related skills — 196
Facilitator's guidelines, tools and techniques — 197
    1. Establishing session climate — 197
    2. Building containment — 197
    3. Building rapport — 200
    4. Providing support to participants — 201
    5. Ensuring full participation — 202
    6. Monitoring and managing group energy levels — 203
    7. Intervening to manage personal, interpersonal & group dynamics — 203
    8. Ensuring good group practices — 207
    9. Managing transference and counter-transference — 208
Conclusion — 209
Personal exercises — 210

CHAPTER 12: MANAGING CONTENT — 211

Managing content overview — 212
    Facilitator's role — 212
    Facilitator's tasks and related skills — 212
Facilitator's guidelines, tools and techniques — 213
    1. Maintaining neutrality — 213
    2. Managing agenda setting — 215
    3. Tracking content — 216
    4. Organising content — 217
    5. Clarifying content — 219
    6. Summarising content — 219
    7. Documenting content — 219
    8. Identifying depth content — 221
    9. Elucidating symbols — 222
    10. Interpreting from a depth perspective — 224
    11. Linking symbolism with concrete content — 226
    12. Maintaining multilevel perspectives — 226
Conclusion — 226
Personal exercises — 228

CHAPTER 13: MANAGING PROCESS — 229

Managing Process Overview	230
Facilitator's role	230
Facilitator's tasks and related skills	230
Facilitator's guidelines, tools and techniques	231
1. Initiating and explaining group surface process	231
2. Facilitating surface process	233
3. Closing surface process	234
4. Tracking the group development process & intervening appropriately	234
5. Identifying depth processes	243
6. Surfacing depth processes	249
7. Completing depth processes	255
Guidelines for the facilitation of specific processes	263
Polarising processes	263
Cathartic processes	271
Reconciliation processes	272
8. Integrating depth processes with surface process	279
Conclusion	281
Personal Exercises	282

BIBLIOGRAPHY — 283

ABOUT THE AUTHOR — 288

SECTION 1
FOUNDATION THEORIES

CHAPTER 1
Introduction to Facilitation

INTRODUCTION

Through the ages, individuals have led, organised, controlled and even manipulated groups in a variety of ways. These processes have resulted in a range of outcomes, from the actualisation of great potential to incidences of massive destruction. As human interaction in groups worldwide generally moves away from hierarchical command and control structures, and decision-making becomes more democratised, the need for using different group leadership approaches has emerged. One of the new leadership approaches is a role now known as "facilitation". Increasingly, organisational groups actively engage and employ facilitators to help them unleash their creativity and solve problems.

Facilitation emerged as a fully fledged business and organisational role in its own right in the 1980s. It arose out of an emerging worldview in the Western world that emphasised participatory processes as being important for organisational functioning. In particular, the idea of facilitation came from the need for people in organisations to have more effective meetings. While the leaders in organisations could rely on individual and group obedience as the major determinant of behaviour, leading meetings was a relatively simple task because participants generally abided by the structure and rules set by the meeting leader.

Although an environment of obedience can result in ordered and co-ordinated group activity, it can be experienced as oppressive and be counter-productive in terms of creativity. It often results in a lack of true buy-in by the participants for the decisions taken in meetings. The fact that individual rights are becoming more important has resulted in a psychological shift in human interaction in organisations. Individuals no longer want to (or have to) be simply obedient to their superiors. Less hierarchy means more participation, and more participation leads directly to more explicit expression of the psychological dynamics between people in groups.

Under a hierarchical structure, dissension in the ranks often goes unnoticed, and so conflict is not resolved because it is not explicit, and may even be thought not to exist. The more participative an organisational culture becomes, the more differing opinions and the resultant conflict and creativity rise to the surface and become explicit. In a participative organisation, leading meetings is not simple at all. The meeting leader needs a whole new set of skills. As a result, organisations have seen the development of the role of "facilitation".

The theory (and practice) of facilitation is still relatively undeveloped, although increasingly work is being done to document the growing knowledge in this area. The different approaches, tools and techniques for working with groups in the world have their roots in sometimes unspecified, but nevertheless greatly influential ideologies. Group leadership of whatever form can be dangerous. So, without the understanding of the ideological principles that are being explicitly or implicitly applied, the actions of an individual doing group work can have a negative impact on the life of a group.

This book was written as the foundation for the first academic programme of its kind in South Africa (a Post-Graduate Diploma in Facilitation). Its aim is therefore to provide a sound and rigorous foundation for individuals who wish to become professional facilitators in organisations, which means assisting groups to achieve their tasks. This, by its very nature, means working not only with the task of the group, but also with the people dynamics that may severely hamper or greatly enhance task achievement. In order to do so safely and effectively, it is important that students of facilitation are exposed not only to tools and techniques, but also to the philosophies and logic behind them.

WHAT IS FACILITATION?

There are many definitions of facilitation. The linguistic root of facilitation is the Latin word "facilis" which means easy. Facilitation means "to make easier"; it is concerned with making a group's task (whatever that may be) easier. It would be accurate to say that facilitation could apply to any situation where you are making something easier, but for our purposes the word is used here to indicate group facilitation. This broad definition needs to be refined further.

Unfortunately, there is no "big rule book" anywhere that defines exactly what group facilitation should be, and so it is left up to individuals working in this area to determine which ways of applying the idea of "making easier" will be most helpful to groups. In my experience (and I will articulate my underlying philosophies later), facilitation does not mean making a group's life easier by doing their task for them, or telling them what to do. That is not sustainable in the longer term. Ultimately, what seems to make a group's life easier is when the following conditions prevail:

- The group has a clear task or objective
- There is a structure that organises the way individuals in the group engage with one another
- The group's activities are coordinated
- The relationships between individual group members do not compromise the successful application of the full resources of the group.

In other words, groups are helped when they are organised and when the group dynamics are managed. These would include, among others, differing participation levels, active or unintended power plays, conflict between different styles and/or preferences, and destructive psychological patterns. Facilitation is not an end in itself, it is a role that assists groups in achieving their objectives.

Facilitation, therefore, can be defined as a role that assists a group in the achievement of its stated and emerging goals as effectively as possible, using the full intelligence of the group and its members as far as possible. The facilitator is not a leader who sets direction, but rather someone who uses a range of skills and techniques to help the group achieve or even find its own direction. A facilitator will work alongside a leader, or the leader may even take up the facilitation role when needed.

A further important idea is that facilitation is a general term and is sometimes used in ways that are confusing. There are several variations possible in the nature of the facilitation role. For example, organisations will speak of a "learning facilitator", which is an alternative term for words like "trainer" or "lecturer". The definition above indicates that a facilitator is concerned with process, not with content, but a learning facilitator does need to have content expertise, whereas a general process facilitator does not. As a result, we will argue here that a learning facilitator in fact holds two roles, one as an expert or a teacher, and one as a facilitator. There is therefore a range of different designated roles that could include the function of facilitation and some examples are given below.

- Chairperson
- Trainer
- Teacher
- Leader
- Participant
- Expert
- Master of ceremonies
- Group counsellor
- Group coach
- Group therapist

Although this book refers to the different variations, it focuses on the "pure" role of facilitation, which emphasises facilitator neutrality in terms of the task outcomes pursued by a group.

THE COMPLEXITY OF GROUP PROCESSES

Most formal (and informal) groups have an explicitly stated task or goal that they are trying to achieve. The group will occupy itself explicitly with the activities and processes needed to move to completion of the task or goal. The difficulty is that when a group works together, there are many things going on other than the stated, explicit goal or task.

The main reason for this is that human groups live in a world of complexity, and there is not always integration or explicit communication between all the complex systems at work in a context, so many processes are going on at the same time. Each of these processes continually affects the others in subtle and overt ways. Also, each context is multilayered and so events and trends occur at a variety of levels, all affecting one another and the people who work in organisations.

Global economic and environmental processes affect everyday organisational decisions. We manage the everyday at the same time as we work strategically towards the long term. Macro- and micro-environmental pressures place practical and psychological demands on individuals. To add to the complexity, the demands themselves on the people of the different levels are sometimes fundamentally opposed to one another, both philosophically and practically.

Therefore, in addition to the task process, it is likely that a working group will encounter a resultant set of psychological processes that are concerned with the "psychodynamics" of the group. In other words, this refers to the "people" processes that occur as soon as there are people together. People processes emerge as a result of contextual influences, power differences, role choices and allocations, our feelings of attachment and belonging, relationships to authority, experiences of marginalisation and discrimination, interpersonal conflict, and also, the split between the conscious and unconscious parts of all human beings.

These additional processes that occur in a group's life have important implications for the facilitation task. Processes that are not directly related to the group's explicit task continually cause complications for the group. The facilitator has to decide whether to allow these processes to "hijack" the group's focus on the explicit task or not. Therefore, in order to better understand the different approaches to facilitation, it is helpful to divide group processes into two broad categories and to consider each of these in more detail. We will therefore make a distinction between "surface processes" and "depth processes".

SURFACE PROCESSES

Surface processes are those that are related to the explicit and consciously acknowledged group tasks and processes. These processes relate to tasks and ideas that are uppermost in the group members' minds and that the group members can talk about openly. Individuals identify with those aspects of their tasks and behaviour that seem most comfortable to them. In business the surface process may well be to make money, either personally or as an organisation. Although the surface process is important, however, it is only a part of the totality of the system. As a practical example, your surface process right now is reading and understanding the concepts that are written on this page, but that is not all that is going on. You are also involved in a number of other processes that you may or may not immediately be aware of, such as feeling tired or excited about your plans for your evening.

Depth processes

Depth processes are the processes that we do not identify with consciously. They refer to interactions and dynamics that are happening beneath the surface of a group's functioning. These underlying dynamics affect the way the group functions, but in a way that is not usually acknowledged or sometimes even noticed by the group. These dynamics could be counter-productive unless addressed, or they could offer the potential for new creativity if brought to the surface. However, because they are usually unknown or at least not openly discussed, they provoke anxiety, and most individuals and groups will initially resist them. Paradoxically, they often hold the key to the group's advancement or survival. Surface and depth processes occur in all personal and group interactions.

"Surface" and "depth" facilitation

At the highest level, there are basically two approaches to group facilitation in organisations. The first is to be a "traffic controller" who assists a group to complete a planned process where the outcome is pre-defined. This will be described as "surface facilitation" in this book. In this case, the facilitator's job is to help the group complete the task as effectively and quickly as possible, ensuring that any distractions are avoided and the planned process is strictly adhered to.

The second approach, described here as depth facilitation, is helping a group to deal with (and benefit from) whatever additional processes may emerge, and in fact ensuring space for these additional processes to come to the surface. The facilitator then needs to be able to help the group successfully negotiate the detour in order to ensure task completion. Sometimes a detour is necessary to enhance the creativity of the group and therefore the quality of task completion. Depth facilitation becomes especially necessary when the overt process is hijacked or compromised by other unresolved and usually more covert processes.

Depth facilitation implies that we are working with under-the-surface material. The most important thing about this is that material is under the surface for a reason. The reason for burying issues and ways of seeing vary in different systems, but there is usually some unspoken injunction or taboo related to discussing or dealing with these issues. Breaking the taboo could be more or less dangerous, but most certainly will feel undesirable or uncomfortable to the majority of group members. Therefore, depth facilitation implies working in an area that feels unfamiliar and possibly unpleasant to the people we work with. As a result, this work has to be done very carefully and with the explicit consent of the participants. The difficulty with gaining this consent is that many people do not understand what it means to work with the under-the-surface material, and so we often have to offer education regarding the nature of the work before we can move into the work itself.

Therefore, in summary, surface facilitation refers to working with what is on the surface and is mainly a structuring and "traffic control" function. The purpose is to meet a group objective as quickly and as participatively as possible. An example would be deciding on the brand of new computers to be bought for the sales team. Depth facilitation refers to working with a process that is under the surface because it is in some way unacceptable at the surface level. An example would be covert racism in a company, or the need for rest in an overworked team. It could also be the opposing or other way of being that is not supported by the culture of that group. An example would be fearfulness in an adventure group.

This book provides a comprehensive description of the theory, tools and techniques that you would need to work as a facilitator in organisational groups. It covers the important aspects of surface facilitation, because the surface aspects of a group's functioning have to be managed even if the facilitator intends working under the surface and it is important that a depth facilitator is competent at the surface level. However, this book goes further in that it considers the principles and practice of depth facilitation in detail.

Finally, but most importantly, the ideas in this book are designed to emphasise caution above all else. A good facilitator works with patience and care, always regarding the needs of the group as more important than his or her own needs, and understands that the facilitation task is one of helping to actualise the full potential of the group in its achievement of objectives. It is always important to err on the side of caution. It is never useful to push against a group's resistance with force. A group can only work at its own pace, and as one of my students once said in class, "You cannot squeeze a banana ripe."

LEARNING FACILITATION SKILLS

If you are reading this book because you would like to learn facilitation skills and work as a practitioner in organisations, then it is important to be aware of a few preliminary ideas as you embark on your learning process.

- As with any new skill, it takes time to really become competent. Good theory helps, but ultimately practice provides the real teaching.

- Good facilitation is a great deal more complex than it may look because people are a great deal more complex than they may at first appear. As a group facilitator, you are managing yourself and your psychology to prevent it from contaminating the group, you are managing the individuals in the group, you are managing the dynamics between those individuals, and you are helping the group as a whole to produce results. This requires a continuous intricate juggling act.

- Facilitation of groups will mean that you continually have to confront yourself, develop your self-awareness and manage your own psychology. This requires courage and emotional resilience.

- Finally, learning to facilitate is in some ways like learning to drive a car – initially it is important that you obey the basic rules rigorously in order to keep yourself and others safe. Once you become more experienced, it becomes possible to break a rule occasionally, in order to be more effective. However, the early part of the learning process can be quite tedious and you may well feel quite self-conscious. As you become more skilled, you will be able to relax and enjoy the scenery, while still arriving safely at your destination.

PERSONAL EXERCISES

At the end of each chapter in this book, there is a set of exercises or questions that you can work through to develop your insight and skills. You can complete them on your own or with a partner, facilitation supervisor or fellow learner. The exercises are designed to stimulate your thinking and there are no definite right or wrong answers. It would be useful to keep your answers in some form of a journal for later reference.

For this chapter, focus on your understanding of facilitation and what kind of facilitator you want to be.

1. If you wish to be a facilitator, consider the following:
   - What is your dream for facilitation and what it can achieve?
   - Who are you currently as a facilitator?
   - Who would you like to be?

2. What do you believe are your current strengths as a facilitator?

3. What kind of groups do you want to work with?

4. What do you see as your role in the lives of your client groups?

Chapter 2:
Underlying Philosophies

INTRODUCTION

There are many broad philosophies that can inform our approach to people as facilitators. Most individuals have developed personal and idiosyncratic philosophies in their dealings with others, based on a mixture of their personal experience and the worldviews they have been exposed to more formally. For example, we can be liberal or conservative or we can have a secular or a spiritual orientation. At a more basic level, we can believe that people are inherently good, or inherently bad. Often, our worldviews are contradictory or inconsistent in some areas, or we can hold one view consciously and the alternative view unconsciously. In my experience, there are some worldviews that are more useful than others when working as a facilitator for organisational groups.

As a facilitator, it is useful to develop some clarity about your views on the general laws of the world, and in particular, your views regarding the determinants of human behaviour. Some background in this area is offered below.

THEORIES OF HUMAN BEHAVIOUR

Much of the world is concerned with the issue of human behaviour – attempting to influence it, control it, manipulate it, protect it, or support it in some way. A great deal of theory has been produced in human history about the origins and determinants of human behaviour. The theories thus produced span many cultures and disciplines: many theory worlds have been created, with varying degrees of overlap and agreement. Some of these worlds have begun to integrate as a direct result of the increasing interconnectedness of social and other systems in an increasingly global environment. Technological, intellectual, social, political and environmental factors have all played a role.

In this process of integration, two of the academic disciplines that have developed over the past 200 years in the Western world – those of clinical psychology and management – have become both passionate and reluctant bed partners. These two disciplines attempted to solve different problems. Broadly speaking, clinical psychology originally concerned itself with understanding mental illness and human development and functioning. Management theory concerned itself with the processes of harnessing human behaviour in the interests of producing wealth. As the disciplines widened their scope and discovered new territory, they started to overlap with one another, and produced a hybrid form – what became known as industrial or organisational psychology.

ORGANISATIONAL PSYCHOLOGY

Organisational psychology studies areas such as communication, roles and responsibilities, group dynamics, teams, motivation, job satisfaction, leadership and power dynamics.

Organisational psychology was deemed to be useful by managers of organisations because, although psychological in nature, its concepts and techniques were apparently scientific and goal-oriented, and therefore could help harness behaviour in the interests of the organisation. It could assist management to solve problems and achieve more organisational goals. In fact, the influence of organisational psychology can now be seen in many areas of current management teaching, even in the specialist areas that were previously regarded as "hard" areas: production, management accounting, and even corporate finance.

Even where organisational psychology did make a contribution, however, the world of management was left with human problems it could not solve. Many of the unsolved problems faced by management were (and still are) characterised by recurring patterns of conflict and chronic disturbance to the system. In most cases, the roots of these problems were invisible to management. Existing theories of organisational psychology were found wanting. Something else was needed.

THE DIFFERENT SCHOOLS OF CLINICAL PSYCHOLOGY

In the meantime, the world of clinical psychology had continued to develop. This was important in terms of knowledge about how to produce healthy behaviour in individuals as well as in groups. Both areas had direct relevance to human behaviour in organisations. Many schools of clinical psychology developed. Each of these schools approached the psyche differently. There are some commonalities, but there are also many differences in the way they choose to intervene in the processes of the mind. All the schools of clinical psychology do, however, believe that they can heal or modify a psyche (a mind) and thereby eventually change behaviour. They just do it in different ways. Some examples of the different schools are given below.

THE BEHAVIOURAL SCHOOL OF PSYCHOLOGY

This school, also known as behaviourism, focuses on changing observable behaviours by means of altering the consequences for behaviour. It regards behaviour as being determined by the reward or punishment the person experiences in response to that behaviour. This is a useful school of thought because individuals do change their behaviour based on the consequences elicited by what they do. It is also limited because other factors also play a role, and at some point consequences no longer have an impact on behaviour.

The Cognitive School of Psychology

This school of psychology emphasises internal mental processes. It focuses on thinking and how to change people's thinking so that their behaviour might change. A variation of this is the cognitive-behavioural school, which broadens the thinking behind the behavioural school and incorporates the knowledge of cognitive psychology to creating, sustaining and changing their problems.

Many of our organisational interventions are based on the ideas of cognitive psychology. Any training course that teaches new mental models or frameworks is essentially cognitive in nature. Like behaviourism, this approach produces results, but also has limitations, as shown by the fact that even when people know what is the right thing to do, they sometimes do not do it.

The Humanistic Perspective

This approach, also known as Humanism, is a conglomeration of several approaches. It is concerned with a system of values and beliefs that emphasises the better qualities of humankind and people's abilities to develop their human potential. It focuses on the idea that if you provide individuals with a positive affirming environment, their behaviour will be productive and constructive. Of course, this basic premise is true up to a point, but again has its limitations in that even individuals in a very supportive environment will sometimes behave counter-productively.

The Developmental School of Psychology

This school is interested in how behaviour is affected by the individual's life stage or developmental phases. The theories in this school describe a variety of developmental phases or stages, both in early childhood development and through the later stages of adolescence, the middle years and old age, and how they affect human behaviour. These stages certainly do provide an indication of the behavioural consequences of certain levels of development, but of course there are many other factors that also play a role.

Depth Psychology

Depth Psychology is a broad term for all the psychological schools that are concerned with the idea that individuals have an unconscious component in their minds, and that this unconscious area sometimes drives behaviour in directions that are in conflict with consciously held perspectives and thoughts. It includes the psychoanalytic and psychodynamic perspectives (as developed by Sigmund Freud and Carl Jung).

THE IMPORTANCE OF THE UNCONSCIOUS

In addition to the development of the different schools of clinical psychology, lay people in organisations were discovering over the last decade or so – in some cases with mixed results – that certain kinds of actions and interventions that deal with the less tangible aspects of human functioning do make a difference. What some members of the world of clinical psychology knew (particularly those who focused on Depth Psychology) and others were discovering was that some factors affecting human behaviour are intangible and invisible. They exist beneath the surface of the conscious mind and so are difficult to get to and to deal with.

It came to be understood that if you can work with this area under the surface, then you can solve a range of recurring problems. Depth Psychology knows this intangible and invisible world as the human unconscious – formally studied predominantly in the realms of psychodynamic and psychoanalytic theory. Lay people often do not have a name for the unconscious, but have discovered ways that provide access to it. Numerous individuals, from both the formal worlds of clinical (and to a lesser extent, organisational) psychology, as well as from less formal backgrounds, have noticed the relevance of working with the unconscious in organisations, and have ventured into consulting, facilitation and teaching in organisations.

THE DIFFICULTY OF WORKING WITH THE UNCONSCIOUS IN ORGANISATIONS

Although well developed theories and practice for working with the unconscious in organisations now exist, and are slowly gaining popularity among managers, this approach has not been widely adopted. Managers of organisations have either been unaware of, or understandably resistant to, notions of working with the unconscious processes within their organisations. The human unconscious is intangible and invisible precisely because it is by its very nature potentially disturbing, and maybe even dangerous to other parts of the (human or organisational) system. The problems that can result from the unleashing of the unconscious can be devastating for a system if they are not managed with care.

Managers need knowledge about the nature and functioning of the unconscious in order to reduce their wariness. Knowledge will help them become more conscious themselves, thus increasing consciousness in the workplace, as well as empowering them to make informed choices when seeking specialist help. The knowledge they need should ideally be grounded in formal theory and practical experience. A comprehensive, accessible and formal bridge does not yet exist between the theory and practice of working with the unconscious and the theory and practice of management for managers, so it needs to be built – through research, through writing, through education and through informed practice in the field. Such a bridge would ensure that the power of working with the unconscious in organisations is unleashed in as safe and effective a manner as possible.

This bridge is slowly being built in organisations. Facilitators who work in the "depth" area, using some of the ideas of Depth Psychology, can help build this bridge by working in a competent and professional manner. The focus of this book is to help develop competent and professional depth facilitators.

SYSTEMS THINKING

In addition to the ideas of Clinical Psychology and particularly Depth Psychology, there is another school of thought that came particularly from the natural sciences, which also informs sound facilitation work. It is broadly known as Systems Thinking.

From approximately 1600 AD to the late 1800s, reductionism dominated scientific thinking. Most problem solving was seen to be within a linear cause-and-effect framework – in other words, a mechanistic system. Thinking mechanistically means thinking of a system as an elementary machine in which problems can be solved by breaking the system into its components and identifying the component that is problematic. It relies on analysing simple linear cause–effect relationships and essentially "fixing" the part that is causing the problem.

In the last 120 years, it has become apparent that not all problems can be solved by adopting a mechanistic approach. Some problems are context-dependent, i.e. the entire system needs to be evaluated. A way of thinking about problems that emphasises the dynamic aspects of a system developed. This came to be known as systems thinking. More sophisticated than mechanistic thinking, systems thinking is a way of approaching systems and their problems that considers the dynamic relationships that exist within complex systems.

Different kinds of problems require different kinds of thinking. For example, when a car breaks down, it is obvious that mechanistic thinking is the appropriate path to take. However, when the problem is how to address growing absenteeism in an organisation, systems thinking provides the more appropriate approach.

Systems thinking is based on some key concepts that are important to keep in mind when working with groups. These concepts essentially challenge a more mechanistic approach and sometimes require the individual to embrace a shift of mind. Some of the key concepts of systems thinking are outlined below.

- Cause and effect relationships in complex systems, which all human systems are, are not linear. This means that outcomes have multiple causes that may be non-linearly related to one another. For example, de-motivation in a group may be as a result of a complicated combination of factors, rather than simply the remuneration they receive.

- Complex systems should always be considered in terms of the context in which they occur. In other words, the larger systems around a group should always be considered. Systems thinking implies seeing actions and relationships in terms of the greater system of which they are part, as well as the sub-systems. For example, when working with a business, it may be important to consider the broader economic climate as well as the immediate business environment.

- The past and future of any complex system is as important as the present. Group events should be seen as part of a process where change is continually occurring. For example, a group that is demotivated may be partially affected by a past retrenchment, or a future merger with another organisation. "Snapshot" views of systems should be avoided.

- Systems thinking means seeing the underlying structures of situations. In other words, events are often the result of underlying patterns, and these patterns are the result of underlying structures. In environmental systems, this could mean that the physical environment may be affecting system behaviour. In a group, an individual coming late for a meeting may in fact be reflecting a greater pattern in which certain members of the organisation feel less included. This may be because the head office is situated far away from the regions, or because a certain part of the system has access to more resources than other parts.

- As a result of the fact that everything is connected to everything else in a complex system, it is possible to use leverage to effect change. The principle of leverage is that you can find simple actions and changes in structure that can lead to significant, enduring improvements. Small changes can produce big results, but

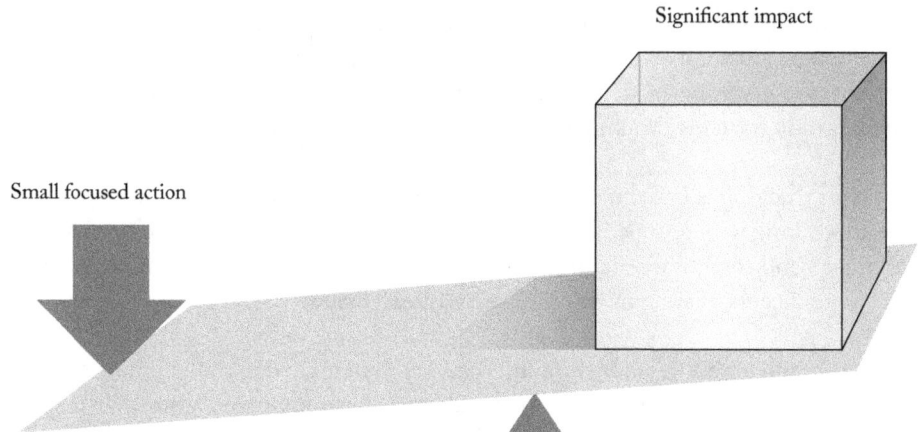

the areas of highest leverage are often the least obvious. For example, changing one high-leverage thing – such as the extent to which the person exercises – may change many other aspects of the individual's life.

- Systems thinking means understanding that complex systems are so both in the nature of the detail in the system and in the nature of the processes. In other words, systems have both detail and dynamic complexity, and both must be managed. Dynamic complexity implies that human behaviour operates in a set of self-reinforcing patterns and these patterns can change over time. For systems to shift, the complexity of the relationship dynamics must be recognised. For example, in a strategic planning session, it is not only necessary to consider the different business areas, but also the overt and subtle influences that the actions of the different areas have on one another.

- If you take a systemic perspective, it also means that there are not always clear right or wrong answers to questions. The answers to various problems depend on the perspective you hold, and many different perspectives are possible in a system. For example, in a group that is facing a dilemma, you often have to explore both polarities at length before a new perspective emerges that encompasses the wisdom of both sides. All members are part of the blame and the responsibility in a group.

- When dealing with complex systems, it is important to realise that quick change is usually not sustainable. It is also not possible to speed up growth and development in a system beyond a certain point. Systems that grow too quickly often develop problems at the same speed. This characteristic of systems means that great patience is needed. For example, for a group to break out of destructive psychological patterns often requires a thorough examination of how those patterns work and particularly how they are maintained by responses that individuals are not necessarily aware of. Occasionally you may find a quick fix that appears to work, but usually it only works in the short term. Beware the easiest, fastest solution because the easiest way out will lead back into the problem, although it may have taken a different form. All systems grow at an optimal pace and real, sustainable change takes time. Systems (and behaviour) may grow worse before they improve.

- Closely linked to the idea mentioned above is the fact that solutions that do not address the core problems in a system may in fact cause further complications. The logic of the solution and the logic of the problem are seldom the same. Analysis alone will not provide sustainable solutions. Synthesis is needed too. Multiple perspectives are required.

PROCESS AND CONTENT

There are two basic approaches to working psychologically with individuals and groups. The first, here named a content approach, is to have a set of notions, concepts and frameworks that guide what you look for and try to interpret for the group. In other words, this is an approach that describes the different types of group interactions and tries to name them as if there is a pre-determined set of interactions. An example would be Wilfred Bion's "basic assumption" groups, where one looks for prescribed patterns of behaviour, and then categorises a group's emerging behaviour accordingly. (We will look at this in more detail in Chapter 4.)

The second approach is a process approach, where there are no or few preconceptions about the emerging patterns of behaviour and you simply follow and allow the process to unfold, without labelling or interpreting the pattern in a particular way. This approach assumes that each situation will be fairly unique, although there may be general trends.

Both are useful. The content approach offers containment and structure, often specifically for the facilitator, and the second offers more freedom for the true uniqueness of the particular story to emerge.

DEEP DEMOCRACY

Deep democracy is an approach to facilitation that believes many of our current approaches to groups do not work in the best interests of the group in the long run. The term "deep democracy" has been used by the group facilitator Arnold Mindell to describe a way of working in which the full wisdom of the group is sought regardless of minority and majority power division.

Approaches to group decision-making and the leadership of groups have varied enormously through the ages. There have been numerous attempts throughout time to create political and organisational systems that are both efficient and just. In the Eurocentric cultures this progression has taken us from monarchy to the present system of representational majority democracy. Majority democracy, as it is now widely practised, creates a situation where 51% of the population can dominate and suppress 49%. This is certainly an improvement over monarchy, where the king may ignore the wishes of his people, but majority democracy to a large extent still ignores the disenfranchised 49%. Sabotage – whether politically expressed in random bombings, or represented in the workplace as strikes, slowdowns or absenteeism – is to some extent a symptom of the failures of majority democracy. Deep democracy does not try to get everyone to agree on the same approach or idea. That would be unrealistic, impossible, and would not value the "conflicting" opinions.

Instead, the practice of deep democracy believes that solutions can only be sustainable if they have recognised and incorporated the wisdom of the conflicting opinions. The practice of deep democracy requires the facilitator to create an environment that will allow and support (not necessarily agree with) all sides. The belief is that each side, no matter how apparently "bad", has within it a wisdom that is needed by the group before it can move on. Denial of this wisdom and repression of the conflicting opinions will result in sabotage and cycles of ever increasing hostility.

Deep democracy differs from traditional problem resolution techniques and majority democracy in that it does not strive for agreement or compromise; it strives for consensus. Gaining consensus means discovering the hidden wisdom in all the sides and gaining agreement, by all sides, to move in a given direction even if the sides still hold conflicting opinions.

Deep democracy is based on the realisation that every person's view is needed in order to represent reality and create sustainable solutions. In the business environment this means that the troublesome, annoying or negative people and views are just as important and necessary as the "good" people and views.

TYPOLOGIES, FRAMEWORKS & DEVELOPMENTAL STAGES

Many of the players in the field of psychology have tried to categorise, generalise and explain the functioning of the psyche and human behaviour in a predictable way. In other words, it is a discipline that has been treated scientifically. The result of these endeavours has been to produce a number of typologies such as personality types and styles. Also, each school of psychology has outlined a framework for viewing the psyche, giving names to certain entities and phenomena. Many theorists have viewed human development in terms of identifiable stages or phases, and have used these to understand adult difficulties.

All of these approaches are useful, but it is limiting to regard any one approach as gospel because an overview of many approaches provides a far more comprehensive overall picture of the complexity of the human psyche. In depth facilitation, an attempt is made to draw from a variety of typologies and frameworks, so that a resulting methodology is a somewhat eclectic mix of a variety of approaches. Many theorists would baulk at the seeming lack of rigour in the combination of the different approaches, but based on experience it seems that the complexity of groups and contexts demands this type of flexibility.

In order to work successfully with the complexity of groups, the facilitator needs the ability to understand what is happening through a variety of lenses. It is important to develop an understanding of a variety of approaches and lenses and to move flexibly between them. Many of us tend to fall in love with one approach and use it to the exclusion of all others, but this leads to a myopia that does not serve our clients in the long run. Also, it is important that you as a facilitator actively test any theories that you may embrace against personal experience.

It is important to supplement the theories and ideas given in this course with any of your own, and to continue developing your theoretical knowledge throughout your work life.

CONCLUSION

Facilitation is a new and evolving field. It does not yet have a comprehensive theory base of its own, and so draws from many related theory bases. However, to ensure that it is based on a rigorous approach, the roots and underlying assumptions of any facilitation methodology should be carefully considered.

PERSONAL EXERCISES

1. Consider what theories inform your general worldview and where they came from. Are your basic assumptions still valid?

2. Consider what type of facilitation you want to do.

3. Consider the philosophical assumptions behind the type of facilitation that you want to do.
    - What are they?
    - Where do your assumptions come from?
    - Are these assumptions still valid?
    - What do you think are the worldviews of the clients that you would like to work with?

CHAPTER 3
DEPTH PSYCHOLOGY – THE INDIVIDUAL

INTRODUCTION

In order to facilitate groups from a depth perspective, it is useful to have an understanding of the individual psyche from a depth perspective. This is a complex area of study, and there are many theories that attempt to explain the functioning of the unconscious and its effect on behaviour. This book does not offer a comprehensive analysis of the various theories, but it does introduce some of the key concepts that will help a facilitator understand individual behaviour, and therefore group behaviour, better.

THE LOGIC OF THE INDIVIDUAL

The human psyche and its functioning can often seem mysterious, but the more we study our psychology, the more it is possible to understand, predict and manage our own behaviour. Depth Psychology sheds light on some of the mysterious aspects of human behaviour because it considers the existence and influence of the less conscious drivers of what we as humans do. One of the premises of Depth Psychology is that human behaviour is logical, and although the detail of the logic is subjective and unique, there seem to be certain general mechanisms at work.

Each person, over time, develops a mental representation of the way that the world works based on the proximity of events and experiences in his or her life. This mental representation or mental map of the world not only records our experiences, but also influences the way we perceive and therefore experience anything new. This mental map will contain a set of logical paths and our experiences and related concepts will be joined by the paths.

An important aspect of these logic paths is that the mind joins together aspects of experience that are not necessarily closely related in terms of space or time, but rather associated with one another as a result of psychological similarity. Therefore, a response you have towards an event today may have its roots in events that happened in other places many years ago. Making those links enables the individual to become aware of associations and therefore responses that are no longer valid.

For example, if a boy is exposed to parents who are distant and aloof, he may expect others to be unapproachable later on in life, even when that is not the truth of their behaviour. His own reticence will make him unlikely to approach others naturally and this, in turn, will affect their availability to him. And so our early experiences to some extent shape our expectations and capacity for our later life experiences.

If we are to escape the influences of our early "programming", it is useful to understand our early experiences as much as we can, and sometimes to be able to "reinterpret" them though adult eyes. Good facilitators will have a reasonable understanding of their own set of logic paths, and recognise when they are not appropriate in the present in their work with clients. This chapter considers the psychological development of the individual in more detail from a Depth Psychology perspective, in order to help facilitators understand not only themselves, but also the members of the groups that they facilitate.

THE ARCHITECTURE OF THE INDIVIDUAL PSYCHE

The diagram on the next page captures some the various influences that determine individual behaviour in the world. It distinguishes between two main compartments in the human psyche – the conscious and unconscious parts of the mind. It indicates that difficulties in the different areas will result in differing symptoms and that, broadly speaking, the different schools of psychology address different root causes. This chapter considers the compartmentalisation of the individual psyche in more detail, discussing some of the key concepts that help to understand individual psychology from a depth perspective.

THE ORIGINS OF DEPTH PSYCHOLOGY

Throughout the 1800s, people in a range of disciplines studied the functioning of the human mind more and more actively and scientifically. Over time, it became clear that some of the functioning of the human mind is not necessarily available to the individual's conscious awareness. Although Sigmund Freud was not the first to consider the idea of the unconscious, he is commonly regarded as the founder of Depth Psychology, which studies the unconscious and its effect on human behaviour.

Carl Jung, originally a student of Freud's work and later a rival, developed Freud's idea of the unconscious further. His work introduced the idea that human beings have an inherent set of "blueprints" or "archetypes", as he called them, and that these blueprints comprise the capacity for the full range of human emotions, thoughts and behaviours.

For easier understanding, the blueprints can be regarded as containing both our biological and psychological pre-dispositions, or to use more technical language, our

ARCHITECTURE OF THE INDIVIDUAL PSYCHE

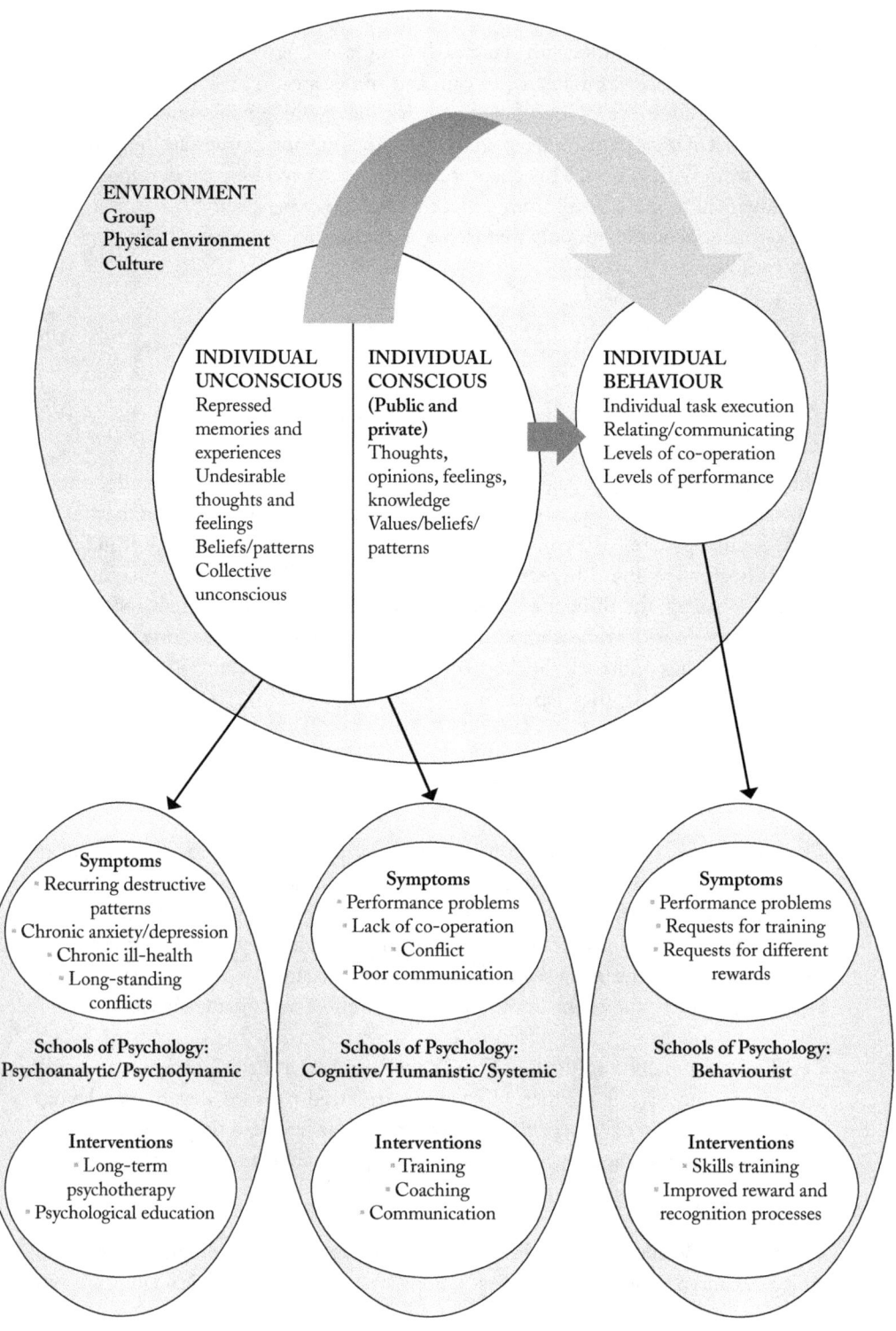

instincts and archetypes. As we interact with the world, these blueprints become activated, and so are personalised and become part of our experiential and behavioural repertoire. Jung argued that the capacity for our full potential (held in our instincts and archetypes) becomes inhibited by our interactions with the world, where we slowly but surely limit our range of thoughts, feelings and behaviours to those that are tolerated and/or encouraged by the world around us.

ARCHETYPES

Archetypes refer to the psychological pre-dispositions inherent in all people. In other words, archetypes are the potential ways of being human that all people are subject to. An archetype is a primordial, structural element of the human psyche and represents an inherent universal tendency to form certain ideas and images and to behave in certain ways. They are important because they shape our interactions with the environment. Individuals will each develop a unique version of these psychological blueprints – in other words, individuals will each develop a unique set of behavioural fingerprints based on their interactions with the world. For instance, the idea of the hero is an archetype, although individual heroic acts will have a unique flavour. Archetypes will be considered in more detail in the next chapter when we look at how they are manifested in groups.

INSTINCTS

Instincts are the biological versions of archetypes. We are all subject to a set of biological imperatives that drive our behaviour. Psychological thought accepts the existence of inherent instincts in all individuals, but theorists differ about the exact nature and priority of these instincts. The biological blueprints or instincts include, among others, our need for food, shelter, safety, rest and procreation.

Our instincts will be activated by internal or external stimuli. When they are activated, instincts will lead to feelings and thoughts, which then lead to behaviour. The environmental response to our behaviour sets off a process of learning and adaptation, and over time, our instincts consolidate into behaviour patterns that then become characteristics.

THE CREATION OF THE INDIVIDUAL UNCONSCIOUS

There are many ways of viewing the architecture of the unconscious, its contents, its language, its dynamics, its purpose. The definition here is broadly drawn from the work of Carl Jung. According to Jung, the unconscious is the part of our psyche that contains everything that could not be integrated into the conscious self. It contains all the disavowed parts of human experience. When activated, all the psychological and biological blueprints, or archetypes and instincts, will produce an internal state in the individual that may lead to behaviour. The environmental response, which is initially usually the response from the primary caregiver, will have a significant impact on the psyche's capacity to integrate the archetype or instinct as a personal characteristic or fingerprint in the individual. The feelings and ways of being that were disallowed or disapproved of either explicitly or implicitly by the early environment, and/or were too overwhelming for the individual, are placed in the unconscious.

However, these parts do not disappear altogether. Instead, they remain active in the psyche and affect our behaviour. They will appear in our consciousness eventually, often when we are more able to manage them. Unaddressed, they will appear at unexpected times and cause unpredictable behaviour. Ideally, we need actively to try to reintegrate these parts by noticing and in a controlled way allowing them into consciousness. According to Jung, we have a tendency to try to recapture the wholeness of our original being and the unconscious will therefore deliberately remain active in all our relationships, whether we are aware of it or not.

The diagram on the next page shows the development of the different compartments of the psyche. The archetypes and instincts are activated and are expressed as behaviour. If the environmental response is one of disapproval or sanction, the psyche cannot integrate that way of being into the conscious public self. The psyche divides into compartments that house different aspects depending on the level of acceptability of each way of being human. There are essentially three compartments: the conscious public self, the conscious private self, and the unconscious.

THE DEVELOPMENT OF THE PSYCHIC ARCHITECTURE

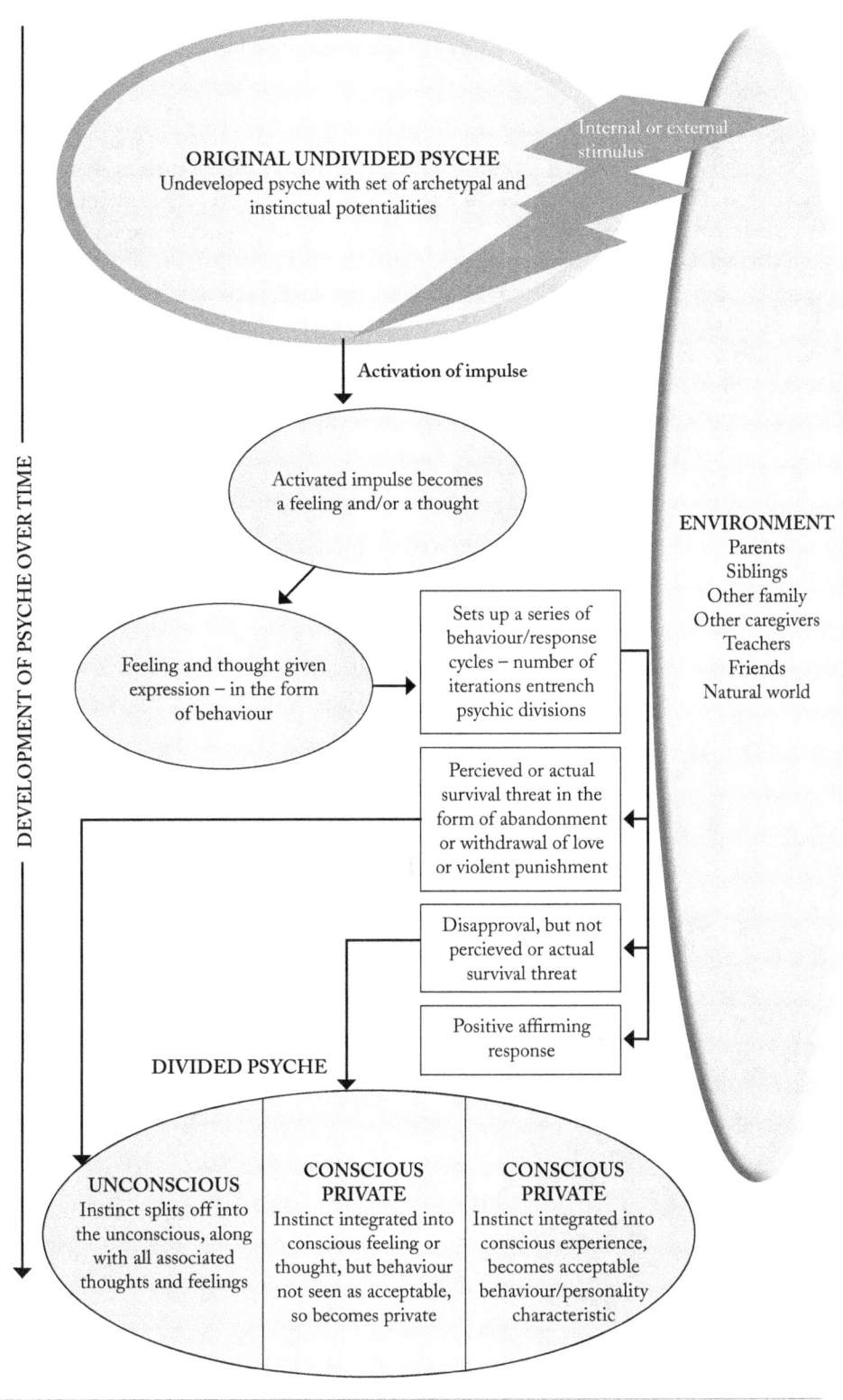

INTRA-PSYCHIC CONFLICT

The compartments in the psyche cause continual tension because the split-off ways of being that exist in the unconscious are active, energy-laden entities that need expression. This causes anxiety, because the psyche on one hand tries to maintain the compartments as it feels safer, but on the other hand the natural drive for balance and wholeness demands reintegration of the disavowed parts. As a result of the two opposing forces, intra-psychic conflict results, and this is very uncomfortable. The psyche has various ways of trying to lessen the anxiety caused by the conflict, as discussed in the following pages. The conflict will be characterised by two different and usually opposite ways of being, such as caution versus recklessness, or a task focus versus a people focus. The diagram below graphically illustrates how intra-psychic conflict works.

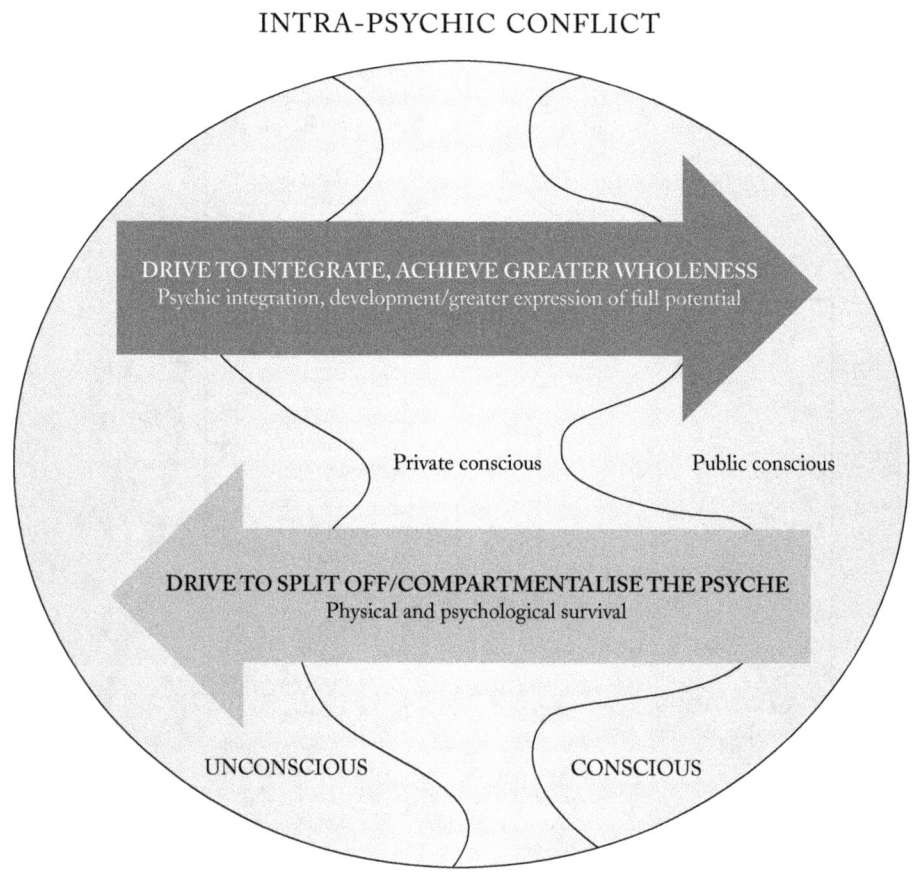

ANXIETY

From the moment we are born, two things seem to be clear. The first is that we are alive (an obvious but nevertheless remarkable idea) and the second is that living is not guaranteed. So life comes with an inbuilt anxiety about its loss, and this informs the human condition at a fundamental level. Anxiety is not only felt about the loss of life, but about anything that threatens a part of the self.

Anxiety is one of the most common human emotions, but it is often hidden or expressed indirectly. Anxiety develops when it is perceived that our survival is threatened. In addition to threats from the outside, a survival threat can also come in the form of intra-psychic conflict – the conflict between the conscious and unconscious parts of the mind. Potential loss will also trigger anxiety, whether it be loss of a desired object, loss of love, loss of identity or loss of love for the self.

Anxiety can be dealt with in one of two ways.

1. It can be dealt with directly by resolving the problem, overcoming obstacles and coming to terms with the loss.
2. It can be dealt with by distortion or denial in the form of a defence mechanism.

SOURCES OF ANXIETY AND HOW INDIVIDUALS RESPOND

There are three broad sources of anxiety. Each potentially elicits a defensive response:

- An external threat. This is when the threat to the self comes from the outside in the form of a physical or psychological attack. Our natural response to this threat is to reduce our anxiety by trying to get away from or eliminate the threat. We respond with a natural biological defence mechanism called fight or flight (or freeze). We eventually psychologically internalise perceived threats to our survival.

- An internal threat, when our private self threatens to reveal itself to the public, or there is a risk of exposure of our private thoughts. We respond with a conscious psychological defence mechanism designed to protect us from public exposure.

- An internal threat in the form of unconscious intra-psychic conflict – disturbing thoughts and/or feelings from our unconscious threatening to come into consciousness. Here we respond with an unconscious psychological defence mechanism such as denial.

In order to manage irreconcilable intra-psychic conflict, the psyche splits into compartments. The diagram below shows the eventual contents of the different parts of the psyche as a result of the splitting process caused by the interaction with the environment. Each time a way being causes anxiety in the individual because it is perceived as threatening, it is relegated to a compartment that allows it to be managed safely in the psyche.

CONTENTS OF THE COMPARTMENTS OF THE MIND

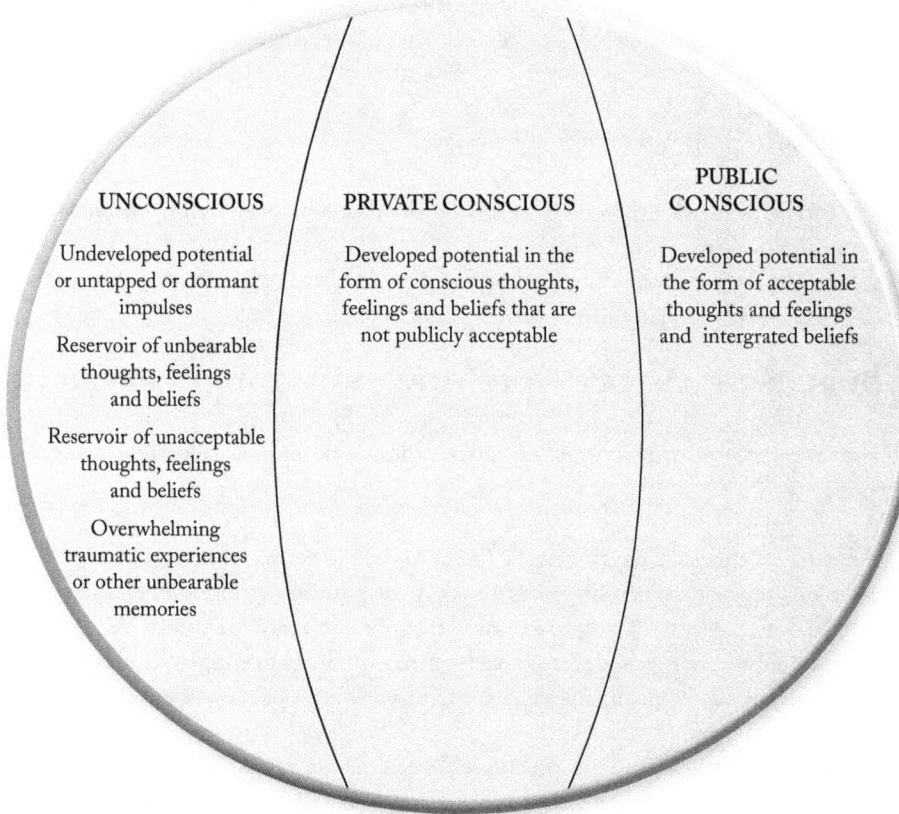

Mindell's concept of the edge

Arnold Mindell, a psychologist who started Process-Oriented Psychology (also known as Process Work), defined a concept that describes anxiety and how it works in the psyche. He called it the "edge". According to him, an "edge" is something you cannot bring yourself to say, to think, to do, to feel or to look at because it causes anxiety. One of our edges would be the dividing line between the conscious and the unconscious.

We all have different edges – what one of us will comfortably do, others cannot.

Examples of edges:

TO SAY: It is often difficult to tell someone that we are upset with him or her.

TO THINK: It often provokes anxiety to think about some things, such as losing your job.

TO DO: Certain actions will provoke anxiety, such as making presentations, engaging in conflict with someone, giving or receiving feedback, or saying no.

TO FEEL: We all have emotions that could provoke anxiety, especially if those emotions were disapproved of by our caregivers. For example, for some people feeling angry or sad is uncomfortable or provokes anxiety.

TO DREAM: It may be frightening to dream of moving to a new city or country; it may frightening to dream of returning to university in an effort to change your career.

TO HEAR: It is often difficult to receive feedback from someone.

TO LOOK AT: For many people, looking at certain things provokes anxiety. Some of us find it difficult to make eye contact with others. Many of us are afraid to look at a creature such as a snake.

As we approach an edge, our anxiety increases and our internal voices inform us that it is dangerous in some way to cross the edge. These internal voices are a mixture of reality and perception based on our previous experiences, our culture, our families and our values. We approach an edge because we choose to, or because life pushes us there. The edge idea in itself does not imply that all edges should be crossed. Some edges should not be crossed because they are simply too dangerous to that individual.

For example, it may be a career-limiting move to tell your boss what you really think of him or her in an unprepared and unprofessional manner. Edges not to cross are those that would hurt you or someone else unnecessarily.

To move over edges, we need support. Without thinking, we can push people over edges and embarrass or hurt them. It is critical that we never push someone over an edge; that we only support and assist a person over his or her edge. Different individuals will approach edges differently. Some of us go leaping over edges; others tread slowly. Most of us find ourselves somewhere in between.

There are some ways of crossing edges in an unprepared and uncontrolled manner:

1. Under the influence of alcohol, because alcohol works as an anaesthetic that silences our internal cautionary voices.
2. Strong emotion may cause people to cross edges more quickly and with less preparation.
3. The peer pressure in groups or crowds may cause people to cross edges more quickly and with less preparation.

THE EDGE
The 'edge' is something that is hard to do, to say, to feel, to think, or to look at.

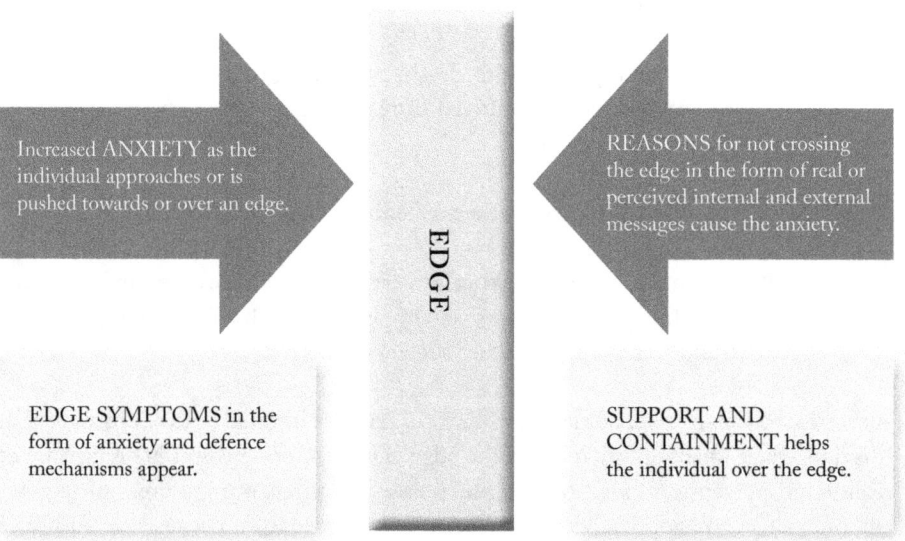

Sometimes life pushes us over edges. Examples include job loss/retrenchment, death of a loved one, sick children, and the end of a relationship. Individuals can decide whether or not to cross an edge by considering their internal voices and checking which of them are real and which are perceptions. If the internal voices reflect reality, then it is sometimes possible to make contingency plans in order to avoid those outcomes.

Edge behaviour

It is possible to notice when you or someone else is at an edge because certain symptoms of anxiety will be present. Also, the individual may have already started moving towards defending him- or herself from anxiety by moving into a defence mechanism. The defence mechanisms will be explored in more detail later. The list below indicates some of the more visible symptoms of anxiety:

- Symptoms of anxiety such as sweaty palms or an increased heart rate
- Cycling – going round in circles
- Boredom
- Uncomfortable silence
- Mixed messages or double signals
- Odd or unusual behaviour
- Confusion
- Nervous laughter
- Incomplete acts or sentences
- Sleepiness
- Gossip or reference to third parties
- Chaos
- Withdrawal
- Anger/frustration.

In the chapters dealing with facilitation practice in Section 3 we will consider how to help individuals and groups manage their edges.

Defence mechanisms

Defence mechanisms are some of the ways in which the psyche manages the anxiety caused either by external threats or intra-psychic conflict. When discussing defence mechanisms it is important to stress that the presence or use of a defence mechanism is not necessarily bad or wrong. Defence mechanisms, or our defences, have many benign functions. They originate as healthy, creative adaptations that allow us to deal with difficult and stressful periods in our lives. We tend to make use of our defences when we need to manage powerful and threatening emotions or when our self-esteem is feeling threatened. We also tend to use our defences "automatically" or without much thought as to what we are doing or saying. We all make use of defence mechanisms at different times, with a greater or lesser awareness of why we are reacting in this way.

There are different levels of defence mechanisms. This is because the type of defence mechanism that an individual develops is related to the general developmental stage at which that person is functioning. The earlier a defence mechanism develops, the more unsophisticated it is. These early defence mechanisms are referred to as "lower order" defences. They tend to be used unconsciously, and are more likely to "remove" the existence of a threatening internal state and place it outside of the psyche. Of course, internal states cannot be "removed", they can only be buried, but once the defence is active, it will seem to the conscious part of the individual as if the uncomfortable internal state no longer exists within.

The "higher order" defence mechanisms that develop later tend to be more mature and are often used more consciously. Rather than "remove" the uncomfortable internal state, they "transform" difficult thoughts and feelings into something more palatable for the individual. The lower order defence mechanisms tend to be more destructive to our sense of self and interpersonal interactions if used continuously. Ideally, the individual needs increasingly to develop the more constructive, higher order defences. A detailed list of some of the more common defences and their explanations is given in the table below.

Defence mechanisms	Explanation	Type of defence
Repression	Essentially forgetting or ignoring, preventing painful emotions and memories related to prior events having an outlet in our consciousness	Tends to be unconscious Lower order
Suppression	Temporarily removing an unpleasant thought or feeling from our conscious mind	Tends to be more conscious Higher order

Defence mechanisms	Explanation	Type of defence
Denial	Distorting our perception of some aspect of external reality, refusing to accept that something is happening	Tends to be unconscious Lower order
Rationalisation	Inventing an explanation to justify behaviours or feelings, generally after we have failed to get something we wanted or when something bad has happened	Can be conscious or unconscious Higher order
Reaction formation	The transformation of a negative, disturbing thought or feeling into a positive, more acceptable response	Tends to be unconscious Lower order
Projection	Attributing our own state of mind, and the internal conflicts it gives rise to, onto someone else, thereby freeing ourselves from it	Tends to be unconscious Lower order
Isolation	Separating the knowing and the feeling out of an experience, such as being able to do something without feeling anything	Can be either conscious or unconscious Higher order if used consciously

Defence mechanisms	Explanation	Type of defence
Splitting	Keeping apart two thoughts or feelings, because only one can be managed at a time; separating the world into parts that are either only "good" or "bad"	Tends to be unconscious Lower order
Regression	Reverting to former and outgrown behaviours in order to avoid an anxiety-provoking, more mature responsibility, feeling, thought or behaviour	Tends to be unconscious Lower order
Minimisation	Discounting the actual importance or effect of an object, event or person	Can be conscious or unconscious Lower order when unconscious
Introjection	Attributing the qualities, aspects and feelings of another person onto ourselves	Tends to be unconscious Lower order
Conversion	Transforming psychic or emotional conflict into physical symptoms	Tends to be unconscious Lower order
Intellectualisation	Applying cognitive analysis to threatening emotional content; using "theories" to manage feelings	Can be conscious or unconscious Higher order

Defence mechanisms	Explanation	Type of defence
Compensation	Masking a perceived weakness, developing other positive traits to compensate for a weakness	Tends to be unconscious Lower order
Displacement	The redirection of an emotion, thought or behaviour from its original object to another less stress-inducing object or person	Tends to be unconscious Lower order
Sublimation	Finding a creative, useful and socially acceptable way of expressing anxiety-producing impulses and drives	Can be conscious or unconscious Higher order
Withdrawal	Retreating from social or interpersonal interactions, often substituting inner thoughts and daydreams for the more stressful experience of relating to others	Tends to be unconscious Lower order when unconscious Higher order when used consciously
Aggression	Resorting to anger when the underlying experience of hurt, fear or vulnerability provokes too much anxiety	Tends to be unconscious Lower order
Humour	Resorting to making jokes or fun about an anxiety-producing situation or experience	Can be conscious or unconscious Higher order when used consciously and constructively

The role of defence mechanisms

The diagram on the next page shows how defences are used to remove, reduce or transform threatening internal responses to external states and events, in order to reduce the anxiety the individual experiences.

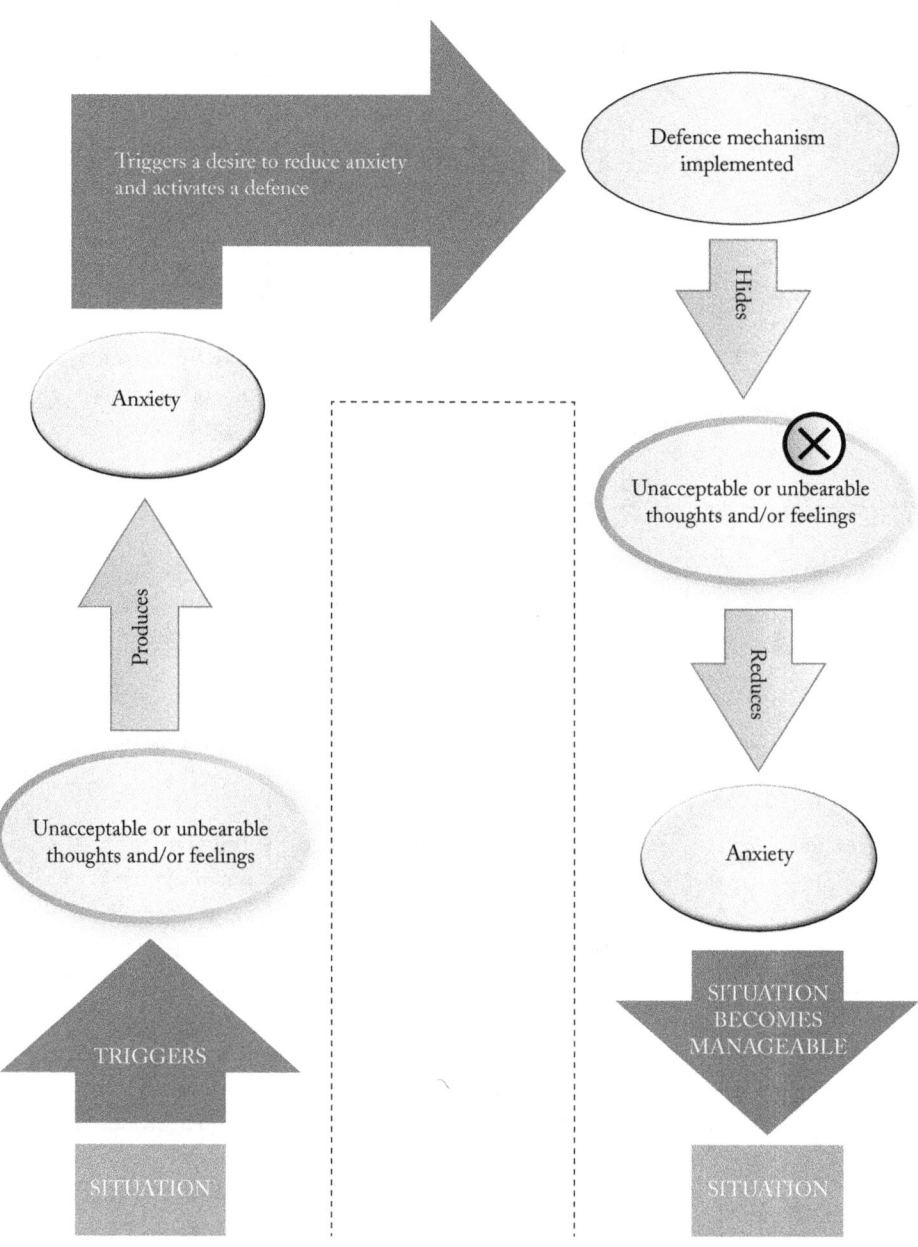

Projection

Although projection is discussed in the table above, it requires further elaboration because it a defence that is so pervasive and has such a great influence on group processes. It is one of the most common defence mechanisms used by all people. It is a defence that develops very early in an individual's life. The individual may encounter a way of being that is intolerable to the self because it represents a significant threat to the psyche. The defence develops in response to the anxiety caused by an internal response or state that is perceived as (or is actually) dangerous to psychic and/or physical survival.

For example, if a young girl feels angry towards a parent, it may feel too threatening to the relationship with the parent, on whom she depends absolutely, to express or even experience the anger. She buries the anger in the unconscious, but because she cannot fundamentally rid herself from it, it needs to "be given away" to someone else. Until she can experience (and possibly express) that anger without it seeming or being threatening to her psychic or physical survival, it will have to be projected onto someone outside of herself. Projection happens automatically, unknown to the person seeing the projected qualities.

There are two different kinds of projection: positive and negative projection. Negative projection is when a quality that is regarded as undesirable is projected onto another person. Negative projection can cause great interpersonal conflict. We project because we cannot integrate the quality directly and therefore experience the projected quality as intolerable in the other person. Positive projection is when we "fall in love" with the other and then suffer huge disappointment when we discover that he or she is simply human and has qualities other than the projected one.

A good indication that projection is present is when the intensity of the feeling seems incongruent with the situation in some way. In other words, our reactions towards people on whom we have projected certain qualities will seem extreme to others not caught in the projective process in the same way.

The diagram on the next page shows how projection works.

THE MECHANISM OF PROJECTION

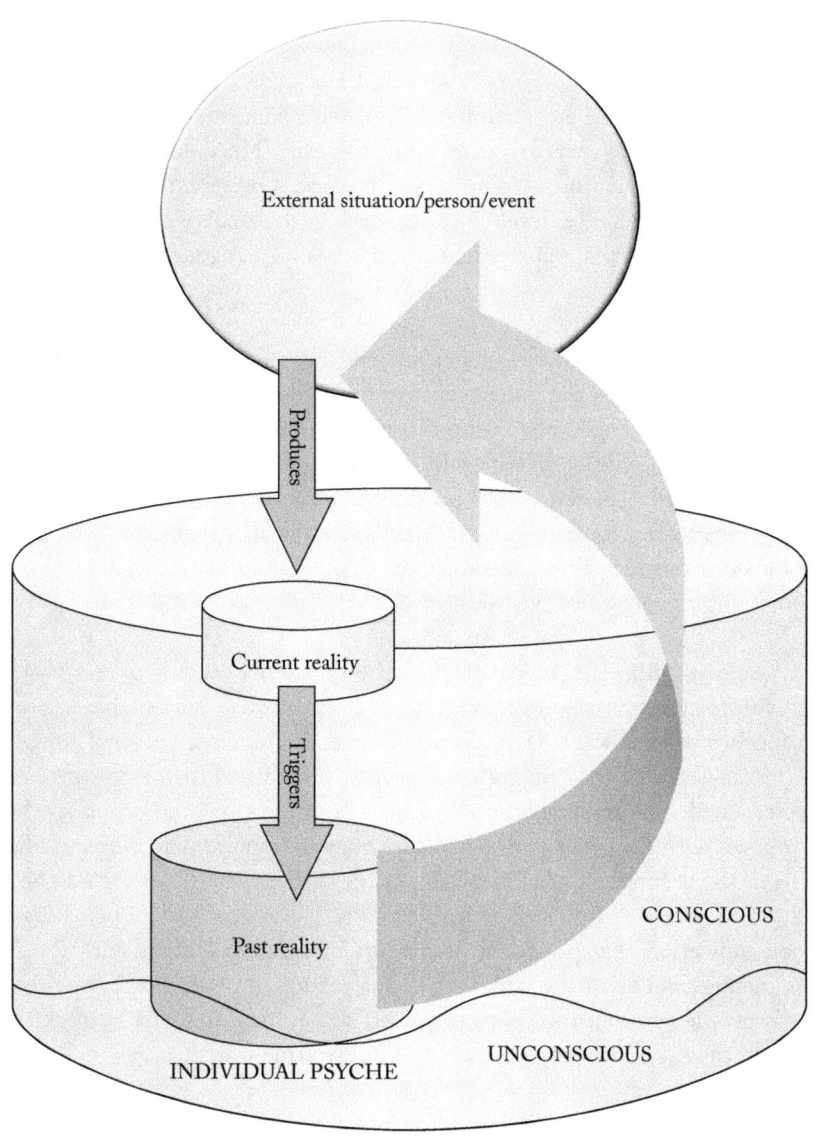

Projective identification

Another defence mechanism worth mentioning in its own right is projective identification. This is a defence that occurs between two people where one is projecting a way of being on to the other, and is doing it so effectively – or the other person is so susceptible to experiencing the projected quality – that a dynamic evolves where the receiver of the projection starts experiencing the quality that is being projected. For example, a man may have felt harmed by his critical mother. The feelings were so intense that he buried them in the unconscious part of the psyche. Unconsciously, as a defence against his own intense and unbearable feelings of being victimised, he becomes extremely critical of his wife. She starts feeling like a helpless victim of his criticism, and starts feeling as if she is not good enough herself. The two are in the grip of projection and projective identification. This dynamic may be strengthened by the fact that the wife may have had a very critical father and is therefore susceptible to feeling criticised, but has consciously not identified her own internalised and self-critical nature. She projects the critical part onto her husband and through a process of projective identification he behaves even more critically towards her. For this type of dynamic to be broken at least one of the parties must become conscious of the feelings that have been buried within.

The diagram on the next page graphically demonstrates the process of projective identification.

THE PROCESS OF PROJECTIVE IDENTIFICATION

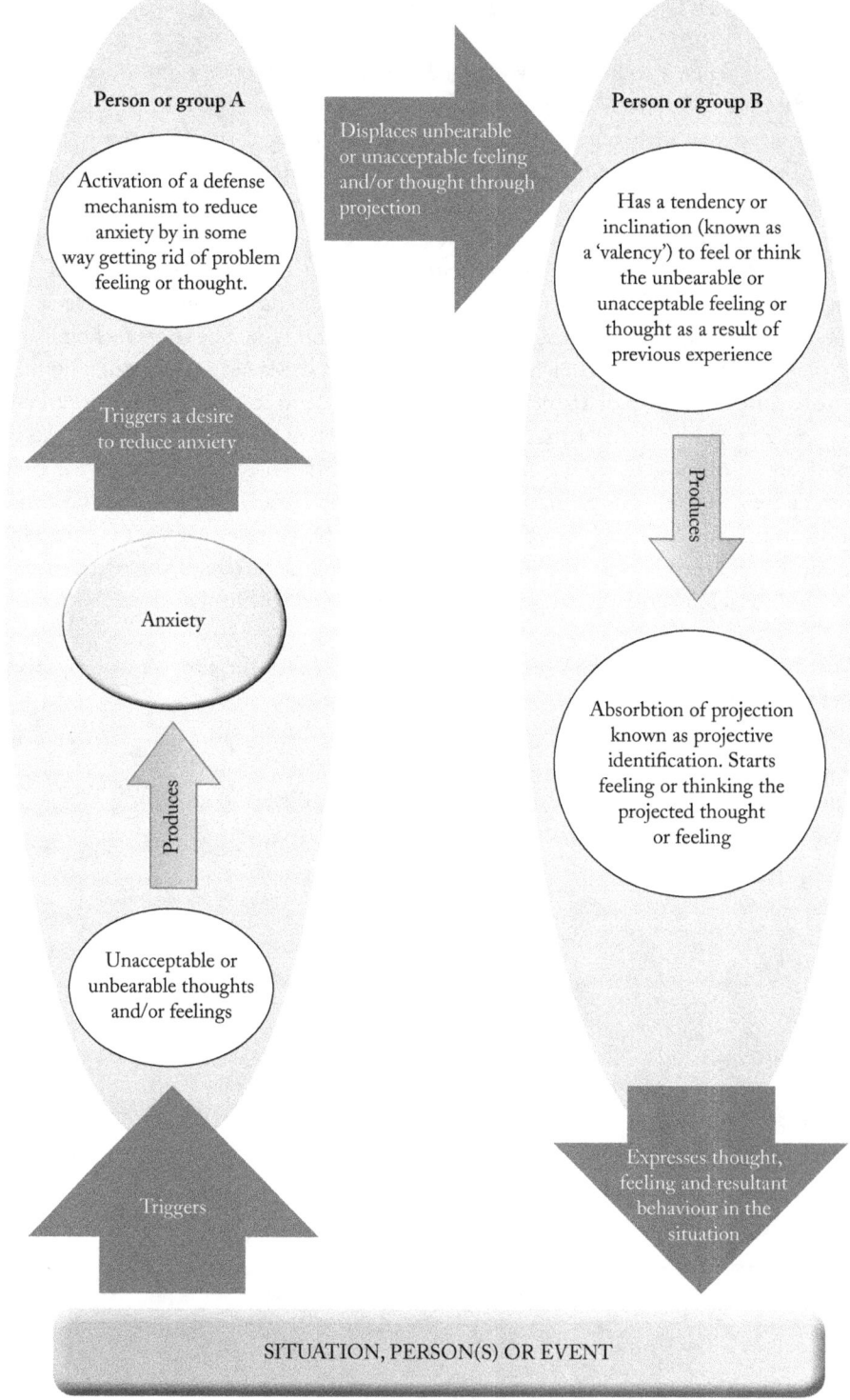

Transference and counter-transference

Transference is a particular case of projection over time, used to describe the unconscious emotional bonds that happen between two people in a long-standing relationship. It refers to the transfer of feelings that originally belonged elsewhere, such as to a mother or a father, or to a different authority figure later in life. Transference is a phenomenon that can occur in the workplace too.

Counter-transference is where the target individual for the transference starts identifying with the nature of the projection and starts behaving in accordance with it. This is a great risk for facilitators or leaders, as you can get unconsciously hooked and start responding to someone in accordance with their transference. For example, if someone is looking for a parental nurturing figure, the facilitator or leader may start feeling compelled to provide more nurturing than would be appropriate for the professional nature of the relationship.

Complexes

A complex is an emotionally charged group of ideas or images. Complexes develop over years and centre around certain images, such as those of "mother", "father", "money", "power" and so on, and arise from our experiences. The activation of a complex is always marked by the presence of some strong emotion, whether it is love, rage, hate, jealousy or joy. We all have complexes, which is to say that we all react emotionally when the right buttons are pushed. We cannot rid ourselves totally of our complexes because they are deeply rooted in our personal history. A complex is emotionally charged because it is usually the result of early trauma or wounding.

The most we can do is become aware of how our complexes influence us and how they interfere with our conscious intentions. As long as we remain unconscious of them, we are prone to being overwhelmed or driven by them. When we understand them, they lose their power to control us. One of the useful ways to think about complexes is that they are like "landmines" in the psyche. Other people may inadvertently trigger one of our "landmines" and we will overreact without them understanding the strength of our response.

Repetition compulsion

Repetition compulsion is a termed coined by Freud. It refers to the psychological tendency human beings have to repeat patterns of early distress or wounding in later situations. Jung further developed the idea by noticing that this behaviour is purposeful because it is in fact an effort to heal the original wounding. In other words, we unconsciously recreate certain situations in an attempt to rewrite the original situation and its painful outcome. Friends, partners and colleagues become unwitting characters in a drama played out by the psyche, where individuals other than the original participants in the wounding become actors in a re-enactment of early problematic interactions and relationships.

This is a largely unconscious process, but will trigger strong and often inexplicable responses in a context that is similar to, but obviously different from, the original context. Projection plays a significant role in this process because representatives for members of the original cast of characters have to be selected from the available members in the new situation. Our complexes will usually be driving forces behind our repetition compulsion.

Repetition compulsion means that individuals will be attracted unconsciously, often in a workplace setting, to dysfunctional behaviour patterns in groups, and thereby fulfil the need for the re-enactment. Unless the individual can become conscious of the repetition compulsion process, he or she is often doomed to repeat the pattern in various settings for a long time.

CONCLUSION

The individual psyche is a complicated system with conscious and unconscious aspects. It is affected by inner conflict, and much of that inner conflict can be unconscious. The inner conflict causes anxiety, which in turn leads to defence mechanisms. The split in the psyche also leads to interpersonal complications caused by phenomena such as transference and repetition compulsion.

As a facilitator you need to be aware of the complexity of your own psyche, and be able to work with the complications caused by psychic complexity in yourself and in others.

PERSONAL EXERCISES

1. Consider you own edges and defence mechanisms. Think about what could be unconscious in you.

2. Consider the edges and defence mechanisms that you notice others using. Remain aware that most people are not aware of their edges and defence mechanisms.

3. Consider your moments of anxiety and identify the symptoms you display at these times.

4. Identify any complexes that you are aware of in yourself. Notice whether you may be caught in a process of repetition compulsion where you continually place yourself in an upsetting situation in the hope of being able to produce a better outcome.

CHAPTER 4:
Depth Psychology – The Group

INTRODUCTION

This chapter considers the functioning of groups from the perspective of Depth Psychology. It considers some of the general principles in groups, and then discusses the way the group manages the tensions between the various aspects of itself. It considers the way the group plays out its "psychodynamics" through the allocation of roles to individual group members, as well as the impact of power and privilege on these dynamics.

THE ARCHITECTURE OF THE GROUP PSYCHE

The diagram on the next page captures some the various influences that determine group behaviour. As with the individual psyche, it distinguishes between two main compartments in what is known as the "group psyche" (a concept that will be elaborated on later in the chapter). The group psyche has a conscious aspect, which refers to the issues and concerns that are dealt with openly in the group, and an unconscious aspect, which refers to the issues and concerns that the group cannot discuss openly. The diagram indicates that difficulties in the different areas will result in differing symptoms and that, broadly speaking, the different schools of psychology address different root causes.

THE NOTION OF THE GROUP PSYCHE

Many theorists have discussed the phenomenon that when a collection of individuals come together as a group, they in fact become part of something which has alternatively been called the "group mind", the "collective mind", or the group psyche. In practice, this means that in a group, one is no longer dealing with a collection of individuals and their psychological processes, but is in fact dealing with an "n"th entity, a new being, with its own unconscious and unconscious processes. The group behaves as a single psychological unit and "uses" the individual members to play out the different parts of the group mind.

Any attempt to deal with the individual members on their own could cause further problems in the group, or will not solve the group difficulties that may exist. The group will unconsciously use different members of the group to play different roles, and to a relatively large extent, individual autonomy may be lost.

ARCHITECTURE OF THE GROUP PSYCHE

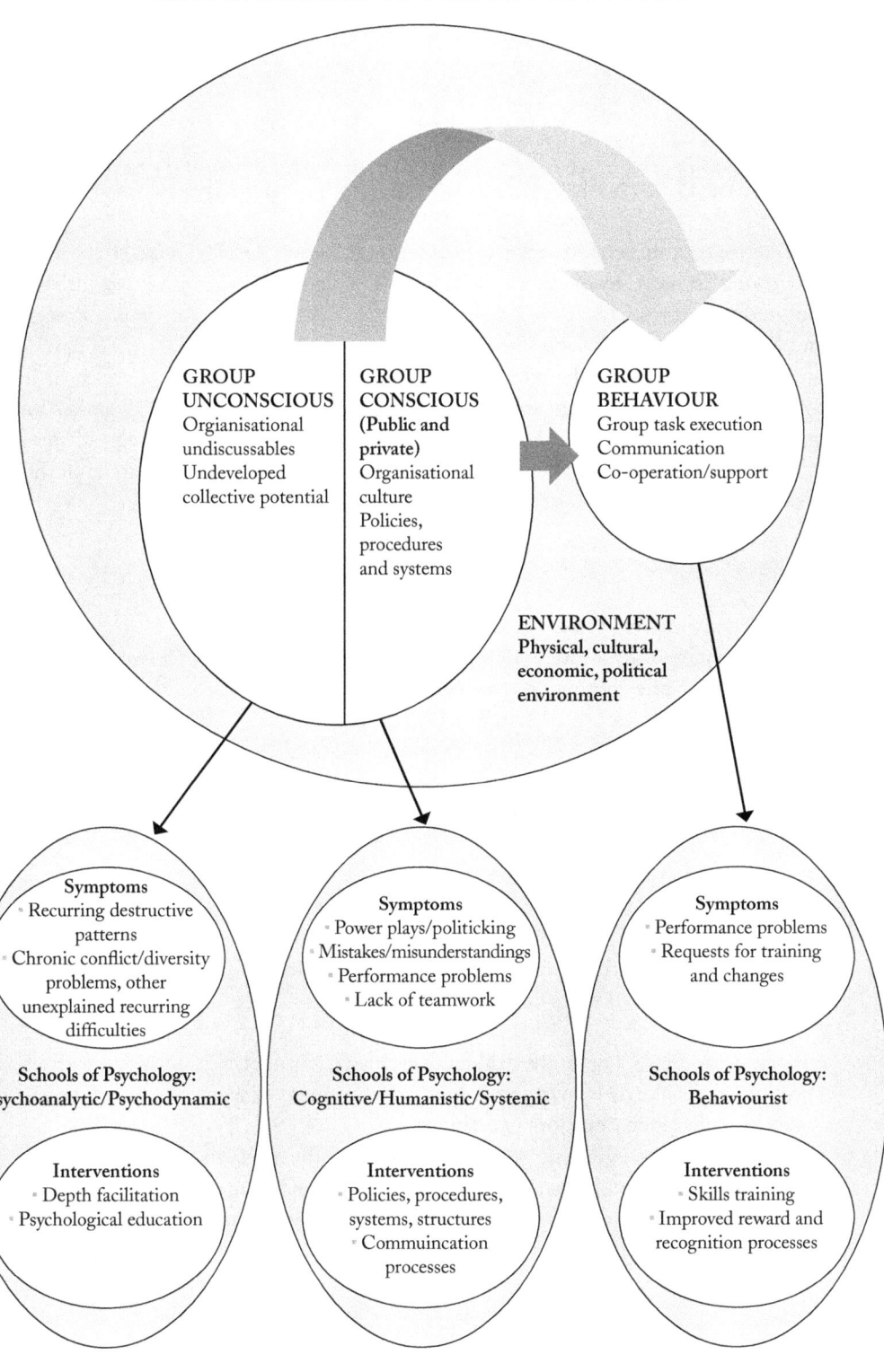

Many individuals will struggle with the notion of their potential subjugation to the will of the group mind, but it is nevertheless essential that groups are worked with as entities in their own right.

WHAT IS A GROUP?

The concepts in this chapter form a foundation of knowledge that a facilitator must understand in order to manage groups well. The concepts add up to a multilevel, multifaceted view of what groups are and, as a result, of how they work. Process and structure are inextricably linked. For our purposes, a group is a collection of individuals who have gathered together to execute an explicit task or tasks, or to achieve explicit goals. There are emerging groups who do not explicitly gather for task execution or goal achievement, but nevertheless end up functioning as if they did. These groups are less likely to be part of a facilitation process as defined in this book because such a process should always be explicitly agreed on.

In more detail, a group is any collection of people who:

- Perceive themselves to be a group
- Are psychologically aware of one another
- Interact with one another on a regular basis
- Have interdependent relationships with one another
- Perceive themselves as a group by reliably distinguishing members from non-members
- Are recognised as a group by non-members.

TYPES OF GROUPS

It is likely that most facilitation interventions will occur in some kind of organisational setting. The two broad types of groups in organisations are:

- Formal groups – These are deliberately created by managers in order to fulfil specific tasks clearly related to the total organisational mission. These groups can be either temporary or more permanent.
- Informal groups – These groups arise out of the particular combination of "formal" factors and human needs. Often such groups come to serve a "counter-organisational function" in that they attempt to counteract any coercive tendencies of the organisation.

FUNCTIONS FULFILLED BY GROUPS

Groups fulfil many functions in organisations and society. It is important to recognise that there are formal organisational functions and more informal psychological functions. In fact, a facilitation intervention relies on recognising that the psychological functions are sometimes far more important to the individual than the organisational ones.

The formal organisational functions of groups include:

- Working on complex, interdependent tasks
- Generating new ideas or creative solutions
- Offering liaison or coordinating functions
- Providing problem-solving mechanisms
- Facilitating the implementation of complex decisions
- Serving as vehicles of socialisation or training.

The more informal, psychological functions for the individuals of a group include:

- Meeting affiliation needs
- Strengthening and confirming an individual's sense of identity
- Maintaining self-esteem
- Serving as a vehicle for establishing and testing social reality
- Reducing insecurity, anxiety and a sense of powerlessness
- Offering a problem-solving, task-accomplishing mechanism for the individual
- Enhancing the individual's power
- Serving as a lobbying mechanism
- Offering a psychological holding environment
- Serving as a vehicle for the individual's projections.

THE GROUP CONTEXT

Understanding the group context is critical when facilitating a group because the group's behaviour will be dictated largely by the nature of the context. The following systems need to be considered when building an understanding of the group field:

- The global situation in all its aspects
- The political environment
- The economic environment
- The technological environment
- The natural environment

- The cultural system in which the group functions
- The religious environment
- The history of the group
- The psychological climate of the group
- The industry sector
- The region in which the group operates
- The organisation of which the group is a part
- The department in which the group operates
- Other related departments
- The organisation's client group (if any)
- Any hierarchical systems, including class systems.

When thinking about these other systems, we need to consider the major events and trends in each system. The human psyche – whether individual or group – continually anticipates, monitors and evaluates the events and trends of the context in order to better position itself for survival. Its behaviour is therefore context-dependent.

THE GROUP HISTORY

Part of the group context will be its history. Each group will have a history that will predispose it to certain experiences or outcomes in almost a mythical way. The history will include both trends over time and critical events or incidences. Of course all human beings share a common ancestry of being human, so we have all the archetypal possibilities available to us. A particular group history will predispose us to a certain set of archetypal behaviours. The way a group story unfolds will be connected to the history of the group, and so the history is significant in understanding and processing depth material. Knowing the group's history will assist the facilitator to anticipate and identify depth processes. As an example, in South Africa, whether everyone likes it or not, groups share the history of apartheid. Often group members will dissociate themselves from an aspect of the history, and insist that they have moved on. Whatever the history, however, it is an integral part of the identity of the group and needs to be kept in the facilitator's mind.

GROUP COMPLEXES

One of the important aspects of group history is that the group may have experienced traumatic events or wounds in its past that may have scarred the group psyche. This type of scarring is referred to as a group "complex". A complex is an emotionally charged group of ideas or images. As we saw in Chapter 3, a complex in an individual arises from his or her experiences over years, and centres on images like "mother", "father", "money", "power", and so on. We also saw that strong emotions (love, rage, hate, jealousy, etc) accompany the activation of a complex. Individuals cannot get rid of their complexes because they are deeply rooted in their personal history, but they can become aware of how they are influenced by them.

Just as individuals have complexes, so do groups. It is important for the facilitator to recognise that complexes are part of group functioning. We mentioned above that apartheid was part of South Africans' group history. It is also a complex in the South African group – an area of wounding in the collective psyche that predisposes South Africans to strong emotion, and affects the group functioning.

THE GROUP FIELD

The group context, history and complexes will determine the group field. The group field is the psychological, mental and emotional force field that exists in the group and is derived from the entire set of systems that have an impact on the group. This force field will be made up of all the archetypal energies at work in the system. These energies will play themselves out in the group and will influence the patterns of behaviour significantly.

An example would be a group functioning within an organisation that is making a consistent loss. This group will be psychologically and practically affected by that context, even if the group itself may be a profitable unit within the organisation. The group will define itself and derive its identity at least to some extent from the identity of the larger system.

It is useful if you as the facilitator have some idea of the group field and potential archetypal energies at work. This information may not be available before the session, but will certainly make itself known throughout the session.

PSYCHOLOGICAL SYSTEMS OPERATING IN A GROUP

We have considered the superstructures that operate in group life, such as the group context, and therefore the systems surrounding the group. It is also important to consider the psychologically coherent systems that operate within the group because these are similarly multileveled.

For our purposes, there are three sets of psychological systems operating in a group: the group psyche, the individual psyches of the members, and the sub-groups. As a facilitator you need to keep all three levels in mind, and attend to the interrelationships between them. Ultimately, you are taking care of the group psyche, but you cannot do this successfully if you are not attending to the other two levels. Special aspects of each of the three levels are discussed in more detail below.

1. The group psyche

The group functions as a psychologically integrated unit in which the individual members become subject to the larger psyche of the group. Individual group members will of course have distinctive psyches, but the human psyche is a permeable and flexible system, and it easily combines with other psyches in order to form an integrated larger whole.

This means that the individual psyche is significantly affected by the larger group of which it is part. We can assume that we are both agents and puppets when functioning in groups. Many individuals claim that they can maintain their independence in a group, but this is manifestly not the case. Just as individual rivers become indistinguishably part of the sea, so individual psyches become part of a larger group psyche. The difference between an individual psyche and a river is that the individual psyche can re-form after the group. However, for the time that the individual is part of the group, the individual psyche is unlikely to function completely autonomously.

The role the individual plays in the group is determined by his or her particular tendency to embody one of the archetypal energies at work in the group. Individuals develop characteristic preferences. Depending on the other members and their availability to take up a particular characteristic of the group, the individual will be "used" by the group to fulfil a particular psychological or practical purpose. Individuals are often not aware of their particular role tendencies or of how the group may use their capacity for a certain role. In fact, the whole notion of playing a role for a group may be a foreign idea to most people.

In order to work successfully from the perspective of roles that are taken up by individuals in groups, it may be important to offer some education regarding these psychological ideas. If you are working with a group in which the members particularly want to learn about group consciousness and how it works, then it is critical to offer psychological education. With more knowledge about how groups work and how their own role tendencies operate, individuals can reflect on their own behaviour in the group and then it becomes possible to operate less as a puppet and more as an agent.

In order not to be sucked into the undertow of the group psyche, any individual needs to maintain a reflective capacity. This is obviously particularly important for the facilitator, as depth facilitation in particular demands a certain measure of psychological independence.

The work of Wilfred Bion was groundbreaking in that it introduced the idea of the group psyche and the idea that individuals have tendencies (or valencies, as Bion termed them) for certain roles in the group psyche. We will look at this in more detail later. The Tavistock tradition, which is based on the work of Bion, emphasises a focus on the "group as a whole". However, it is important not to focus on the group as a whole to the exclusion of the individual. The individual psyche still exists and needs to be cared for in a facilitation situation. If the facilitator focuses only on the group, ignoring the individual psyche, it can become extremely stressful for the individual – and this can be counter-productive to the group process.

2. The individual psyche in the group

The individual psyche is one of the sub-systems of the group, but needs special treatment because it operates as a psychologically coherent sub-system. There is a trend in some methodologies where the facilitator regards the individual as merely instrumental in the group psyche, and therefore treats all individual behaviour as an expression of the group psyche. It is true that the individual is expressing an aspect of the group psyche, but the facilitator needs to remember that ultimately the individual psyche has to remain intact beyond the group's life. A facilitation methodology that depersonalises the individual completely may be useful in a training situation where individuals are learning about group life, but is not desirable in general facilitation situations.

The challenge therefore for the facilitator is to manage the tension between treating the individual as an individual in his or her own right, and simultaneously remembering that the individual is operating as an aspect of the group psyche. The individual must be treated as an individual, but not as a special member of the group. Any conversations with individuals outside the group should ideally bear no relation to the individual's functioning in the group, other than to encourage the individual's authenticity in the group. Ideally, though, the facilitator should avoid personal contact with individuals during sessions, if this can be done without becoming rude or cold or unnecessarily distant.

3. Sub-groups

All groups are part of larger groups (the largest being the entire human race) and any group larger than two members will have the tendency to further divide itself into sub-groups. Group power relations and group dynamics will influence the nature of this subdivision and these mechanisms will be discussed in more detail later. Unlike the individual psyche, the sub-groups need to be managed only as part of the group as a whole. Sub-groups will try and demand special attention from a facilitator. Although this may be practically impossible not to give, as in the case of a leadership sub-group, it is important that the facilitator remains psychologically equally attentive to all of the sub-groups. Sub-groups represent aspects of the group psyche and it is important to maintain an integrated view of sub-group functioning. It is sometimes tempting to be drawn into a sub-group, especially if the facilitator identifies with certain aspects of that sub-group, but guard against this at all costs.

THE GROUP IDENTITY

The group identity will be formed by a complex set of factors. The group will overtly identify with the explicit context and task of the group, but there will also be an emergent identity based on the psychological development of the group and the psychological needs that the group meets for the individuals. Often this emergent identity will become more important than the explicit identity. This will be because the emergent identity will resonate unconsciously, often with deeply held unconscious needs, and may well be more powerful than the explicit identification. It is important to understand what the explicit identity is, and to relate to that identity as closely as possible in order to build rapport. The group will be interested primarily in how others relate to the explicit identity, and will need to feel that that identity is accepted and valued.

GROUP POWER

Many things determine a group's power, particularly the sum of the power held by individual members and the combination of the variables of the group in its context. A Research and Development group, for instance, will be powerful if the larger organisation is in need of new technology. That same group will lose its power in an organisation where the current technology is very profitable.

The larger the group, the more powerful it is, both in terms of its own members and in terms of the surrounding systems. However, the sheer number of members is not sufficient to determine the levels of power. Other factors such as economic clout, intellectual levels, education levels, access to force and psychological influence will add up to determine the power of the group.
In relation to the facilitator, the group will tend to be more powerful. If you as the facilitator are more powerful, then you have to work very carefully so as not to assume tacit leadership of the group. You do need to have power in the group, but that power must be related to credibility, and you need to establish this early on in the session/s.

A group's power in relation to its members is something that needs to be kept in mind. This will be discussed in more detail later, but it is important to say here that psychologically, groups carry power because they meet or frustrate the unconscious needs of individuals, and often the individual is unaware of this at the conscious level. The facilitator who is not sufficiently aware will also be subject to this power and may often be taken by surprise at the extent of it. Never underestimate a group's power, and remain vigilant to avoid being unduly influenced by it.

GROUP SIZES

Facilitators tend to work with groups that range in size. In this case, size does matter, as the number of members has an impact on how the group works.

Group size has an impact on the following:

- The degree of face-to-face contact that is possible in the group and with the facilitator
- The amount of psychological energy available to be expressed
- The impact of proportional relationships between the minority and majority sub-groups
- The psychological dynamics that are triggered, e.g. family dynamics versus herd instincts
- The relative powerlessness experienced by individual members
- The relative levels of anonymity experienced by the individual members and therefore the levels of responsibility taken.

Different methodologies differ in their definitions of group sizes, but there tends to be agreement that a small group has a maximum of 15 members, a medium-sized group consists of between 15 and 25 members, and a large group has more than 25 members. Only a small group can reliably have face-to-face contact, which will mitigate the more destructive aspects of the anonymity that the individual experiences in a large group. If you are an inexperienced facilitator you should not work with a group of more than 15 members if you intend doing depth work.

GROUP ENERGY

Many things determine the psychological, mental and physical energy available to a group. This is an important element to be considered in the facilitator's work. There are many sources and blockages to the energy available in groups, and it is useful to be aware of the different possibilities and work with them if necessary. The physical sources and blockages are relatively easy to work with and need to be tackled as quickly as possible. Having some control or say about the environment in which group sessions are held is important from an energy perspective. Monitoring and working towards optimising the group energy levels is particularly important when doing depth facilitation because a group's energy level is usually the best indicator of the degree of integration experienced by the group.

Sources of energy	Blockages and/or consumers of energy
Physical sources Adequate light Adequate space Fresh air Food and beverages	**Physical blockages** Poor temperature control Inadequate ventilation Confined spaces Overcrowding Lack of refreshments Poor lighting Time of day
Mental and psychological sources Sufficient stimulation A non-judgemental atmosphere Sufficient rest Sufficient time for reflection Role switching and sharing Process resolution Catharsis	**Mental and psychological blockages and consumers** Tiredness Anxiety Unexpressed emotion or opinions Unresolved dynamics Role over-identification Defence mechanisms Conflict

THE GROUP TASK AND INTENTION

Groups have both explicit and emerging tasks. The explicit task will be the conscious and openly identified one. As a facilitator, it is important to ensure that you are working towards helping the group achieve this task. The explicit task is, in fact, the most important one. However, if emerging tasks in the form of underlying processes interfere with or prevent the achievement of the explicit task, then the facilitator may need to alert the group to the lack of progress and help it to decide whether to address the underlying issues before resuming the work towards the task itself. Depth facilitation is a way of helping a group explore depth material so that it may achieve its explicit task. Without a detour into the underlying processes, the group may not achieve its stated task. Unless explicitly stated, depth facilitation is a means to an end, not an end in itself.

Without an explicit task, the group may easily fall into exploring the emergent intentions of the unconscious minds of individual members and the group. This takes the group into a depth process that it has not agreed to tackle. The most likely outcome of such a process is great dissatisfaction among members and frustration or even anger towards the facilitator.

According to Wilfred Bion, of the Tavistock approach, a group will be successful in an organisational context only if it remains able to stay in touch with the need to perform a joint task, and with the external reality, its constraints, its moderating factors on group functioning, and the inflows in terms of information and resources offered by the external environment.

Failing the existence of a group task that is consciously understood, acknowledged and actively pursued, the group will resort to what Bion terms a "basic assumption group", which is more occupied by its psychological needs and will remain organisationally unproductive. Bion divides basic assumption behaviour into three types, called "dependency", "pairing", and "fight/flight". (We will look at this in more detail later in this chapter.)

As a facilitator, it is therefore very important to help the group clarify its explicit task and to ensure that there is agreement from all the members about this task as this will ensure that the group intention is aligned with the task. If there is misalignment between the group's task and its intention, then a depth process is necessary to achieve alignment.

GROUP BEHAVIOUR

If the group has a psyche that functions as a whole, then its psyche will have thoughts, feelings and behaviours just as an individual does. These thoughts, feelings and behaviours will be derived from the same archetypes and instincts discussed in terms of the individual psyche in Chapter 3. The archetypes and instincts are the biological and psychological imperatives that drive human functioning, and in groups, the medium of expression of these imperatives is a complex one.

An individual has thoughts, feelings and behaviours that identifiably belong to that individual. In a group, the individuals become parts of the whole and so the group can only express itself through those individuals. The group uses the individuals to express itself, and so the human functions of feeling, thinking and behaving for the group psyche are carried through individuals who operate in roles for the group. Therefore, whenever you witness individual behaviour in a group, it is important to remember that the individual is, at least partially, in a "role" for the group. Observation of the roles individuals take for the group is critical to understanding the functioning of the group psyche.

Archetypes and instincts

In Chapter 3, we discussed that human beings have the potential for all ways of being human encoded in their beings at birth. These ways of being include instincts, which are our biological predispositions, and archetypes, which are our psychological predispositions. Which of these predispositions will be activated within a group depends on the context in which the group finds itself and the task that the group has in that context. The context and the task are far more important in determining which predispositions will be activated than the nature of the individuals that make up the group. We like to think of the individual behaviour in a group as being personal, and determined by the personality of that individual, but this is not the case. If the group were stranded on a desert island, the likely ways of being would include some of the following:

- Protector
- Hunter
- Leader
- Clown
- Rebel
- Explorer
- Nurturer
- Entertainer
- Nurse
- Pragmatist
- Observer
- Builder
- Strategist
- The person who panics
- Organiser

The exact patterns of behaviour that will emerge may differ from group to group, but many of the essential elements would be the same. One of the ways to think about these archetypes and instincts that function in a group would be to view them as roles in the group. The individual members take up roles for the group in order to express the group psyche. As a facilitator, it is vital to remember that you are not dealing with individuals in a group, but rather with how individuals represent the playing out of human predispositions in that group.

Bear in mind that the archetypes and instincts are in themselves responses to environmental demands, and are therefore ways of being that are designed to ensure survival, rather than good or bad in themselves. There is usually logic behind the activation of a particular role, often as a response to a situation that is out of balance. The instinct or the archetype will manifest itself as an attempt to balance the situation. For example, in a group that is working too hard, the archetype or instinct related to rest and relaxation will start manifesting itself. It is useful to remember that there is some essential wisdom at work when a new role appears in a group.

Role types

It is useful to have an overview of the different types of roles. Broadly speaking, there are four types of roles: task roles, political roles, psychological roles and emotional roles. They can be correlated with the categories of doing, thinking, relating and feeling.

1. Task roles

Task roles refer to the roles in which something is done. There are activities that contribute to task completion. In some ways they are the least contentious roles, because they are the clearest of all the roles, and groups are usually comfortable discussing task roles openly. Examples of task roles are:

- Project manager
- Cleaner
- Scribe
- Programmer
- Operator
- Decorator
- Builder
- Planner
- Designer
- Cook
- Porter
- Troubleshooter
- Coordinator
- Trainer
- Facilitator

2. Political roles

Political roles derive from our opinions, thoughts and judgements that pertain to power arrangements. Often these opinions and thoughts derive from belief systems created as mental constructs in order to better understand and manage the world. The political role takes a particular position on a subject. For example, a conservative role would work towards protecting a system in its original state, whereas a revolutionary would work towards transforming that system. Some examples of political roles are:

- Populist
- Democrat
- Liberal
- Conservative
- Rebel
- Feminist
- Activist
- Pacifist

3. Psychological roles

Psychological roles refer to the different ways human beings have of relating to one another and themselves from an interpersonal and psychological perspective. A psychological role will often lie beneath a political role, and its roots are most likely to be found in the unconscious. Psychological roles tend to operate in reciprocal patterns. For example, a critic will almost always elicit a victim, and a leader needs a follower in order to lead.

- Critic
- Victim
- Rescuer
- Peacemaker
- Disturber
- Perpetrator
- Nurturer
- Protector
- Parent
- Leader
- Follower

4. Emotional roles

Emotional roles are related to the feelings we have as human beings, which are the ways in which we value our experiences. Emotion is distinct from the other two phenomena of the mind, that of cognition and of the will. Emotional roles are different from the other types of roles in that they cannot be actively chosen, but rather are a result of other choices. In some ways emotional roles are the hardest to fulfil in organisational settings, and there may be many defensive processes that prevent the experience and articulation of emotional roles.

- Sadness
- Anger
- Grief
- Jealousy
- Envy
- Affection
- Lust
- Vengefulness
- Bitterness
- Relief
- Anticipation
- Excitement
- Joy
- Love
- Frustration
- Satisfaction

Role differentiation

In groups, the archetypes and instincts in action take the form of roles. Role theory has been a part of traditional sociological thinking for at least half a century. A role is a thought, feeling or behaviour that is expressed in a group context in order manifest the mental, emotional and psychological life of the group. Roles are the archetypes and instincts in action in a group. In order for the group then to express itself, role differentiation is required among the individual members of the group.

The group context and task will provide a script for the required roles, and the individuals in the group become actors who often easily slip into the roles available. The roles provide the pattern according to which the individual should be acting in the particular situation. Certain roles, such as physician or clergyman, require very specific mannerisms, speech patterns, postures, and so forth. The roles themselves carry these emotions and attitudes, and when an individual adopts a particular role, he or she is influenced by it and takes on its characteristics. For example, a person becomes wise by being appointed a professor. The person not only begins to act wise, he or she actually feels it.

From the depth perspective, a role is regarded as being greater than an individual, and the individual is also recognised as being greater than the role. In a group, an individual is part of a larger psychological field and is used by the field to express an aspect of its essence. In this way, an individual becomes a vehicle for the group process.

Roles, not individuals, constitute the basic organs of the group's body. Role theory also contains the idea that while functioning in a group, the group itself is psychologically whole or complete and therefore the individual need not always be whole. Each individual plays a role, which contributes to the group's wholeness, but each individual unit is not expected to be complete in itself.

The roles will have a longer life span in a group than the individuals who occupy them, and over time they change more slowly than individuals do. If no individual is available to fill a certain role, the group will have to invent or produce a person who fulfils the required specifications.

Individual role valency

Role allocation is determined by a combination of individual tendencies and group requirements. As we have mentioned, each individual has what Wilfred Bion termed a "valency" for a particular role. Individuals may have more than one valency, and different contexts will activate different valencies. A valency refers to the conscious or unconscious preference or tendency that an individual may have for a certain role in a group. This preference or tendency develops in an individual as a result of a variety of factors in their early chidlhood, such as:

- A need in the individual's original family
- Birth order
- Inherent talents
- Role models
- Parental complexes and projections.

An individual's valency for a particular role may be incongruent with the individual's active and conscious choices. A person may become the "rescuer" in a group even when he or she really does not want to. However, the group's needs and the individual's unconscious preferences will be stronger than the individual's capacity to make rational choices.

Role casting

Matching the person to the role can be thought of as role allocation or role casting. Sometimes role casting is a conscious, active process, where a group leader or the group members themselves actively allocate a role to an individual. The individual may be explicitly consulted and then voluntarily take up the role. This type of role casting is probably the best way to allocate roles. It is easy to allocate task roles explicitly; but it is harder to allocate political, psychological or feeling roles. Most role casting happens in a very different way, without the explicit consent of either the group or the individual, but rather as an unconscious collusion between the individual's psyche and the group psyche. The collusion happens because the group has a need and the individual has a valency that communicates itself subliminally to the group.

Role suction

When there is no one else to fill a role, an individual may become subject to what can be thought of as "role suction", where the individual is subtly (or not so subtly) coerced to take up a particular role for the group. Through the complex interaction of projection and projective identification mechanisms, the individual will be sucked into playing a particular role within the group. This may feel quite uncomfortable and an individual may resist it, but the group will tend to be stronger than an individual's will in this situation. What this means is that if there is a variance between what the individual wants to do and what the group wants that individual to do, the group's requirements of the individual may prevail.

Role identification

The opposite of role suction (where the individual knows that he or she does not wish to take up a particular role or that the role does not suit) is that of role identification, where the role "fits" the individual so well that the person becomes identified with the role. In other words, the person feels very comfortable in the role and starts equating it with his or her own identity.

In this situation, the collusion between the group and individual becomes complete, and everyone starts believing that the role is the person, and that the person is the role. This will feel comfortable to everyone in the group, or almost everyone. In the long term, however, it will be destructive to group development because it does not acknowledge the complexity and diversity of the system or the individual.

Scapegoating

After a person has been selected to fill a role, the rest of the group tends to identify the person with the role. This can easily become a form of scapegoating and its prevalence is one of the reasons why people are often afraid to speak out in groups, especially when they are in minority positions. Scapegoating refers to the situation in which everything that is wrong or bad with a group is considered to belong to one individual. The group believes that if it can rid itself of the problematic individual, all its problems will be solved.

This is not true because groups are interconnected and dynamic systems in which the interactions between all the individual psyches result in functional or dysfunctional behaviour. As long as parts of the group – certain individuals or sub-groups – are available to take the minority role, the rest of the group can scapegoat that part and avoid the experience of the position themselves. A holistic view of the individual recognises that all the roles are present in all of us.

The diagram on the next page shows how the person with the greatest tendency to express a particular thought or feeling does so for the whole group.

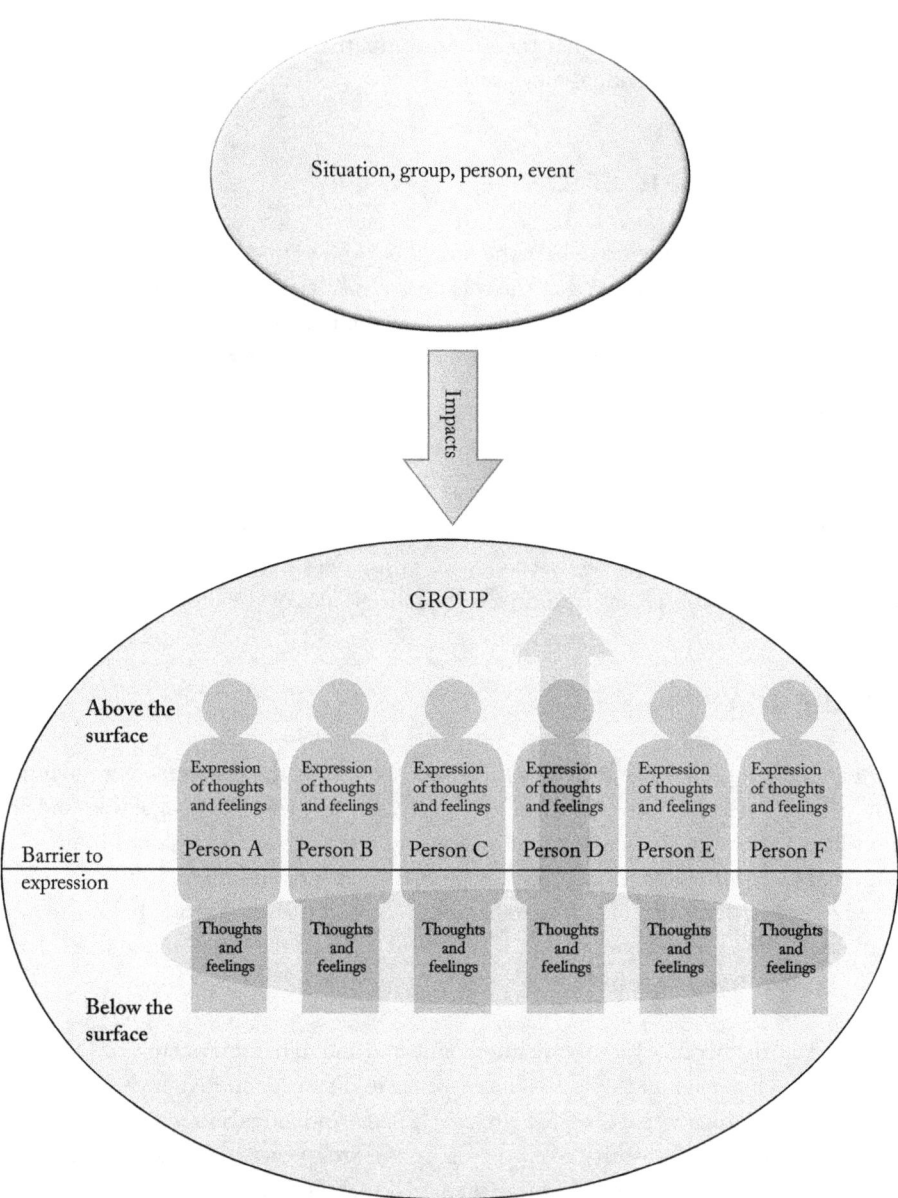

Person D has the greatest inclination or tendency for expression of particular thought or feeling, or lowest barrier and therefore expresses thought and/or feeling with the combined force or energy of his/her own and everyone else's unexpressed thoughts and/or feelings.

The ghost role

Sometimes, a role is so unpopular or so unacceptable that no one in the group feels able or willing to take on that role. Usually such a role is then allocated to someone or something outside of the group. For example, a family can decide that all members within it are fine, but that the in-laws are problematic. Psychologically, however, the role is still part of the group psyche and affects the entire functioning of the group. The way of being or archetype represented by the role will be talked about by the group and will have a significant psychological impact on everything the group does. Because the role is not occupied in person, it becomes difficult or almost impossible to successfully integrate that role into the group psyche. In this instance, the Process Work methodology (as developed by Arnold Mindell) refers to the role as a "ghost" role in the group. The facilitator's task is to ensure that the ghost role is in some way actively expressed so that it can be addressed if necessary and integrated into the larger psyche.

Roles and positions

The moment someone takes on a role, that person is effectively taking on a position, particularly in the case of political or psychological roles. Taking on a role or position is one of the ways in which an individual differentiates himself or herself in order to have a sense of identity. All roles or positions can be placed somewhere on a continuum. The minute you take a position, you are creating a "position" pair. In other words, every role can be paired with its opposite. So, the moment you take a position, its paired position is activated (e.g. criticiser and victim) and a discourse develops. Sometimes the discourse will develop under the surface and remain there for a while before it can be dealt with openly.

Each culture, whether organisational or national, will have series of discourses that define how members of that culture can make meaning for themselves. In each discourse, there is a limited number of positions, each with a particular value-base. We both position ourselves and are positioned by others. Each position defines our identity and, by implication, our degree of membership, as well as our rights, duties and responsibilities. These factors assist us in deciding how to act and what goals to pursue because they offer a way of making meaning out of our choices, being able to derive value from those choices, and ultimately being able to experience self-esteem.

A position determines to a large extent what a person is able to say. It also leads to a situation where what is said is interpreted even before it is said. Individuals can become stuck in a position or a role within a discourse in an organisation. This theory suggests that roles always lead to discourses or dances, and these will be explored in more detail below.

Role dances

Psychic life tends to be interactive rather than a unidirectional. As a result of the split between the conscious and unconscious parts within us, psychic processes are characterised by duality, in which a particular way of being elicits its opposite or complimentary way of being. The more one-sided a way of being is, the more likely it is to unconsciously evoke the opposite way of being in the self or in another.

When a way of being or behaving in the world is simplistically one-sided, the psyche will, often unconsciously, search for or manifest the other side in order to allow for the possibility of a more integrated position. The more the psyche is split, the more unacceptable the other way of being will tend to be. In a more integrated position, polarities are complementary rather than adversarial. In order to resolve the conflict caused by adversarial polarities, the psyche needs to encounter the value of the other way of being and find a way of integrating it.

The group psyche seems to work according to the same principles. But contrary to the psychic dance that is created between the conscious and unconscious in an individual, the group can play out the psychic dance between individuals occupying opposing roles. The purpose behind the dance is to allow a conversation and interaction between the polar opposite ways of being so that a more integrated position can emerge. For this to happen, though, the tension between the two ways of being needs to be held long enough and with sufficient containment for the more integrated position to emerge.

Harriet Lerner describes these role dances very well in her series of books about psychological dances. One of the most common psychological dances is one in which one of the roles is critical, and the other role is at the receiving end of criticism, and therefore becomes the victim. This dance is illustrated in the diagram on the next page.

CRITIC-VICTIM DANCE

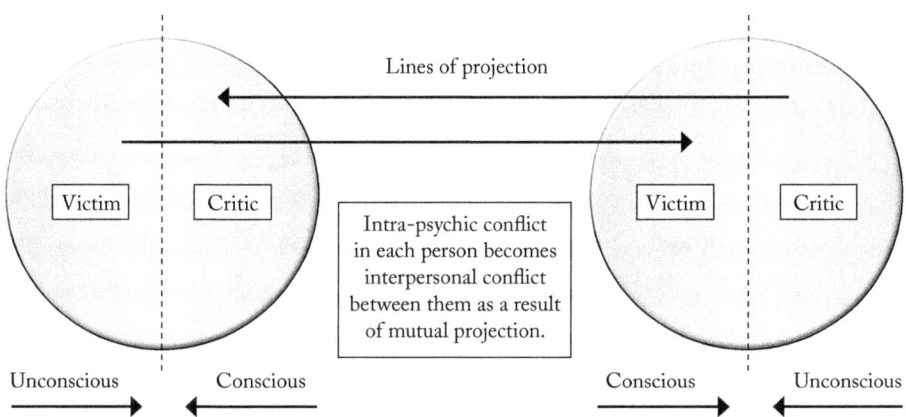

Person A with intra-psychic conflict Person B with intra-psychic conflict

The diagram illustrates how the role of critic has its pair in the role of victim. The role of critic cannot exist without the role of victim, so the minute there is a critic, a critic–victim dynamic develops. In a group psyche, an individual or sub-group will take up the critic role. Similarly, in response, a different individual or sub-group will occupy the victim role. However, whatever role an individual takes up, the unconscious carries the opposite archetypal possibility unconsciously. The dance is only complete when the critic–victim dance transcends into a transcendent third position, in which a new way of relating becomes possible – which is developmental rather than defensive. This process will be described in Chapter 13. There are many examples of these dances, and in each case they reflect the duality of one way of being versus another. Some examples are provided below:

- Pursuer – distancer
- Hard-working – lazy
- Independent – dependent
- Responsible – irresponsible
- Playful – serious
- Task-focused – people-focused.

Paradoxically, opposing roles reinforce one another's existence. The more one person takes up one role, the more the other is forced into the opposing role. Many group processes will end up, especially in a polarising process, in a role dance. The facilitator needs to help the full expression of each role, allowing the wisdom behind each role to emerge. This allows the other side to begin to see the value of the opposing side and is therefore move to a position of integrating the opposing role.

GROUP PROCESSES

Here we consider the group processes that result from the psychological dynamics described above. Obviously, there are as many group processes as there are groups. To have a meaningful discussion about some key concepts of group processes, therefore, it is useful to define some categories. From a depth perspective, at the broadest level, there are essentially two sets of processes in groups:

1. Defensive processes
2. Developmental processes.

Both of these types of important processes are needed in a healthy group. Although a facilitator will be more interested in the second set of processes, it is necessary to appreciate the value of defensive processes too – and sometimes actively support them. The two sets of processes are discussed in more detail below, after we look at anxiety, which is one of the most important driving factors behind these processes.

Defensive processes

Groups will use defensive processes when they are in situations that are threatening and provoke anxiety. The nature of group anxiety and group defence mechanisms is discussed in detail below.

Group anxiety

In Chapter 3 we discussed in detail how individuals manage anxiety. Here we are concerned with how groups manage anxiety, because as facilitators we need to help groups move through states of anxiety in order to achieve their tasks.

Individuals experience anxiety in groups on two levels. The first is individual anxiety about group membership and group issues; the second is anxiety on behalf of the group as a part of the group psyche. Regardless of the level at which the individual is experiencing anxiety, it is important to remember that anxiety is always uncomfortable and that the psyche will do everything it can to get rid of it. This means getting rid of the source of anxiety. Groups and individuals in groups will use a variety of more and less sophisticated means to get rid of sources of anxiety. We consider these group defensive processes in detail in the following pages.

Group defence mechanisms

Just as individuals have defence mechanisms, as we learned in Chapter 3, so do groups. Defence mechanisms are strategies that the group uses to reduce anxiety, essentially by obscuring, hiding or ignoring the source of the anxiety. Any impulse, way of being, feeling, or set of ideas that the group finds difficult to deal with – and therefore could cause anxiety in the group – will be suppressed or eliminated in some way if possible.

For example, openly discussing issues of incompetence could cause anxiety, so the group may defend itself against such discussions by focusing on the problems caused by demanding clients. The cause of non-delivery is then laid at the door of the clients rather than the staff members themselves. There are many more or less sophisticated ways in which groups will unconsciously or consciously work together to avoid confronting painful, embarrassing or difficult subjects. Everyone in the group will be involved in these self-deceptions, but they will not be openly planned or discussed.

Organisational defences vary, but will often be reflected in organisational processes and systems, and will determine what can and cannot be spoken about openly. Organisational defences are difficult to dismantle. These defences will interfere with task achievement and are often reinforced by the power arrangements in the organisation.

Examples of organisational defences are:

- Continual restructuring, rather than addressing power blocks
- Having a culture of meetings that seems to suggest an organisation that communicates well, but is in fact not communicating about any of the important issues
- An unbalanced focus on one part of the organisation, such as the Finance Department
- Continuing with unproductive activities, such as closing meetings with "next steps" that are never implemented.

Different methodologies have different ideas about the nature of group defences against anxiety, as well as the sources of anxiety. The Tavistock methodology (Bion) is concerned with the fact that individuals experience groups as being similar to parental figures, primarily mother figures. Individuals in a group situation will therefore experience a state of regression, in which they are plunged back into an infantile state. Depending on the nature of the infantile experiences, they may need to activate a variety of mechanisms to protect themselves in that regressed state. As we saw earlier, Bion suggested that without a clearly defined task and accessible external reality, the group would resort to dealing with this anxiety through what he calls "basic assumption" functioning. He described three basic defensive structures that groups would use.

1. **Pairing** – here the group will divide itself into sets of pairs where, in one or more instances, two group members bond together. The group will view the sets of pairs as important to survival, and there is hope that the pairs will produce an "offspring" that in some way offers salvation for the group.
2. **Fight or flight** – in this defensive process the group chooses an enemy from which it needs to withdraw or flee in order to survive, or which it needs to fight in order to survive. The group will choose various things to be defined as the enemy. It may be someone outside the group, or in fact the group task itself.
3. **Dependency** – here the group looks for one individual on whom they can depend in order to reduce the anxiety. They will look for a particular person who has a strong leadership capacity, who they hope will protect them from potential or actual threats that cause anxiety.

Bion's defensive processes listed above are interesting to keep in mind. Some facilitators work specifically with this formulation, but other theorists have added to Bion's list, and there does seem to be a variety of other ways in which groups deal with anxiety. Nonetheless, the principle that groups will find psychological defence mechanisms in order to deal with anxiety is important.

From a Jungian standpoint, people will develop defensive processes to manage the anxiety caused by the conflicting demands on an individual – usually to manage the conflict between inherent drives and the assurance of perceived or actual survival. Therefore, groups and members of groups will find ways of avoiding confrontation, either with their inner worlds or with the systems around them.

Some groups will be preoccupied with intra-group defences, while others will be pre-occupied with inter-group defences. The differences are listed in the table on the next page.

Intra-group defensive processes	Inter-group defensive processes
The group regards problems as being within the group	The group regards problems as being outside the group
A member or a sub-group is held responsible for difficulties	Individuals or groups outside the group are held responsible for difficulties
The group will struggle with its diversity	The group will regard itself as homogeneous in important aspects

Essentially, defensive processes will either place the undesirable way of being on one individual or sub-group, or will help the group to pretend in some way that it is not a problem. These can be categorised broadly into projective and denial processes. Sometimes both processes are used together. Some details of these processes are given below.

	Projective processes	Denial processes
Main activity	Scapegoating	Avoidance
View of the problem	Someone is to blame	It does not exist
Main symptoms	Conflict Lack of cooperation Membership turnover	Superficial harmony and covert tension Rigidity in behaviour Incongruities
Main defensive mechanisms	Projection Projective identification	Denial Groupthink

Mechanisms for group projective processes

There are two essential mechanisms at work in projective processes, and they operate in conjunction with one another and are dependent on one another. They are described below.

Group projection

Projection is the process by which anything that is unacceptable to the psyche is attributed to something or somebody outside of the psyche. Groups will identify with a certain set of values and ways of being, and any way of being that is seen as unacceptable will be identified with someone or some sub-group that is viewed as outside or contrary to the identity of the group. This can apply to an individual within the group or to someone or something outside of the group. Projection is the mechanism that underlies scapegoating. If we can view an undesirable way of being as belonging to somebody else, and that somebody else can be eliminated, then the problem is solved. Groups regularly choose scapegoats as ways of dealing with the existence of undesirable ways of being.

Projective identification in groups

The difficulty with projection is that it operates in conjunction with a twin mechanism called projective identification. In this mechanism, as we have seen, the recipient of the projection cooperates with the mechanism by living out the behaviour that is being projected onto him or her. It is particularly likely for projective identification to work if the recipient identifies with some aspect of the projection. Together, the projecting party and the recipient collude in the success of the defensive process. Projective identification is often present in a group that is engaged in projecting undesirable ways of being onto one individual in a group. This mechanism makes the individual susceptible to the projection, and in a way, the individual "volunteers" (albeit unconsciously) to be the scapegoat.

Mechanisms for denial processes

Similarly, there are two mechanisms at work in order to ensure the success of denial processes. Firstly, the group has to deny the existence of an undesirable way of being and, secondly, everybody has to agree.

Denial

In some way, the group has to have the ability to maintain the illusion that a way of being, or a set of thoughts or impulses does not exist. Some groups do this by focusing excessively on the opposite of that way of being. This will often be visible in a consciously constructed culture, such as: "We are all family here." These groups will actively construct a belief system and an identity that excludes unacceptable ways of being.

Groupthink
For denial processes to be successful, everyone in the group has to agree. This agreement will take the form of a voluntary process, where everyone is seen as like-minded, and it would be unthinkable and certainly undiscussable to disagree. There will be a strong unspoken taboo against questioning the validity of the identity. Belonging and agreement become the overall driving forces.

Groups that use denial processes are less likely to volunteer for depth work because the very agreement to do depth work would nullify the defence. A facilitator has to work very carefully when encountering denial processes in a group.

Maintenance of defences over time

Of course, no defensive strategy will work indefinitely, so many of the strategies have an inbuilt conclusion for which a new strategy is needed. One example is that idealisation (the making of somebody into a "messiah") cannot last indefinitely because inevitably the "messiah" turns out to be a real person. The psyche copes with this by going through continual cycles of idealisation and denigration, or in organisational terms through a messiah/scapegoat cycle. Therefore, group defences will play themselves out in patterns over time. In learning about the history of the group, the facilitator can start to see the pattern and help the group to see the pattern.

Group developmental processes

Group defensive and developmental processes do not operate in isolation from one another. Groups will often vacillate between the two, as their anxiety fluctuates over time. Also, there will be many varieties of group developmental processes, and so any ideas offered here will be generalisations at best. From a depth perspective, however, group developmental processes can be broadly described in terms of four types: relationship building processes, polarising processes, cathartic and reconciliation processes. These four broad categories are described in more detail below. In each case, the group process is described. The facilitation practices for each are described in detail in Chapter 13.

1. RELATIONSHIP BUILDING PROCESSES

All groups go through a variety of stages in terms of the development of their relationships and their ability to function cohesively. These stages can be understood in terms of the natural progression of the relationships between them, and of course closely tied to that is the development of trust and acceptance between the members.

When individuals initially come together, they come together as strangers. This means that they do not know much about each other, and certainly do not trust each other yet. Any knowledge they may have about each other will be based either on the opinions of others or on their own stereotypes that will be activated by the superficial information about one another. For example, group members may draw conclusions about one another based on their gender, race, age, profession, general appearance and a myriad other clues that may be misinterpreted when viewed subjectively.

Most models of group development indicate that if the group is to become a fully functioning unit, it will need to go through a stage of conflict. This does not have to involve overt and acrimonious conflict, but it will involve disagreement and a negotiation between diverse points of view and ways of doing things. In order for the group to pass successfully through this stage, there has to be a sense that there is mutual benefit in continuing through the difficulty together. The existence of an objective task can provide the sense of mutual benefit.

The other important stage in a group's development is the time where individuals move beyond individual viewpoints and opinions to showing their feelings and areas of vulnerability. It is very unlikely for a group to achieve tasks successfully over time if group members have not been able to acknowledge and respect each others' vulnerabilities.

Once a group has reached the fully functioning stage of group development, it will not stay there indefinitely. If it functions within an open system where change is inevitable, then new issues will continually arise. New issues will present new challenges in terms of possible differences of opinion, and the group may have to resolve these to become fully functioning again.

Importantly, every time the group gains a new member or loses a member, the group has to form as if it is a new group. The group dynamics will be affected by changes in membership and the stages will have to be negotiated from the beginning.

The different stages are summarised below:

Courting
This is the stage of politeness, where the group members do not know one another.

Individuals may avoid being confrontational at this stage. The task of this stage is for individual members to get to know one another.

Asserting
This is the stage where individuals start asserting themselves and expressing their differences in terms of opinions and beliefs. The task here is for members to risk expressing difference and see whether their differences are included in the group's functioning.

Revealing
In this stage, the group members move beyond opinions and beliefs and start revealing their preferences and feelings in a personal way. They also provide the underlying reasons for their preferences.

Fully functioning
In this final stage, the group members have accepted one another and their differences, and have found an inclusive way of working together.

2. POLARISING PROCESSES

One of the sub-processes of relationship building is that groups will encounter situations in which the group members have differing opinions. This refers to the dynamic in which groups develop two opposing viewpoints in their membership regarding particular issues, which then causes tension.

This is a direct result of the defensive processes discussed earlier (usually in the projective processes). As a result of the projections onto one another, the group will tend to divide itself into two groups: the sub-group who is right and one who is wrong (at least in the mind of the sub-group). Although this is a result of the defensive process, it provides the opportunity for development. In fact, without this polarising process it is hard to ensure that transformation happens.

The group seems inevitably to head into a dilemma, disagreement or conflict and then possible resolution. The dilemma is a necessary precursor to innovative solutions.

Obviously, the actual steps taken by each group will differ, but there are similar elements between groups. A rough guide to the steps in such a process is as follows:

1. A general discussion of the situation, the task, establishing and/or maintaining relationships
2. Surfacing or introduction of issues/listing of preoccupations

3. Sorting of issues, prioritisation of one issue either directly or indirectly
4. A move either into avoidance, which takes the group back to step 1 or 2, or deeper into the issue, which makes resolution possible
5. Development of views on the issue – many different views initially
6. Polarisation into two opposing views
7. Exploring further, defining the polarities (the two different views in the dilemma or conflict), entering into awakening of what Jung called the "transcendent function" (which produces the "transcendent third" position) and results in innovative solutions, or a quantum breakthrough of some kind.

In order to move beyond this polarisation, the group may need the help of a facilitator. The depth theory discussed in Chapter 3 suggests that whatever else we may be engaged in our conscious lives, there exists an invisible autonomous process inside us, in which the psyche is trying to integrate the split between the conscious and unconscious parts of ourselves. This underlying split inside all of us means that there tends to be two possible parts or views on any given issue. The psyche wants to resolve the dilemma and will produce ways of interacting that manifests the duality inside us. This often results in a conflict where there are two sides. In a group, the split between the two opposing views manifests as a group conflict. This brings the possibility of integration or, to use the technical term, the possibility for a transcendent third position to emerge, which resolves the conflict in a win-win way. This third position is only possible if the opportunity is allowed for a deeper conversation in which the tension of opposites is allowed. Usually groups need some support to manage such a process, but the results can be truly transformational. Depth facilitation is one way of providing this support.

3. CATHARTIC PROCESSES

Catharsis comes from the Greek word "katharos" meaning pure. It refers to a process whereby an individual or a group releases pent-up emotions and repressed thoughts by bringing them to the surface of consciousness. This is a very important process for groups because without it the group life can become septic and ill.

The human psyche (and body for that matter) has an inbuilt ability to process experiences, or digest and metabolise the things that happen to it. If we are able to express emotions, we are able to move on to new activities. However, many of the more modern cultures have chosen a way of being that discourages the expression of emotion. In particular, injunctions to "think positively" or "move on" may prevent the appropriate expression of emotion. Our capacity to heal depends on the "metabolising" function of emotions.

For many reasons, the ability to express emotions or certain thoughts may cause anxiety in a group and lead to the activation of defensive processes. The resulting suppressed thoughts and feelings become problematic for the group and will interfere with task execution. An important group process, then, is to allow for and encourage catharsis so that the group can "purify" itself. Cathartic processes may be related to past events or situations, or to the here and now that the group finds itself in. The facilitator needs to identify that a cathartic process may be needed, and provide a suitable environment and set of facilitation interventions to ensure that such a catharsis can happen.

4. RECONCILIATION PROCESSES

Sometimes a group surface process becomes blocked because group members have been harmed by each other and the relationships between them have been damaged. In this instance, the group has to enter a reconciliation process before the group can successfully complete its task. A reconciliation process will include cathartic and polarising processes, but it has additional stages that are outlined in Chapter 13.

POWER DYNAMICS IN GROUPS

One of the biggest complicating factors in groups is the fact that different people or sub-groups hold power and others hold less or none. Power differences result in complex dynamics in groups. Facilitators will invariably encounter the dynamics produced by power and difference. This section considers the key concepts that a facilitator needs to consider when working with power and difference in groups.

SOME DEFINITIONS

There is much theoretical literature written about power and authority and related concepts. Many definitions are given, and there is great complexity in the field. For our purposes, the terms below will be used in the following way:

Power:	The capacity to have an effect or an influence.
Privilege:	An advantage, right, favour or freedom from a burden.
Authority:	Power derived from office, character or prestige.
Difference:	Dissimilarity, carrying a distinguishing quality.
Rank:	The differentiated status afforded to an individual or a sub-group in a group as a result of the combination of power and privilege.

The impact of power and difference in groups

Here we consider in detail how power inequalities and other differences impact group dynamics. Most under-the-surface processes are related in some way to the complexities caused by power and difference.

If power is defined as the capacity to have an effect or influence, then it is easy to see that human beings are at their most vulnerable when they are surrounded by others who have more power than they do. Power differences evoke very strong feelings, and create a dynamic that may completely obliterate the group's capacity to fulfil a task. Group behaviour is so greatly influenced by differences in power that a facilitator can regard it as a given that power dynamics exist.

Importantly, power dynamics that are not managed consciously almost always cause conflict, and in many instances can cause wars. It is therefore a critical but difficult task to help groups manage power dynamics.

Types of rank

We can think of rank as the effect that the power and privilege held by an individual or sub-group has on its status in the group. Rank gives an individual or a sub-group influence in a group. There are many types of rank possible in groups, and rank is a relative term. An aspect that will give an individual or sub-group rank in one group will not necessarily do so in another group in a different context. There are some differences in how types of rank will affect group functioning that are useful to consider here.

Psychological rank

Confidence	Self-awareness	Sense of humour
Spirituality	Emotional literacy	Intelligence
Experience	Creativity	
Assertiveness	Authority	

Social, cultural and organisational rank

Race	Language	Expertise
Gender	Sexual orientation	Connections to networks
Culture	Class	Connections to
Religion	Economic	influential people
Age	Education	Organisational position

Physical rank

Attractiveness	Health	Able-bodiedness
Ability	Strength	

Of the above types of rank, the social, cultural and organisational rank is the most context-dependent, and the type of rank most likely to play itself out in a group situation. Group members will usually seek out sub-groups to join in terms of their social, cultural and organisational rank. Psychological rank is the most reliable form of rank, and the one over which the individual has most control.

THE PSYCHOLOGICAL IMPACT OF RANK

All people have an experience of rank differences. However, depending on early experiences, where an individual was at the mercy of a powerful caregiver, he or she may be more or less comfortable in the presence of somebody who has more rank. Individuals whose early experience was of being well cared for by a powerful figure are likely to be more comfortable with rank differences. If, however, an individual had a general experience of frustration of his or her needs and general lack of care, or even an abuse of care, then the individual would be less likely to accept rank differences. Also, whatever the individual's experience, human beings instinctively know the incredible danger of large power differences. Power differences cause anxiety and therefore invariably cause defensive behaviours, which have a massive psychological impact on all the members of the group.

THE DYNAMICS OF RANK DIFFERENCES

Rank differences are responsible for relationship dynamics in groups. The individual or sub-group that has more rank will tend to be the decision-making body in the group. Individuals or sub-groups with little or no rank will be excluded from decision-making processes, if not actively, then by a lack of inclusion. The group with little or no rank experiences the exclusion as problematic, rightly so, and eventually starts taking action in order to address the exclusion. The excluded sub-group may begin by waiting to see if the exclusion is temporary, but after a certain period it will decide to start acting to rectify the situation. However, because the individual or sub-group does not have power, it is difficult to confront the exclusion directly.

The first step towards gaining some power would be for members of the sub-group to band together or to seek out individuals who are having a similar experience. They will start having off-line (out-of-group) discussions about the exclusion and how to rectify it. Sub-groups may also start banding together more formally.

The most common example is that a group may unionise. Once a sub-group has banded together, the members may try to challenge the group with rank in order to be included in the decision-making. A sub-group may also resort to passive aggressive behaviour, resisting the decisions of the group with rank. If these strategies do not work, the sub-group may turn to some form of sabotage or terrorism to alert the dominant group to the problem.

An added dynamic in a situation of rank differences is that individuals with little or no rank may exclude themselves from decision-making processes because they do not feel confident enough to make themselves heard. This form of internalised oppression can be as debilitating as explicit oppression. Sometimes the group needs help to develop the confidence to speak up. It is important that the facilitator does not provide artificial strength in the situation. The sub-group should only be encouraged to speak up if it will be able to sustain its challenge in the absence of the facilitator.

RANK AND RESPONSIBILITY

Rank differences are a fact of life: there will always be taller and shorter people in the world. However, the way individuals with rank handle rank differences makes a big difference to the psychological impact on those with less or no rank. For rank differences to be palatable to those with little or no rank, the individuals or sub-group that hold rank need to use that rank responsibly. An example of irresponsible use of rank is when a parent enjoys beating a child at a simple game, such as a card game, or a game of sport. Another is when people who have resources waste them. People or sub-groups that use their rank responsibly do some of or all of the following:

- They are aware of the rank they hold and the privilege that it gives them
- They value the privilege that it gives them
- They are conservative with the use of the privilege

- They do not flaunt the use of their privilege
- Where possible, they share their power and privilege
- They work towards developing power and privilege in others
- They are aware of the psychological impact of the privilege.

Rank awareness

Many people, in fact most of us, are not aware of the privileges we hold. Human beings are more interested in the areas where they do not hold privilege and are more aware of feelings of deprivation than they are of feelings of satisfaction. We all tend to focus on the areas we do not hold privilege and to be acutely aware of those people around us who have rank.

When working with groups, you can expect that rank awareness and responsible use of rank may not exist. As a result, one of the key depth dynamics that you as the facilitator would work with is the psychological impact on the group of a lack of rank awareness.

Creating rank awareness

In order for a facilitation process to be successful, it is important to minimise the negative impact of rank differences on the group. The only way to ensure that this happens is to try and make those with rank aware of the impact that their rank has on the group. As facilitator, you can offer psycho-education and teach people about the rank concept, or gently try to lead the individual or sub-group to its awareness of privilege in the situation. You need to use your own psychological rank in order to bring awareness in an acceptable way to those who are exercising unconscious rank in a group.

Minorities and majorities

One of the ways that rank can exist in a group is through the existence of a majority sub-group and a minority sub-group. Arnold Mindell's Process Work methodology uses the terminology of "minority" to denote the group with less or no rank, and the term "majority" to denote the group with more rank. This use of terminology is somewhat confusing because rank does not always belong to the sub-group that is greater in numbers. In many instances, the group with more rank is in fact a smaller group. Sometimes, the minority in numbers will also be the minority in power, but this is not reliably the case. It is therefore useful to be explicit when using terms like minority and majority.

Rank inversion

One of the most difficult situations to work with is that of rank inversion. This is where someone or a sub-group that has previously held rank loses that rank, and someone or a sub-group that had previously held little or no rank, now gains rank. Effectively, there is an inversion between the two parties. Not only will the parties have the difficult thoughts and feelings normally associated with the rank position that they occupy, but they will also have to deal with change in rank and its psychological implications.

Formal versus informal rank

Another area of complication is when some members of the group have formal rank and some members have informal rank. The formal rank is often more known and visible than the informal rank, yet the informal rank could be more powerful. Formal rank refers to explicit, designated group positions that have power attached to them, such as the position of CEO or Chairperson. Informal rank usually refers to an intrinsic quality or a particular connection that an individual has in the organisation that is not explicitly recognised as providing influence, but nevertheless holds great influence, such as the staff member who has been at the organisation the longest. From a depth perspective, informal rank is likely to be more problematic because it is often related to under-the-surface processes that cannot be discussed. Unless the informal rank is acknowledged and discussed, the group is unlikely to move past the conflict caused by the rank difference.

The role of rank in projective processes

Rank differences have a major impact on the direction and success of projective processes. Unpopular ways of being will always be projected onto others if possible, and this projection is more likely to be successful if the receiving group or individual is lacking in rank. A powerful individual or sub-group will usually successfully resist the projection of an unpopular role. However, a sub-group or individual who is already carrying the role of less or no rank is sufficiently disadvantaged psychologically to become a target for other unpopular projections. It is therefore important to notice how a difference in an individual or sub-group that can become a distinguishing feature will be used by the rest of the group for the allocation of unpopular roles if possible. This will predispose the individual or sub-group to potential scapegoating. In order to protect that individual or sub-group, it is the facilitator's job to try to prevent this kind of situation or alert the group if it has already embarked on a scapegoating process.

Rank and group constitution

If you as facilitator have an option to guide a group in terms of its membership – particularly if the group is to be divided into smaller sub-groups for the purposes of task completion – then it is important to keep in mind the impact of rank and difference as discussed above. Two major depth processes exist in any South African group.

1. The issue of racial discrimination, because of our history. The political environment is now more equal, but huge economic divisions still exist between races.
2. Gender, which is the most obvious fundamental difference between people, and exists in all groups worldwide.

A debate about these two issues will appear, almost without exception, at some stage in the group's life. When it does, the representatives of the different demographic groups end up having to speak from the position of the grouping to which they belong. If there is only one person representing that demographic grouping, that person has a very difficult task – either being totally silenced, or burdened with having to carry the position alone. The person is often targeted with all the feelings the other members in the group may have about his or her particular grouping, and that is a particularly heavy burden to carry.

In South African society in general many strong feelings exist about race, and to a lesser extent gender, so facilitation sessions become complex. These kinds of depth processes, particularly of race, have the potential to hurt people enormously, and facilitators are often used to help people who have been hurt in this way. It may be impossible to address the damage once it has been done.

Ideally, group membership situations in which there is one person from a particular demographic group should be avoided if at all possible.

Conclusion

This chapter described the core ideas of a depth or "psychodynamic" view of a group. It highlighted the fact that a group will work as an integrated entity, thereby lessening the autonomy of the individuals in a group. Individuals become parts in service to the whole, rather than important in their own right. Some key group processes were discussed and group dynamics such as those caused by power or rank imbalances and scapegoating were described.

PERSONAL EXERCISES

1. Consider a group of which have you have been a member.
   - Document the group as a case. Describe the group size, the group members, the group context, the group history, the group task and intention and any other salient features.
   - Create a timeline of the group's life, listing particular trends and critical incidences or events. Imagine what would be the next logical step in the group's history.
   - Consider the group dynamics that may appear as a result of the group context and history.

2. Notice your own particular role inclinations or valencies in groups. Experiment with choosing different roles in groups.

3. Make a list of group complexes that you have seen in operation. Consider the group complexes in your family.

4. Consider the difficulties caused by rank differences in groups. Identify three examples of problematic situations and document the rank dynamics that occur. Suggest possible ways the facilitator can help the group overcome the problems caused by rank differences in these situations.

5. Consider your own areas of sensitivity in terms of rank. How do you respond when those sensitivities are triggered? Try to develop compassion for the other side, and develop a capacity to speak on behalf of the other side.

SECTION 2
YOU AS FACILITATOR

CHAPTER 5
MANAGING YOUR OWN PSYCHOLOGY

INTRODUCTION

This chapter concentrates on the process of managing yourself as a facilitator. You are a permeable human system, with your own intra-psychic conflict, role preferences and rank levels, so you will be affected by everything that happens in the groups that you work with, and they in turn will be affected by you.

If you are choosing to work as a depth facilitator, you need to be able to work with yourself at the depth level first. You cannot help groups to move below the surface if you have not experienced the challenges and difficulties of this kind of work first hand. Even if you remain at the surface level with most of the groups you work with, you will not be sensitive to the issues at the depth level that may be hampering group progress unless you have explored yourself in depth.

THE DEMANDS ON A FACILITATOR

The role of the facilitator is always potentially difficult, even if you are only working at the surface process level. Whatever the level of work, the full psychological system of the group will be active and making demands on you. Group members will project various roles onto you and have a range of psychological expectations of any group process.

These demands are even more complex when working with below-the-surface issues. There is a significant risk that the facilitator becomes part of the group process, and becomes drawn into the psychodynamics of the group. This will not serve the group in the long run.

The facilitator needs great consciousness to intervene meaningfully in the group process and there are many components to group facilitation. These range from trying to understand the emerging process of the group psyche, the power arrangements in the group, and the level of organisational readiness for working under the surface, to the work itself, which involves intervention with either the whole group or sub-groups in the organisation. These complex tasks require that facilitators can manage themselves and their own psychology very carefully. This chapter discusses various aspects related to managing yourself as a facilitator and provides some tools to help you do so.

THE IMPORTANCE OF SELF-AWARENESS

Self-reflection and the self-awareness that comes from it is a critical part of a facilitator's role. Without self-awareness, great muddles occur. Self-awareness means greater consciousness of what you are doing, and what you are trying to achieve at the deepest level. Often we are unaware of our impact on others, and so may not understand why others are being difficult. We may unwittingly be eliciting anxiety, and it is only with self-awareness that we can address this. Often we feel compelled to achieve something and may be driven by our complexes. The power of the complex blinds us to the need for and validity of other perspectives. The diagram below shows the value of self-reflection and self-awareness.

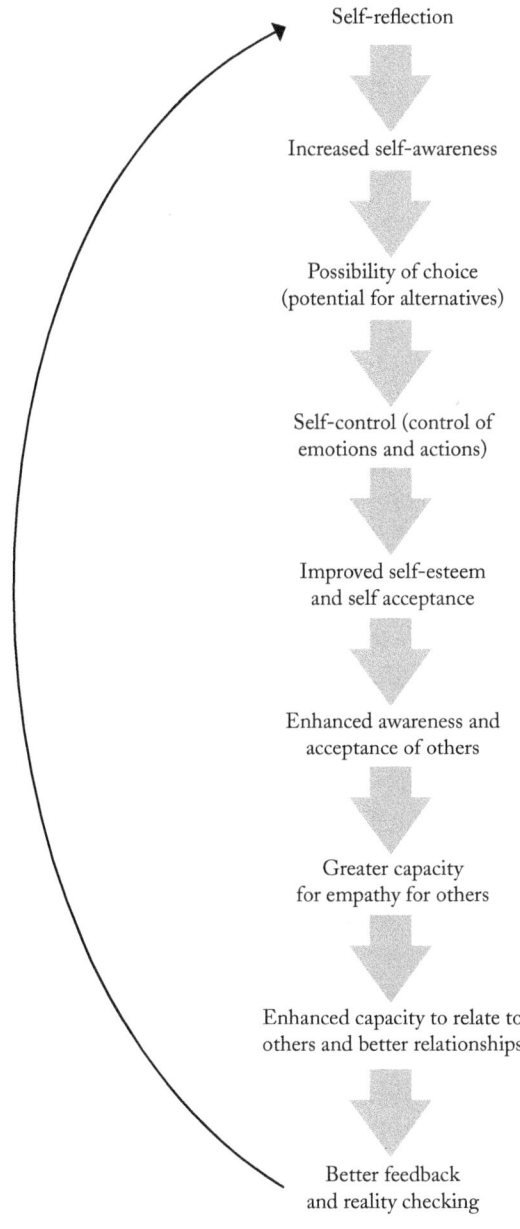

The diagram indicates that self-reflection and the capacity to relate well to others are linked and work in a self-reinforcing loop. However, because self-reflection is often hard and painful, it is often avoided. In order to be a good facilitator you must be prepared to confront the difficulty of self-reflection, because without it you are likely to contaminate the group with your own psychology.

Self-reflection means continually investigating your own behaviour, and understanding what is driving you to do what you do. It requires being aware of your own responses and particularly your own feelings. Many of us distract ourselves unwittingly from our experience, especially if we were never taught how to understand and manage ourselves. It is particularly important for facilitators to explore their unconscious processes because these will affect them in often unpredictable and counter-productive ways if ignored.

AN ATTITUDE OF NEUTRALITY

We briefly mentioned the importance of neutrality in the definition of facilitation in Chapter 1. If you are occupying the role of a "pure" facilitator – in other words you are not holding dual roles such as leader and facilitator or trainer and facilitator – then it is central to your role to be neutral about the outcomes that a group is pursuing. This does not mean that you do not express opinions about the appropriateness of the process the group is following, rather that you are neutral about the content and outcomes.

We can only facilitate human depth processes if part of the self remains neutral and maintains enough awareness to follow the process impartially as it unfolds. Neutrality is much harder in practice than in theory. Many people misunderstand the notion of neutrality. Neutrality does not mean not caring about an issue, or not having an opinion about it. It does mean personally exploring both sides of an issue fully, so that you can identify the logic and even wisdom of both sides of the issue. In order to ensure this, it is first necessary to allow yourself to experience your lack of neutrality as fully as possible. This does not mean expressing it in front of a group, but allowing yourself to think and feel as much as you can about your position on an issue. The more you allow your experience, the easier it will be to eventually see the other side. This requires extensive psychological agility and means exploring as broad a range of archetypes as possible within yourself and your life experience.

Loss of neutrality can happen for many reasons. You can become identified with a role in a group and/or become caught in a projection from the group or a sub-group. You can be caught in one of your own complexes. You can develop or hold an opinion about the "right" course of action for a group and not be able to relinquish your opinion sufficiently in order to serve the group well. Most facilitators will be caught by a lack of neutrality at some point in their work with groups. It is not too serious if you lose neutrality, but it is important to recognise it quickly, and recover your neutrality. Moving back towards neutrality quickly is an advanced skill that develops only through active inner work and a great deal of practice. Although neutrality is an ideal to strive for, rather than a steady state, it is important to hold an attitude of neutrality – at least intellectually – and to notice if you are moving away from it.

The inner work exercise that follows will help you develop your capacity to maintain neutrality.

INNER WORK

Inner work is the process by which we confront our own difficulties, identify and allow our own underlying processes, and realise our own potential. Every time we work with a group or an individual, our psyche will engage with the individual's or group's psyche and new processes will emerge. In order to maintain our neutrality and thereby be able to truly facilitate, we continually need to do inner work. It requires working with our thoughts, feelings, body experiences, symptoms and fantasies. Inner work requires attention, perseverance and a great deal of time for reflection. It also takes practice.

INNER WORK EXERCISE

The following steps for doing inner work in almost any situation combine different psychological theories. The questions are designed to help you think through a particular situation in which you find yourself. It may be a facilitation situation, or it may be a personal relationship situation. It allows you to analyse what may be happening for you and the other person from a depth perspective. You can also use these questions to analyse past situations. Although it may be too late now to change their outcomes, it could give you insight about your own psychological make-up and potential vulnerabilities as a facilitator.

Given an interpersonal situation:

1. What is the situation? Who are the characters (the people involved) and what are the issues?

2. What are you feeling, thinking, experiencing? Try to describe your responses in detail.

3. Have you experienced a heightened emotional, mental or physical reaction? What is it?

4. What are your edges?

5. Are you using any defence mechanisms? What are they?

6. Who has rank in the situation and why?

7. What is happening for the other(s)? Try not to interpret, but describe their reactions, behaviours, observable emotions.

8. What could be their edges?

9. Do you notice whether they are using any defence mechanisms?

10. What could have been done or could still be done to make both parties feel safer and less anxious? What could be done to manage the rank differences in the situation? Try to establish what the pattern of behaviour is between the two parties. What are the two (or more) differing viewpoints in the situation? What are the roles/positions/archetypes that each party is taking? What is the plot? What is the drama being played out? What archetypal story is being played out? (We discussed earlier that patterns tend to consist of two polarities that are opposing, but intrinsically linked, such as persecutor – victim; unheard minority – autocratic authority; pursuer – distancer; overfunctioner – underfunctioner; emotional expression – unemotional withdrawal. There are many potential patterns, and they function in a self-reinforcing way.)

12. Try to identify whether you have seen this pattern before. Could this be repetition compulsion? (This idea refers to the fact that individuals will continue to recreate personal and relationship patterns that resemble those established in earlier situations where emotional complications occurred, in an attempt to heal the wounds caused by those situations.)

13. What part of yourself are you maybe not acknowledging or possibly giving to or projecting onto someone else? (We argued earlier that these patterns exist intra-psychically, with one part or role of the pattern remaining unconscious, and the other more palatable role existing as a conscious characteristic. For example, you will identify with the "unheard minority" part, but be unconscious of the part of you that is an "autocratic authority". The part that remains unconscious and that you do not identify with consciously will usually be projected or "given to" the other.)

14. How could the part that you are projecting onto the other be useful in your own life? (For example, the other person may irritate you because he or she is too silly and irresponsible. You may in fact be too serious and may need to develop your playful side.)

15. How can you integrate that part of yourself? In other words, how can you develop the previously unconscious part of yourself (which you may have been projecting onto the other) in a healthy and useful way, in order to achieve more balance in your life?

16. What could be done now to address the situation?

Inner work is even more important when a facilitator is engaged in depth work. When working with depth processes, the facilitator is actively engaging with unconscious dynamics and is therefore much more susceptible to being affected by them. The task of the group is not as clear as in surface facilitation, and there is no clearly defined process to follow. These factors complicate the work, and make it far more demanding for the facilitator. In depth processes, the mechanisms of projection and projective identification are actively employed by group members to manage the challenges of working with potentially threatening unconscious processes. It is highly likely that as the facilitator you may become a target for these mechanisms and because they are very powerful, you may easily be caught up in them.

Getting hooked

To reiterate, the facilitator needs to avoid getting caught up in the psychological dynamics of the group in order to remain attentive to the whole of the group psyche. The term "getting hooked" is one way of describing getting caught in projective processes. Getting hooked means to be drawn into an unconscious dynamic through the mechanism of projective identification, and therefore being drawn into fulfilling a role for the group. The following are signs indicating that the facilitator has got hooked:

- Experiencing a stronger than usual emotion and not being able to move through it
- Feelings of protectiveness towards certain members of the group
- A desire to repeat yourself, or actual repetition of a certain point of view
- An inability to observe without intervention
- Feelings of dislike towards individual group members or a sub-group
- Arguing with the group
- Offering unsolicited services
- Stepping outside of your brief
- Breaking agreements

- Justifying behaviours to yourself or the group
- Heightened feelings of anxiety when working with the group
- Feeling "right" or being "right"
- Feelings of investment in a particular decision or process.

In order to avoid getting hooked, you as the facilitator need to go through an inner work process to understand your susceptibility to a particular projection or role.

INNER WORK IN FRONT OF A GROUP

Often the facilitator gets hooked without having the benefit of a break in which to spend time doing the necessary inner work. In order to manage this, the facilitator has to take action to prevent contaminating the group. As a facilitator you have the following options:

1. Avoid any further interventions that emphasise your one-sidedness.
2. Actively take the other side to the one with which you over-identified, in order to provide balance.
3. Do the necessary inner work in front of the group without involving the group.
4. Practise self-disclosure and share with the group your awareness of having been hooked.

Which of the options above you choose depends on the group's experience of depth work, the sensitivity and depth of the process, and your capacity to do inner work. A group that is experienced in depth work will be more likely to understand and appreciate self-disclosure and will be able to use it to further the process. A less experienced group may feel uncontained with that level of self-disclosure.

ONGOING INNER WORK

It is imperative that a depth facilitator is actively engaged in ongoing inner work. Continual work on your self-awareness is necessary because new situations may produce new blind spots. Try to maintain as accurate a picture as possible of:

- Your complexes and the roots of these complexes
- Your chosen defence mechanisms
- Your edges
- Your own symptoms of anxiety
- Your role inclinations
- Areas where you hold rank

- Areas where you do not hold rank
- Mechanisms that contain you
- The developmental processes of your life stage and current situation

It is useful to have a professional partner for your inner work process. This can be a therapist, a coach, a supervisor or a peer. It is helpful to have a formalised relationship with this partner, in which the boundaries and scope of the work are specified. If you expect groups to commit resources to you as a facilitator, then you need to be able to commit resources to your own depth process. If you have a particularly traumatic or difficult psychological history, then it is recommended that you engage in long-term therapy.

MANAGING TRANSFERENCE

Regardless of the facilitator's capacity for neutrality, group members will not necessarily feel neutral about the facilitator. The facilitator will be a likely target for group projections. Like any of the other defence mechanisms, projection is a way of coping with the unconscious material or subject matter that feels threatening to us either because it is not in keeping with our self-image or because it is considered a social taboo. With projection, we take an inherent or potential characteristic (or experience, feeling or thought) and in order to minimise its potential impact on us, we view it as being part of the "other" rather than ourselves. We can of course have instances of positive or negative projection.

As we saw in Chapter 3, transference refers to projection that happens over time in a relationship – a transfer of feelings that originally belonged to a parent or other authority figure. Any long-term relationship in which feelings or experiences associated with an earlier relationship are replayed between two people could be considered transference. It has been shown that our unconscious minds will find situations in which those relationships can be replayed in order to allow for healing of the psyche.

As a facilitator you are a very likely object for transference from individual group members or the whole group psyche. You hold a position of authority in the group and this is one of the key triggers for transference. The likelihood of transference onto you is even higher in depth work because unconscious material is being tapped into and you are playing a containing role. This may lead to a similar transference process as would occur in a therapeutic setting.

Group members may start relating to you as if you are the perfect parent, the guru or the distant, withholding parent. The difficulty with transference in a relationship is that it distorts individuals' perceptual ability, and they will only see what they want in the facilitator, which will confirm the transference. This mechanism is useful in a therapeutic process where it can be used bring understanding. In a facilitated session, however, transference cannot be used in the same way to serve individual group members; it is more likely to cause difficulty for the work of the facilitator.

To avoid unhelpful transference as much as possible, you as facilitator need to be as authentic as you can be without compromising your neutral attitude. This lessens the potential idealisation of the facilitator. You can carefully practice self-disclosure to balance and neutralise the type of transference that has developed.

Transference tends to consist of either a set of fairly negative projections or a set of fairly very positive projections. The one-sidedness is characteristic of projection, as a real relationship will have both negative and positive components. More information is given below about how to deal with either of these options.

MANAGING COUNTER-TRANSFERENCE

Counter-transference refers to the facilitator's psychological response to transference. As we mentioned in Chapter 3, if someone views you as very nurturing, it is highly likely that you will start feeling an urge to nurture that person. Because transference arises from the unconscious, it triggers very intense feelings in the person who is experiencing transference. Similarly, the person who receives the transference may start experiencing an intense response. Invariably, these subtle psychological processes occur between two individuals who each have a need, and because a certain complementarity exists between them. A facilitator is therefore always vulnerable to a strong counter-transference response. You cannot necessarily avoid a counter-transference response, but is really important to handle it correctly.

The most important thing to do when experiencing counter-transference feelings is to remember the purpose of the facilitation role. As facilitator, you are primarily there to assist the group to meet its own objectives, so any experiences or events need to be used to further that purpose. This means that any feelings of counter-transference should be seen as information about what is happening in the group and used to assist the group to achieve its tasks. More detail about how to handle counter-transference is given in the specific situations discussed below.

Managing positive projections

You might imagine that it would be easy to manage positive projections. In many ways, though, a positive projection is much harder to manage than a negative projection.

Common language for the psychological phenomenon of positive projection would be terms like "falling in love", or "admiration", or "hero worship". I do not know of any human being who does not enjoy being viewed positively, and so it is very hard to be neutral when this happens.

If the group member has a very strong, positive transference onto the facilitator, the facilitator will be tempted to over identify with the role that is being projected. The facilitator will be seen as all-good, all-powerful, completely fair or in some other way an ideal figure. It is important that the facilitator dispels these one-sided notions. Some of the following guidelines may help.

- Remember that there are aspects of the positive projection that are true and based on reality, and that the facilitator possesses a legitimate and genuine response to positive qualities. However, it is not the full picture; any facilitator is human and also possesses qualities that are problematic or unedifying.
- Ensure that your self-esteem is intact (or as intact as possible), and do inner work until you can comfortably accept a realistic picture of yourself.
- Practise careful self-disclosure that offers some reality testing for the unrealistic projections. In other words, carefully reveal your clay feet.
- Actively assist the group member to explore his or her projected material as aspects of him- or herself.
- Avoid interpersonal interactions that could fuel the positive projection. Do not treat the person as special in any way.
- Avoid claiming any particular way of being as exclusively your own.
- At all times remember the contract that defines the interaction between you and the group. You have an ethical responsibility to fulfil the contract and avoid interpersonal interactions that could jeopardise it. Maintain your professionalism.

MANAGING NEGATIVE PROJECTIONS

Managing negative projections and a strong negative transference also has its challenges. It is very painful when someone is unable to see any of your positive qualities and only focuses on the negative qualities. As a facilitator, your inner critic may be evoked in such a situation, and you could start feeling ashamed and become debilitated by the projections. Some guidelines on how to work with negative projections are given below.

- Ensure that your self-esteem is intact (or as intact as possible), and do inner work until you can comfortably accept a realistic picture of yourself.
- Do not take the negative projection personally. The group member is caught in a mechanism that most likely has its roots in childhood, and therefore the opinion or judgement is not an accurate adult assessment of your qualities as a person.

- Use the feelings that are elicited as information about the group and how it functions.
- Ensure that you treat all group members consistently and with equal care, regardless of their behaviour towards you.
- Avoid any urge to discuss the individual carrying the negative projection with any other members of the group.
- Maintain your professionalism.

Managing the demands of individual members

Occasionally, individual group members will demand special attention from the facilitator. This could happen because the individual has a strong transference onto the facilitator or because the individual is having difficulty with the group and is seeking support from facilitator. As a facilitator you need to engage with the individual in a professional and friendly way, but avoiding any special treatment of that person. If an individual comes to you with a particular problem or request that relates to group functioning, you should always encourage the individual to bring the problem into the group directly.

Sometimes an individual seeks advice on a personal level that is not necessarily directly related to the group. In this instance, you may be able to provide the advice, but always need to check first that it is not a group issue in disguise. Ideally, you should try to defer contact with an individual on unrelated personal issues until after the session.

THE INNER CRITIC

As a facilitator, one of the most difficult inner voices to manage is that of your "inner critic". This constitutes a voice inside that is continually berating you for your poor performance or numerous inadequacies. If you grew up in an environment where your self-esteem was not supported and you were continually criticised, you may have internalised this situation by developing a harsh (and unrealistic) inner critic. This inner critic will often be projected onto the group and you will become defensive about your imagined inability to meet the needs of the group. It sometimes happens that the inner critic coincides with an attack from the group. This situation can only be navigated if you become aware of the projection and introduce a neutralising or transcendent voice, such as that of compassion. In other words, try to have a balanced view of yourself and your abilities. If your inner critic is so severe that it becomes debilitating, then it is usually out of balance and inner work.

BARRIERS TO AWARENESS

Awareness is one of the most important tasks of a facilitator – being aware of yourself and of others. Continual reflection is necessary to maintain awareness.

There are many things that could become barriers to awareness, and your own psychological make-up is a large factor. Beware of the following barriers to awareness:

- Feeling tired. Try to avoid facilitating if you are tired and ensure that you get enough rest before, during and after facilitation work.
- Losing your neutrality because you have a vested interest or a strong opinion about the group and its process.
- Thinking that you know what to expect from a group and not leaving room for surprises. All groups have the capacity to behave in an unexpected or unusual manner.

PAYING ATTENTION TO DEPTH PROCESSES

It is important as a facilitator to pay attention to signals from the group that are different from the surface process. "Surface" attention is the awareness needed to accomplish goals, to do your daily work, to appear the way you want to appear. "Depth" attention focuses on things you normally neglect, on external and internal subjective, irrational experiences. This means paying attention to the messages from the unconscious, to incongruous behaviour, and the accidents and slips of the tongue that happen every day. A facilitator needs depth attention (an ability to notice messages that occur just below the surface) in order to work with a group holistically. It is only possible to have this depth attention if you can be quiet within yourself.

PROTECTING YOURSELF

Although playing a facilitation role is often rewarding and enriching, it can be dangerous or destructive to the self if not managed carefully. One of the skills of a good facilitator is the ability to sense underlying processes, but this is only possible through an attitude of openness, which makes you potentially vulnerable. As discussed, a facilitator is frequently the target of projection for all feelings and ideas relating to authority, leadership, and therefore parenting. These projections are of the most powerful of all interpersonal processes, and need to be treated with care.

Very strong negative projections have the capacity to produce symptoms in the facilitator. In other words, without a strong sense of self, someone else's strong negative projection can make you sick. It is therefore vital for a facilitator to do inner work when becoming aware of a negative projection, and consciously to avoid falling into a dance that will feed the projection.

ATTACKS ON THE FACILITATOR

Groups and individuals will attack facilitators in various ways. These attacks often stem from the projections held by the group members. It is important always to remember that it is the role that is being attacked and/or demanded of and if a facilitator gets "hooked" and becomes defensive, the attack or the underlying conflict will be perpetuated. It is also important to resist any pressure to feed or rescue a group member because this simply feeds the projection. If the facilitator chooses to fulfil a role, it must be done consciously, openly and with awareness. Without consciousness, there is a great risk, as we have mentioned before, that the facilitator will be treated either as the "messiah" or scapegoat.

POPULARITY AS A FACILITATOR

As a facilitator you may sometimes need to be unpopular. Since you are taking care of the whole group, and sometimes even the whole system, you will sometimes appear to be working against a particular view or sub-group or even person. Sometimes that person may be the leader.

It is important to be able to relinquish your need to be liked, approved of and admired in the short term, and sometimes even in the long term. Sometimes you have to hold a group back from entering into a depth process because not everyone in the group is ready. Here, you can be unpopular and hold the group at its edge or you can do what the dominant part of the group wants which may cause the group to hurt itself. The reason to hold the group at its edge is to ensure that everyone is ready and thereby eliminate unnecessary pain. During conflict there is often reluctance for group members to stand strongly for an unpopular role or opinion. If the facilitator takes that unpopular role, then the minority can attack the facilitator instead of an individual group member. Otherwise the minority is forced to attack the majority group or become saboteurs. As facilitator you must be clear and congruent in taking the unpopular role.

Sometimes resolutions cannot be reached. If for time reasons you need to move on from a conflict before both sides feel comfortable, it is your responsibility as the facilitator to tell the group you are moving on, but that the issue is not resolved and will surface again.

LEADERSHIP AND FACILITATION

A facilitator differs from a leader in that the facilitator is interested in the well-being of the entire group, not just for the group's sake but for its relationship to the world. A leader will set direction in terms of the tasks of a team. A facilitator will only set direction in terms of process. A facilitator should never inhibit the emergence of leadership within the group.

THE FACILITATOR'S NEED FOR CONNECTION

In order to manage the above situations and potential problems correctly, it is suggested that you, the facilitator, primarily need to manage your own needs for connection and relationships outside of your professional engagements. Actively pursue your social and interpersonal needs in a private, personal arena, and do not use facilitation work for this purpose. Everyone is lonely sometimes, or in need of company or affirmation, and sometimes it is very tempting to have your needs met by your clients. You are there to meet the client's needs, not the other way around. Here are some guidelines to ensure this:

- Make sure you meet your personal needs outside of the groups you facilitate.
- Do not mix personal and professional relationships.
- Work hard to acknowledge your own needs, so that they do not take you by surprise.
- Actively develop interests outside of facilitation, so that facilitation does not become the primary vehicle for establishing your self-esteem.

REST AND RECOVERY

In order to manage the interpersonal arena well, you need to make sure that you rest and recover after facilitation sessions. It is extremely psychologically burdensome to facilitate a depth process. You need to be able to contain and simultaneously experience what the group is going through. This means you cannot resort to normal defensive processes that the psyche would use to protect itself. One of the ways we protect ourselves against the pain of others is to use the defence mechanism of isolation, where we separate the feeling from the thinking in a situation. Facilitators who practise isolation or other similar defences will not be sufficiently compassionate about what the group is going through. You need to remain undefended and be able to contain yourself through potentially strong emotions. You can only do this if you are well-rested and well cared for psychologically.

It is therefore important to prepare yourself well before doing this work, and to ensure that you are well rested after it.

CONCLUSION

Inner work is a critical part of being a facilitator. It needs to be an ongoing process. At some times in your work life, you may need to embark on a more intensive course of inner work and use formal processes such as therapy. The process of inner work and self-reflection is often painful and harrowing, but it can also be delightful and playful. Either way, it needs to become part of your life as a facilitator.

PERSONAL EXERCISES

1. Consider your inner critic, and document what it might say. Investigate the validity of the accusations. Reframe those accusations in a compassionate way.

2. Identify possible barriers to your awareness.

3. Consider you need to be liked. How can you manage your potential unpopularity as a facilitator?

4. Reflect on the extent to which you do inner work currently. Is it working? Plan an inner work regime for yourself.

5. Make a list of all the archetypes you can think of that you actively play out in the world and then consider the specifics below in more detail.
   - Consider the roles that you are most comfortable taking up in a group.
   - Identify the roles that you are least comfortable taking up in a group.
   - Identify any roles that you take up in a group but that you would prefer not to.
   - Identify the roles that you never take up but would like to.
   - Identify three behavioural patterns that you find yourself being part of.

6. Identify a relationship in which you experienced a strong transference with a figure of authority. Consider how you felt in that relationship and how you treated the other person. What were your expectations? What changed the transference?

7. In what way does a real relationship feel different from one based on transference?

8. Identify the signs to look for in order to identify the presence of transference.

9. Identify areas of vulnerability that may complicate your work as a facilitator. Devise an action plan for addressing the vulnerable areas.

CHAPTER 6:
THE ETHICS AND METASKILLS OF A FACILITATOR

INTRODUCTION

This chapter considers the general attitudes that a facilitator should have in order to work with integrity with groups. The area of ethics is considered the primary attitude that ensures the group is fundamentally cared for so we will discuss this first. We will then consider a variety of metaskills, or general philosophies and attitudes, that form a strong foundation for the tools and techniques discussed later under facilitation practice.

THE ETHICS OF FACILITATION

Ethics refer to the values that a facilitator holds, and to the capacity to implement those values in all interactions despite difficulties. A facilitator needs to have both "an ethical attitude", which is described below, and to abide by specific ethical guidelines that relate to facilitation. In this section, we describe the idea of an ethical attitude in detail, and then consider some of the ethical rules or standards that are appropriate to facilitation.

An ethical attitude

The term "an ethical attitude" (a term used by Hester McFarland Solomon, in her book The Self in Transformation) is used to describe an approach whereby the individual feels bound to examine his or her motives and ethics in a given situation. In order to integrate some of the elements of the unconscious, it helps if the individual has the ethical drive to avoid the path of least resistance, and rather look beyond the obvious in order to observe the negative impact of his or her behaviour. This only happens if the individual has sufficient empathy for others to have developed a moral centre. Empathy, although a potential in all of us, needs to be developed. However, if the primary care-giving in an individual's life is inadequate, the capacity for empathy may be underdeveloped, which could compromise the functioning of the individual's moral compass.

An ethical attitude implies that as a facilitator you take responsibility for your impact on others and investigate whether you are behaving in ways that may unconsciously or even consciously exploit or take advantage of others. If you are a good facilitator, you consider whether your actions are in line with your feelings and your words. You notice if you are giving mixed messages or your behaviour is confusing to others. You are open to feedback and take it seriously enough, regardless of its source, to check whether it may have some validity for you. To move towards greater psychic integration it is important to take responsibility for your actions and to bear the burden of having hurt others, even unwittingly, and do the necessary reparation.

There is a positively reinforcing cycle that becomes possible if you work on developing your morality. In other words, the stronger your ethical attitude, the greater your capacity for increased self-awareness, and the greater your self-awareness, the greater your capacity for an ethical attitude. It is therefore important to do inner work regularly, as described in the previous chapter.

Ethical guidelines

In any profession there are certain ethics that are important to maintain professionalism and protect recipients of the service. The guidelines offered here apply to facilitation generally, whether you work as an internal or external facilitator. No formal universal code of conduct exists as yet for facilitators, but the following underlying ethics should form part of all facilitation work.

1. All facilitation work should be kept confidential unless otherwise agreed between all parties. This includes not giving feedback to a leader or manager who commissioned the facilitator if such a leader was not present in the session itself. Feedback can only be given to the leader if there was an explicit contract to do so and the group gives it agreement about the nature and content of the feedback to be given.
2. As a facilitator you should behave professionally at all times, including practicing sound time-keeping, record-keeping and administration.
3. There should be openness between you, the client and all session participants about the agenda of any given session. You should not collude with any hidden agendas.
4. You must be honest with the client and the participants about their own levels of competency and practice self-disclosure when it is required. If the group requires a depth intervention and you are not experienced enough to do so, you needs to inform the client.
5. You must be honest about the underlying motivation for any given facilitation activity. If group members ask about the reason for a specific intervention, you need to explain the thinking behind the chosen intervention. This ensures facilitation rather than manipulation. Facilitation techniques may only be used if they are deemed to be in the interests of the client group as a whole.
6. You must uphold any agreements you make with a client and group members. Ideally, major agreements should be documented, but a lack of documentation does not provide the license to break agreements.
7. You need to be committed to ongoing inner work, self and professional development. This includes inner work when you feel that your neutrality may be compromised.
8. In the case of difficulty, the facilitator must be available for conflict resolution processes in order to address client concerns.

METASKILLS

A skill is a practised ability. A metaskill is a subtle, yet fundamental way of being that influences all facilitation behaviour, and ultimately separates successful from unsuccessful facilitation. The idea of "metaskills" comes from Amy Mindell's book called Metaskills. Metaskills are the attitudes that the facilitator brings to the use of any skill or technique and are therefore more important than the individual technique or skill. Individuals and groups respond first to your metaskill and only then to the skill or technique. The same technique applied with different metaskills can have very different results. Metaskills will shape the way that you, as a facilitator, apply all the skills, techniques and methodologies that you ever learnt. Without the right metaskills, the tools and techniques will not unleash the potential in a group.

It is important as a facilitator to continually do inner work in order to discover what attitude or metaskill you are bringing to an intervention. Some important metaskills are listed below.

Compassion

Compassion is probably the most important metaskill. It refers to the capacity to genuinely understand another person's point of view without judging the merits of that point of view. It is also critical that as a facilitator you enter this kind of work with an open mind. In other words, you know that you do not in fact know what the group will do and that anything is possible in the group. You need to be open to the unfolding of a story that you have never seen before. The atmosphere of a facilitation session is to a large extent determined by the level of compassion available in the session.

Compassion is an attitude in which you appreciate all the aspects of group life. Among others, these may include productivity and a lack of productivity, conflict states and reconciliation. Favouring certain group ways of being and subtly or overtly disapproving of others could mean that a group does not follow the process that may move it to resolution or creativity. Also, any feedback given to an individual group member or the group as a whole without compassion will leave them feeling attacked rather than helped.

Compassion can also be described as having empathy for the full variety of human experience. According to Amy Mindell, in her book entitled Metaskills, compassion involves nurturing, caring for and attending to those parts of ourselves that we like and identify with, while attending equally to and appreciating those parts that we do not like, that we disavow and that are far removed from how we identify ourselves. Therefore, compassion means allowing all aspects of our experience and allowing each to unfold. A compassionate facilitator also shows compassion for the self, embracing the vulnerability of being human and mortal.

Playfulness

Playfulness is a helpful metaskill in certain situations. It allows a sense of freedom from our ordinary identities and societal rules. Play expert Fred Donaldson says that true play has two rules:

- Everyone is invited
- No one gets hurt.

Playfulness sometimes helps the facilitator to approach in a safe way experiences that provoke anxiety. As children, we initially approached the world with an amazement and joy in the magical and unpredictable elements of life. Through play, we again have access to this worldview. Playfulness means using our senses and acknowledging the sensual information we gather from the world all the time. This gives us access to our broader identity and often provides valuable feedback about depth processes.

Humour and laughter often characterise play, bringing forth emotions and thoughts that relieve stress and reduce conflict. The energy behind playfulness is best captured if you watch small animals play. Nevertheless, it is important to judge when playfulness would be appropriate or not. Humour is sometimes used inappropriately as a defence mechanism. If you are unsure whether humour would be a good idea, then it is usually better to refrain from it.

Humour is a powerful metaskill if you as facilitator can use it to manage yourself and your own idiosyncrasies and foibles. It helps to reduce transference if can be playful about yourself and your difficulties in the world.

Detachment

Detachment is the ability to maintain clarity and direction amid chaos. It does not, however, only mean being uninvolved, as it is so often interpreted. A more accurate view of detachment is the ability to experience the present so fully that it moves through you swiftly and completely. This may sometimes mean that the facilitator will experience emotions with great force. Amy Mindell says that detachment is a feeling in which we are released from the apparent situation, when we step back and discover a "meta" (or outside) point of view. Detachment becomes possible when you have moved through a feeling or "processed" it, not when you have avoided it.

Fluidity

Fluidity refers to the facilitator's ability to flow with the group's process rather than to control it tightly. This is particularly important when working as a depth facilitator. If you become rigid about achieving a certain outcome, it is likely that the group will sense your resistance and start to push against you as the facilitator. The energy in a group ebbs and flows, and you need to be able to manage this movement without becoming anxious and trying to direct the path that the group takes.

Of course, if you are facilitating a surface process only, then it may be important to direct the group more firmly in terms of the path it takes. Depth facilitation, however, requires a far more non-directive style, especially in the early stages of a group's exploration beneath the surface. The unconscious processes in a group are often circuitous, precisely because they provoke anxiety and the group is negotiating an "edge". If you become too directive, the anxiety of a group will rise and become debilitating.

Intelligence

Here we are not referring to the traditional definition of intelligence, which emphasises intellectual competence. Intelligence can be seen as a holistic ability or metaskill that includes all kinds of knowledge and wisdom. It is the ability to combine resources in new and innovative ways. It involves the capacity to learn though trial and error. Intelligence comes from a breadth of experience and is enhanced by the depth of that experience. The more we expose ourselves to the ways of the world, the better we will live within that world. Intelligence involves all the senses, as world information comes in many forms. Intelligence is essentially the ability of the organism to self-organise in the interests of survival. Therefore, the broader our life experience, the better our ability to self-organise consciously. Intelligence does not refer to an isolated skill. Also, it seems, intelligence can be learnt.

Discipline

Discipline is the ability to manage the self and to do what needs to be done in any given situation. It is the ability to harness the self for appropriate action and be able to follow through with a chosen course of action even if it becomes difficult to persevere.

Discipline involves having clarity of purpose and a sense of personal responsibility and power. Discipline needs to be self-centred, as an action arising from integrity and therefore an integrated self, rather than the practice of mindlessly adhering to rules. Discipline is not compromised by a lack of resources or a lack of cooperation from others. It is the result of commitment. However, discipline includes careful self-maintenance to ensure balance and sustainability.

Courage

Courage refers to the ability to approach difficult group situations and not shy away from conflict or intense emotions. Groups are often particularly demanding emotionally and they require the facilitator to be strong in the face of challenging interpersonal interactions. With depth work particularly, you are exposed to under-the-surface material that sometimes appears in an explosive way. It is important that you have the ability to stay calm in these situations and maintain a neutral position. This requires a quiet and centred sense of self amidst potential chaos.

Humility

This metaskill refers to the capacity to let go of the need to be the expert in a situation. The facilitator needs to remember that others ultimately know best what is good and right for themselves, or at least they know best what they can or cannot manage.

As a facilitator it is important to remember how to learn, and that we never know everything. It is important to let go of a need to be the knowledgeable one. Approach a group with an open mind (what Arnold Mindell calls a "beginner's mind") because each group story is, at least to some extent, new and unique.

Patience

The metaskill of patience is best captured in the concept of fishing. True fishing is done when you cast your line into the water and then wait, knowing that eventually, if a fish is there, it will bite. It also means knowing and accepting that sometimes there are no fish. Having the ability to be patient means having the knowledge that the process is unfolding at its own pace. Often a group may become impatient because of the anxiety that is involved in group interactions. It is important that the facilitator holds the group back until everyone in the group is ready to confront difficult situations. You must avoid being pushed by the urgency of a group. Often it will seem as if the group is stuck, but sometimes this indicates a period of incubation before the depth material can surface.

Ruthlessness

In all of our lives, it sometimes becomes necessary to kill. Without the ability to kill we would not survive ourselves. More moderately, we sometimes need to cause pain to others in order to protect the group as a whole and sometimes to protect ourselves. In order to create sustainability around us, we need to set limits. This will always mean denying the fulfilment of someone's need. Especially in situations of strong transference, it is important to resist meeting needs that will ultimately be detrimental to the group as a whole. Open, but well considered, ruthlessness benefits the group when it is exercised alongside the skill of compassion.

Imagination

Imagination includes seeing the possible and the impossible. It means anticipating the highs and lows of a group's life. The ability continually to question and shift the boundaries of the present produces the innovations that improve our quality of life, but we need to imagine the full cost and benefit patterns that can result from our actions. Our imaginations specifically need to include the experiences of others in our world. We need to ask: What is it like from over there? How could it be different? What am I refusing to see? Imagination is most important when ensuring empathy and compassion.

Collective consciousness

Being conscious of our collective experience implies understanding that we are connected to everything around us, that we approach situations with an appreciation of all the parts, even those we cannot sense. Collective consciousness means noticing the intricate patterns of the relationships all around us. It also means allowing the disavowed parts in ourselves and others to have a voice. Consciousness of our collective experience reminds us that ultimately we cannot isolate ourselves completely from the experiences of those around us.

Harnessing energy

Our energy is our power. It is the quantity of life force that we have available to live our lives. Without energy, we cannot live. The ability to harness the energy that is available for our lifework needs to be honed. It is not sufficient to conserve energy. We need to find ways of replenishing our stores and generating enough energy to provide sufficient containment for the groups we are facilitating. We waste energy when we are unaware; we use the energy of others unnecessarily. We waste energy when we push against a system blindly. We waste energy when we do not embrace the fullness of our experience. We waste energy when we do not confront ourselves. Unresolved and chronic symptoms consume our life force rapidly. When we find and encourage new parts of our identities, energy is released and becomes available. Continually expanding our consciousness generates new power.

Curiosity

An attitude of curiosity is essential to the practice of facilitation. We need have a spirit of enquiry, to place curiosity and intelligence ahead of action. Curiosity means genuinely wanting to know and not minding being wrong. When we only use the skill of advocacy or telling others what we think, we waste the opportunities offered by relationships. Curiosity means having a genuine interest in what is going on that is not directly related to the self. Facilitation means prioritising the processes of others above our own pre-occupations. If you are not genuinely interested in the details of a group life, the group will sense it and start resisting you as a facilitator.

Renewal

An attitude that embraces renewal brings the ability to let go of something when it needs to die or end. The life–death–life cycle is found throughout nature, yet we cling to the present and the past. The ability to embrace renewal as part of our existence frees us from the obsession with death. Following the natural cycles of the world ensures continuity. Allowing death brings new life.

Groups will usually resist endings and employ a range of defence mechanisms to avoid facing the necessary grieving processes required. If a group has worked together successfully they will often try to prolong their life together in artificial ways. While they may be able to find a situation that allows them to continue being together, it is important that they confront the ending of their current process together. Ensuring that a group faces an ending allows them to acknowledge and honour their common experience explicitly, which allows them closure and an ability to move forward freely. You as a facilitator need to help a group accept endings, so it is important for you to be able to tolerate ending and the feelings of loss that are evoked in your own life.

Reverence

Having reverence means being able to feel awe at the miracle of life in all its forms. It is often linked to loving nature. Reverence powers the breath of life and connects us to our world. Reverence means knowing that regardless of how much we know, we do not know everything and that a great deal of mystery runs beneath our human experience. As a facilitator, you need the capacity to be moved by the experiences of the groups that you work with. Without this, you will find it difficult to create an environment in which groups can encounter their own capacity to be moved by the group process.

CONCLUSION

This chapter considered the necessity of an ethical orientation to facilitation, showing that without sound ethics, facilitation will destroy anything it might set out to achieve. It also considered the less tangible and more philosophical aspects of facilitation in the form of metaskills. In some ways, metaskills cannot be taught. They can only be developed by individuals themselves, or embraced through life experience.

PERSONAL EXERCISES

1. Consider your own ethics. Under what circumstances is it hard to remain ethical? What can you do to ensure that you do not compromise your own ethics?

2. Evaluate yourself in terms of the metaskills listed in this chapter. Develop an action plan to further develop your metaskills.

CHAPTER 7
THE ROLES AND TASKS OF THE FACILITATOR

INTRODUCTION

Facilitation work can be divided into four main roles:

- Managing structure
- Managing process
- Managing people
- Managing content.

In this chapter we consider the roles more closely and discuss the main tasks and skills required to fulfil them.

FACILITATION ROLES

The four facilitation roles are described in more detail in the table below, which includes the roles required for both "surface" and "depth" facilitation.

Area of responsibility	Roles
1. Managing structure	To design and implement the structure of a group interaction, which means managing the form and boundaries of a facilitated intervention. To maintain a strong structure within which a group can work.
2. Managing people	To ensure that people dynamics enhance rather than detract from the achievement of objectives and to help a group to manage its dynamics by supporting and appropriately challenging all the members within the group as a whole.

Area of responsibility	Roles
3. Managing content	To keep track of content while holding a substantively neutral position. If needed, to maintain this neutral position while interpreting and exploring the deeper meaning of content during a depth process.
4. Managing process	To initiate and manage group processes whereby the group reaches their objective(s) and, if needed, to facilitate the emergence of group depth processes, supporting and ensuring completion of those processes.

Clarifying the facilitation role

Since facilitation is a fairly new organisational role, sometimes the participants do not quite understand the facilitator's role. Sometimes they expect the facilitator to be a leader or an expert. In order to ensure that participants are clear about your role, the following actions are helpful.

- Make known to the group the difference between facilitator and leader
- Clarify appropriate role expectations
- Stress group responsibility and that the group must feel comfortable
- Stress that the facilitator is there to help and support but that the facilitator is not part of the group and should remain neutral at all times
- Help lay and maintain ground rules for the group
- Discuss examples that could clarify the role of a facilitator.

ROLES, TASKS AND SKILLS

In the section below, each of the roles is analysed further in terms of the tasks and skills or knowledge required in order to perform the role successfully. There are some overlaps between the skills or knowledge required for each area. Details regarding the skills and knowledge are given in the next chapter.

MANAGING STRUCTURE

Facilitator's role

To design and implement the structure of a group interaction, which means managing the form and boundaries of a facilitated intervention. To maintain a strong structure within which a group can work.

Facilitator's tasks

1. Analysing client requirements
2. Contracting with the client
3. Designing a group session
4. Organising a session
5. Clarifying session objectives and structure
6. Clarifying session roles
7. Gaining group agreement for objectives, structure and roles
8. Providing information and education about depth facilitation if needed
9. Ensuring task completion
10. Setting and maintaining boundaries and limits, including those of time and space
11. Ensuring that group agreements are adhered to
12. Managing housekeeping

Facilitator's skills/knowledge

1. General psychology knowledge
2. Depth psychology knowledge
3. Systems thinking
4. Metaskills.
5. Self-management skills
6. Communication skills
    - Presentation skills
    - Awareness and observation skills
    - Listening skills
    - Language skills
    - Feedback skills
    - Stimulation skills
    - Support skills
    - Control skills.
7. Process design skills
8. Planning and organising skills

9. Exercising authority
10. Managing boundaries

MANAGING PEOPLE

Facilitator's role

The facilitator's role is to ensure that people dynamics enhance, rather than detract from the achievement of objectives, and to help a group to manage its dynamics by supporting and appropriately challenging all the members within the group as a whole.

Facilitator's tasks

1. Establishing session climate
2. Building containment
3. Building rapport with group members and group as a whole
4. Providing support to participants
5. Ensuring full participation
6. Monitoring and managing group energy levels
7. Intervening to manage personal, interpersonal and group dynamics
8. Ensuring good group practices
9. Managing transference and counter-transference

Facilitator's skills/knowledge

1. General psychology knowledge
2. Depth Psychology knowledge
3. Systems thinking
4. Metaskills
5. Self-management skills
6. Communication skills
    - Presentation skills
    - Awareness and observation skills
    - Listening skills
    - Language skills
    - Feedback skills
    - Stimulation skills
    - Support skills
    - Control skills.

7. Containment skills
8. Exercising authority
9. Relationship skills
10. Group intervention skills

MANAGING CONTENT

Facilitator's role

The facilitator's role here is to keep track of content while holding a substantively neutral position. If needed, to maintain this neutral position while interpreting and exploring the deeper meaning of content during a depth process.

Facilitator's tasks

1. Maintaining neutrality
2. Managing agenda setting
3. Tracking content
4. Organising content
5. Clarifying content
6. Summarising content
7. Documenting content
8. Identifying depth content
9. Elucidating symbols
10. Interpreting from a depth perspective
11. Linking symbolism with concrete content
12. Maintaining multilevel perspectives

Facilitator's skills/knowledge

1. General psychology knowledge
2. Depth Psychology knowledge
3. Systems thinking
4. Metaskills
5. Self-management skills
6. Communication skills
    - Presentation skills
    - Awareness and observation skills
    - Listening skills

- Language skills
- Feedback skills
- Stimulation skills
- Support skills
- Control skills
7. Group intervention skills
8. Detachment and neutrality
9. Conceptual skills
10. Data classification and organisation skills
11. Content documentation skills
12. Depth analysis skills

MANAGING PROCESS

FACILITATOR'S ROLE

To initiate and manage group processes, whereby the group reaches their objective(s) and, if needed, to facilitate the emergence of group depth processes, supporting and ensuring completion of those processes.

FACILITATOR'S TASKS

1. Initiating and explaining group surface process
2. Facilitating surface process
3. Closing surface process
4. Tracking the group development process and intervening appropriately
5. Identifying depth processes
6. Surfacing depth processes
7. Completing depth processes
8. Integrating depth processes with surface process

Facilitator's skills/knowledge

1. General psychology knowledge
2. Depth Psychology knowledge
3. Systems thinking
4. Metaskills
5. Self-management skills
6. Communication skills
   - Presentation skills
   - Awareness and observation skills
   - Listening skills
   - Language skills
   - Feedback skills
   - Stimulation skills
   - Support skills
   - Control skills
7. Group intervention skills
8. Exercising authority
9. Process design skills
10. Process management skills
11. Group intervention skills

Skills and Knowledge Development

It takes time and experience to develop your knowledge and skills as a facilitator. It is important that you understand the various tasks required and identify the skills and knowledge you currently lack.

Many of the skills mentioned are general in nature and should be developed on an ongoing basis. These include your self-management skills, your general communication skills, your metaskills, your understanding of systems thinking and your psychological knowledge, including your knowledge of Depth Psychology. The facilitator is expected to work on all of these areas in a planned and consistent way.

In the next chapter, we look more closely at the essential components of the skills categories that are common to all four facilitation tasks.

PERSONAL EXERCISES

1. Think about your knowledge and skill levels in the different areas.

2. Identify areas in which you may have weaknesses.

3. Develop specific learning processes in order to develop the areas that require work.

CHAPTER 8
ESSENTIAL FACILITATION SKILLS

INTRODUCTION

In previous chapters, we discussed systems thinking, general psychology, with an emphasis on Depth Psychology knowledge, the metaskills you need as a facilitator and the skills you need to manage your own psychology (in other words, self management). This chapter considers the skills and knowledge that are common to all facilitation tasks and they are broadly grouped under the title "Essential Facilitation Skills". These skills include: presentation, awareness and observation, listening skills, language, feedback, stimulation, support and control.

In Section 3 we will consider each or the four areas: structure, people, process and content and the skills pertaining to them in more detail

PRESENTATION SKILLS

Although facilitating is very different from making a presentation, you, as the facilitator, still need basic presentation skills because you will be working in front of a group. This section covers some basic presentation skills.

As a facilitator you need to be able to manage your presence in front of the group so that you inspire confidence. It is important to be confident, relaxed, clearly audible and physically at ease in front of a group. Several aspects of your personal presentation that need to be considered are outlined below.

CREDIBILITY

It is important that the group accepts your authority as a facilitator and so you need to establish your credibility with the group. Once you have greeted the group, welcomed them to the gathering and introduced yourself, you need to outline your credibility as the facilitator. It is important to reassure the group about your qualifications and experience and that you will not be managing the process without the ability to do so meaningfully. This does not mean that you boast about your achievements, but that you state facts. It may be useful to outline your role as a facilitator at the same time.

MOBILITY

A facilitator needs to be able to be physically relaxed in front of a group. It is advisable that you develop a relaxed style of moving around and using your hands to illustrate points you wish to make. Movements should not be hurried or agitated but should flow naturally. For this reason, the layout of the room in which you work is important.

If feasible, a U-shaped seating arrangement is recommended. It allows you to move comfortably inside the U and to move closer to the group to build better rapport.

Confidence projection

You may not feel very relaxed internally because it is always nerve-wracking to be in front of a group. You need to learn to manage your own inner agitation in order to ensure that the group can feel relaxed. You can practice with the help of a group of colleagues or friends, or in front of a mirror. Some guidelines are given below to help you develop your confidence.

1. Be well prepared.
2. Give special emphasis to the first five minutes (super-preparation).
3. Start involving the group as early as you can in the process.
4. Learn participants' names and use them.
5. Use eye contact to establish rapport.
6. Exhibit your advance preparation (for example with a printed agenda).
7. Anticipate potential problems (and prepare probable responses).
8. Check the facilities and audio-visual equipment in advance.
9. Develop relaxation techniques that work for you. Different techniques work for different people. Examples are deep breathing, meditation, and visualisation.
10. Manage your appearance (dress comfortably and appropriately, in other words dress in a style that would be acceptable to the group).
11. Ensure that you are well rested so that you are physically and psychologically alert.
12. Use your own style (do not imitate someone else).
13. Use your own words (do not read).
14. Accept some anxiety as being productive.
15. Introduce yourself to individual group members in advance as they enter the venue.
16. Identify your fears, categorise them as controllable or uncontrollable, and confront them.
17. Imagine yourself as a good facilitator.
18. Practice responses to tough questions or situations.

Voice projection

It is important to ensure that your voice can be comfortably heard by everyone in the room. It is useful to address everyone in the room, speaking both to participants that sit further away and those who are closer. It is sometimes useful to listen to your own voice on a recording so that you can determine whether it is too soft-spoken, too strident, too deep and inaudible, or too monotonous. Ask colleagues or friends to give you feedback if you are unsure. Finally, it is useful to ask the participants whether they can hear you clearly, and if they cannot, ask them to be specific. Check for feedback if you alter the way you speak to accommodate the group.

Mannerisms and bridging sounds

Become aware of any mannerisms or bridging sounds that you may be using unconsciously. For example, you may not be aware that you have a habit of using "hmms" between your words or sentences, or you may have a habit of bouncing your foot when you speak. Some facilitators use words like "actually", "in any case", "in fact", or "okay?", continually. These little habits can become irritating to the participants. It may be useful to make a visual recording of your facilitation presentation style if you have the equipment to do so. It may again be useful to ask colleagues and friends to give you feedback. Being aware of the habit goes a long way to helping to break it.

Eye contact

This is the single most important method a facilitator uses to establish whether group members are comfortably engaged in a process. It is important to make light and brief eye contact with everyone in the room on a continual basis. It is useful also, when listening to one individual member, to have eye contact mainly with that person, but also to glance around in order to gauge the responses of other participants. Often participants communicate with their eyes before they communicate verbally. Eye contact is a useful of noticing someone who may be at an edge about speaking up, and may need some encouragement (even if it is simply gentle eye contact) to do so.

AWARENESS AND OBSERVATION SKILLS

These skills refer to your ability to be attuned to others and the environment, and to be able to make sense of the messages you are getting. As a facilitator you need the ability to notice even small changes around you, and be able to pick up information in a variety of communication channels. These refer to your ability to notice what is happening in the group on various levels: verbally, body language, atmosphere, interpersonal relationships and energy level changes. You may need to remain conscious of several different processes at once, and to pick up subtle information about the group's state of mind and the dynamics between the group members.

Although you will be mainly concentrating on the group, to be an effective facilitator, you should also keep an eye on your own behaviour. Try to recognise emotional and other reactions that may be developing in you. Some detailed observation guidelines are given below.

Observation guidelines

Some of the aspects of group life that need to be observed are listed below.

Participation issues
1. Who are the high participators?
2. Who are the low participators?
3. Do you see any shift in participation, for example, do participative members become quiet, or do quiet members suddenly become talkative?
4. How are the silent members treated? How is silence interpreted?
5. Who talks to whom, and at whom do they look when they talk?
6. Who interrupts whom during interactions?
7. What is the style of communication used in the group?

Content issues
1. What content does the group pay attention to?
2. Does the group keep changing the subject?
3. Do group members become impatient at the mention of certain content issues?
4. Do group members use, support or build on worthy ideas?

Rank issues
Who has influence or rank in a group is not necessarily the person who talks a lot. Some guidelines for observation are:

1. Which members seem to have a great deal of rank or influence?
2. Which members have less rank or influence?
3. Is there rivalry in the group, a struggle for leadership?
4. Are group members aware of their rank in the group?

Decision-making procedures
1. How are decisions made?
2. Do individual members make a decision and carry it through without checking with the other members?
3. Who supports the decisions or suggestions of others?
4. Are attempts made to get all members participating in a decision?
5. Do certain individuals make suggestions that receive no response at all?
6. Are decisions arrived at by calling a vote?

Membership issues
1. Are there any sub-groups?
2. Do some people seem "outside" the group?
3. Do some members move in and out of the group?

OTHER AWARENESS PROMPTS

Some other things that should prompt awareness include:

- Body language and changes in body language
- Gut feel, hunches or intuitive signals
- Individual tone of voice, volume and changes in tone and volume
- Eye contact
- Incongruence of any kind
- The appearance of a new role, particularly if the role is disturbing to the group
- Any changes in the climate or "weather" in the room (this refers to the emotional atmosphere in the room).

It is always useful, if you are unsure, to check your perceptions with the group. For example, you can say: "I am sensing a change in atmosphere in the group. Am I the only one, or is anyone else picking it up too?"

LISTENING SKILLS

Among the most important skills that a facilitator needs to have are good listening skills. This refers not only to being attentive to group members and understanding what they are saying, it also means developing the communication by using the technique known as reflective listening, which is described in more detail below.

REFLECTIVE LISTENING

Reflective listening is a very important skill for building a relationship with a group and helping the group members to clarify their meaning. It involves listening to what is being said and then restating what the person has said. The restatement cannot be mere repetition, but needs to reflect the core meaning of the participant's message. In order to become proficient in this skill you have to listen very carefully to the other person. While listening, try to discover the underlying meaning beneath the person's statement. Once you discover the underlying meaning, restate that view using words that pinpoint the underlying meaning. On hearing the restatement the person will realise that you are listening to the "real" issue and will then be willing to elaborate on it. The different aspects of reflective listening are outlined below.

REFLECTING THE CONTENT
Here the facilitator attends to the content of what the participant is saying and reflects back the basic idea of what has just been said. The participant will usually elaborate on his or her thinking. The facilitator follows the flow, again reflecting the content by using other words and this ensures that the person will move a little further into the issue.

REFLECTING THE EMOTION
Here the listener notices the emotional tone of the issue. The words used in the restatement should exaggerate the emotional tone, trying to take it a shade deeper. For example, if a person says he or she is "anxious regarding the exams", a reflective comment could be: "You're feeling a bit afraid." Note how the "anxiety" was exaggerated in the reflection to become "afraid".

SUMMARISING CONTENT AND EMOTION
As a facilitator, start with content and wait for the participant to begin talking about feelings before picking up on the emotional tone. Let the participant lead. Sometimes it is useful to use a metaphor if an apt one springs to mind. The use of metaphor in restatement is a form of combined content and emotion. Metaphors are ambiguous and allow the person to focus on what is important for him or her. For example, if a participant is discussing the recent leadership changes in an organisation, you may check whether the participant experiences it as moving into a new house. If the participant likes the metaphor, he or she may develop it further and add that it is like moving into a rented house, after he or she had owned the house previously.

REFLECTIVE LISTENING GUIDELINES

Some specific guidelines for reflective listening are given below.

Use different words
It is important when you reflect that you use words different from those used by the person. For example, if a person says, "I'm feeling miserable about the job," and you restate the exact words, the participant will wonder if you have really heard, you are not interested, you do not really understand, or if you are playing games with him or her.

Do not introduce your own views
Limit yourself to the views expressed by the other person.

Listen for the issue that has weight
Issues that have weight are emotionally charged and they have more relevance than others. If you have emphasised the wrong issue or view, do not be concerned – the participant will bring you back to the issue or view that he or she wants to talk about.

Do not steer the conversation
Follow the participant, and only reflect back what has been said.

As a result of using and developing this technique your ability to empathise with people will grow. Empathy is having genuine understanding of what the person has said, together with genuine concern. Empathy is not sympathy. Sympathy is similar but contains a component of pity. Sympathy implies that the person is helpless, cannot cope and is in need of assistance. In most situations sympathy will undermine the person's self-worth and does not acknowledge his or her own strengths.

LANGUAGE SKILLS

Language skills refer to the ability to use language in a way that both makes a group feel comfortable and maintains the neutrality of the facilitator.

GENERAL LANGUAGE GUIDELINES

- The metaskills discussed in Chapter 6 should inform all your use of language.
- Remember that language is powerful and what is heard is often not what is meant. Do not use exaggerations like "fantastic" or "awful".
- Do not use judgemental language with words like "should".
- Do not use limiting language – use "will not" instead of "cannot"; use "want" instead of "need".
- Always invite and suggest, rather than demand and insist. It is always useful to be slightly tentative when making observations, which allows the group to correct you if you are wrong.
- Speak in the first person – use "I" statements.
- Do not de-personalise language – avoid "it" and "one".
- Do not ask questions instead of making statements, if in fact you intend to make a statement.
- Use people's names if you know them (get to know them as soon as possible).
- Avoid jargon or colloquialisms. If you use colloquial or slang expressions, make sure that you translate them for the group.
- Be aware that there are often individual participants for whom the chosen language of the session is not their mother tongue. Keep your language usage simple, and check for understanding.

- Soften feedback by referring to the positive view of a behaviour rather than the negative interpretation: use "forthright" rather than "aggressive", and "independent thinker" rather than "troublemaker".
- Be aware of cultural biases in your language usage.

FEEDBACK SKILLS

A facilitator needs to know how to give feedback so that it can be absorbed, and how to receive feedback without becoming defensive. Feedback refers to the communication of our responses to others. As a facilitator, it is important to be able to give a group feedback about how they are functioning as a group, and this must be done carefully. The rationale for the importance of feedback is discussed first.

THE FUNCTION AND VALUE OF FEEDBACK

If we regard ourselves as living open systems, it is clear that we can only survive in the world if we continually read changes in our environment and respond to them appropriately. The alternative would be death. A snake that ignores the new bird of prey in its territory would soon get eaten. Wildebeest who do not notice a dwindling food supply and therefore do not migrate, do not survive. A puppy that irritates its mother gets bitten. Getting and responding to information about our world is vital in the true sense of the word.

Human beings seem to be the only living creatures that regularly obscure feedback to others or ignore feedback from their environment. This is often to our detriment. We cannot learn or develop without accurate and timely feedback. Withholding feedback for fear of hurting someone does him or her a great disservice in the long run, but giving information out of our own frustration or anger is also an injustice. Feedback is useful when it is regular, well thought out, specific, accurate and given with compassion and humility.

BASIC GUIDELINES FOR GIVING FEEDBACK

For feedback to be of value to a group, a few simple rules must be observed. In applying the following guidelines when giving feedback to a participant or a group, remember to maintain eye contact, but in a relaxed way, not looking as though you are embarrassed to give feedback, but not staring the person down either. Also, keep feedback brief and clear, avoiding extra phrases to pad it out and make it more "comfortable".

Some guidelines for giving feedback are listed below:

1. **Always give feedback compassionately, trying to focus on the positive intention behind the behaviour.** For example, if someone is being disruptive in the group, give feedback that you are aware that this participant may be uncomfortable about the process being followed or the content that is being discussed.

2. **Do not generalise, rather comment on specific observable behaviour.** When giving feedback, specifically describe the event that you are commenting on. Follow this up with reasons for your comments. This is helpful whether the comments are positive or negative.

3. **Take ownership for the feedback you give.** Use "I" statements. Do not speak as if the feedback is given from a position of the greatest authority in the group.

4. **Feedback should be concerned with those things over which an individual or a group can exercise some control,** and/or be given in ways which indicate how the feedback can be used for improvement or planning alternative actions. Feedback on behaviours or characteristics that are difficult to change can make a participant or a group anxious and self-conscious.

5. **Allow people to give input throughout the feedback process.** When encountering rising defence or emotional reactions, deal with these reactions rather than trying to convince, reason or supply additional information.

6. **Give feedback in a manner that communicates acceptance of the participants as worthwhile individuals, and of each individual's right to be different.** The motivation of feedback must be to help and not to hurt. In other words, ensure that you are building someone's self-image.

7. **Remember your neutrality when giving feedback.** If the group has only agreed to surface facilitation, individual feedback can only be given if an individual member is hampering the surface process. If the group is in a depth process, then the group members should be left to give feedback to individual members. Always allow the member who has received the feedback an opportunity to respond. In a depth process, feedback must be given to the whole group, and both sides (if there are two sides) should be given feedback about their one-sidedness.

Guidelines for receiving feedback as a facilitator

The following guidelines will help you receive feedback in your role as a facilitator:

1. **Listen carefully to the feedback you are given** and allow the participant to finish before you respond.

2. **Remember that the feedback is being given to you in your role as the facilitator** and not to you as an individual.

3. **Paraphrase what you think you hear** to check your perception.

4. **Ask questions for clarification if needed,** and ask for examples in those areas that are unclear. Paraphrase the answers again.

5. **Carefully evaluate the accuracy and potential value** of what you have heard.

6. **Do not become defensive or argue with the participant or the group giving the feedback.** Remember that the feedback may be a role in the group and may involve projection if it is not accurate.

7. **Consider aspects of the feedback that may be accurate** and modify your facilitation appropriately.

8. **If you do disagree with some of the feedback, you may say that you disagree.** Do not defend yourself further. If the participant or the group starts arguing with you, say that you will consider it further and move on with the process.

9. **Remember that receiving feedback always offers the possibility of learning something valuable** that can serve as a basis for future improvement.

Defensive behaviour as a result of negative feedback

It is important to keep in mind that all negative feedback can be perceived as an attack on the individual or the group and produce anxiety that then leads to the activation of defence mechanisms. Individuals or groups can use any of the defences mentioned in Chapter 3, and if you as the facilitator notice a defensive reaction it is necessary to realise that the feedback may have been given in the wrong way or that the individual or group is not ready to hear it. If this happens, you need to move away from the feedback and acknowledge that the feedback may have been wrong.

STIMULATION SKILLS

The facilitator needs to stimulate the group members to participate in a group process. To begin with, you do this by providing information on the problem or situation being discussed. It is necessary for the facilitator to provide the objective of the discussion and some of the basic facts. You can remind the group of the objective of the session if necessary.

The effective facilitator stimulates the members throughout the discussion by asking questions and exploring ideas, and by occasionally summarising the contributions made. Use expressions like, "Let us get this clear. Are you suggesting that …?" or "Could you give us an example to help us understand your point?" and "It would be helpful to get the views of a few others on this. How do you feel about John's idea, Rosa?"

Open questions

One important way to stimulate group members is to use open questions. These are questions that encourage others to contribute their ideas and experience. Open questions begin with the following words: how, which, when, who, why or what. A few examples are given below.

"How would you like to begin this part of the process?"
"Which of these items are the most important to discuss in this meeting?"
"When would you like to get together again?"
"Who would like to investigate this more carefully?"
"Where would be the best place to try this out?"

Closed questions

Closed questions are useful in guiding a group in a more directive way because they shorten or discourage further contributions from group members. This may be necessary if you are coming to the end of the agreed time period and need to complete tasks. Closed questions are questions that can be answered with a simple "yes" or "no". They may start with: "Do you?" "Will you?" or "Have you?" Here are a few examples.

"Does anyone have anything further to add before we close?"
"Have we forgotten anything?"
"Is everyone in agreement about the decisions so far?"

Verbal techniques for stimulating discussion

These techniques encourage the participants to engage in the process.

Questions and statements	Appropriate use
Open questions "Tell me about … " "What do you think of… ?" "Could you describe… ?" (How, which, when, who, why, what)	For introducing topics and encouraging participants to talk at length, thus avoiding simple "yes" or "no" answers
Probes "Could you tell me more about… ?" "What do you mean by… ?"	Generally follow open questions to elicit more information about a particular topic or event
Closed questions "How long did it take?" "Did you receive my report?" (Do, have, did, etc)	Establishing precise information (dates, numbers, etc) and receiving simple "yes" or "no" responses; useful when dealing with a talkative, unfocused participant or when closing a session
Comparisons "How does the new system compare to the old one?" "What are the relative merits of… ?"	Getting participants to explore and reveal their own needs, values and opinions
Hypotheticals "What would you do if… ?" "If x happened, how would your job be different?"	Getting participants to think about a new topic or area or getting clarification of what a participant is saying

SUPPORT SKILLS

The facilitator should provide support for every member of the group. You do this by maintaining the right of each individual to express his or her own opinion and by continually drawing attention to the value of considering different points of view. For example: "Peter may have good point here. Let us give him a chance to explain what he has in mind." The effective facilitator will also provide support to group members by keeping any disagreement or evaluation centred on the problem rather than the individual.

Verbal techniques for supporting participants

The following verbal techniques ensure that you understand what has been said, will reveal any inaccurate assumptions and assist in establishing trust.

Questions and statements	Appropriate use
Reflecting "It sounds like you were angry when…" "That must have been quite frustrating."	To show that you understand and empathise; to get participant to acknowledge the emotional content
Restatements "What you seem to be telling me is…"	To confirm or crystallise ideas and to check that you heard correctly
Summaries "What we seem to have discussed and decided so far is…"	Drawing together the main points of a discussion and avoiding the discrepancies; it can also help in gaining commitment to action and be a good precursor to bridging

CONTROL SKILLS

The facilitator should control the group process to ensure that the objectives are achieved. Group participants become impatient if the group is not making progress and this is likely to occur in surface facilitation if the facilitator fails to keep the discussion on course. This does not mean that you must strictly or abruptly control the discussion. Rather, keep the discussion moving forward by gently redirecting members who have strayed from the point and by periodically summing up the progress that is being made.

From a depth perspective, it is important to notice that a lack of progress may be a sign of an unresolved underlying process. In this case, you may feed your observation back to the group by stating that you notice a lack of progress, and that you are wondering what it may be about. More information about this will be given when discussing the facilitation of depth processes in detail in Chapter 13.

VERBAL TECHNIQUES FOR CONTROLLING THE DISCUSSION

The verbal techniques listed below are used to keep the conversation going, to encourage the participants to talk, and to provide structure to the conversation.

QUESTIONS AND STATEMENTS	APPROPRIATE USE
Lubricators "Ye-es", "Go on", "Mmmm", "Uhuh", "Ah ha"	Indicating to participants that you are listening and want them to continue
Inhibitors "Oh, I see", "Yes but ..."	Signalling that enough has been said; of use with talkative participants
Bridges "I think that I understand now; can we move onto... ?" "How does this link in with the issue we are discussing?"	Providing a smooth link between one topic and another and indicating clearly what the next one is

CONCLUSION

This chapter provides information about the general communication skills of facilitation. It is important to note that sometimes the best facilitation comes from your intuition, and what you do that works will not necessarily be described anywhere in these pages. Although there are many skills for a facilitator to acquire or develop, the skills mentioned in this section are important basic skills. As a facilitator you need to remember that you have an audience at all times, and that the well-being of the group participants needs to be supported by your actions.

PERSONAL EXERCISES

1. Consider the impact of your presence on a group. What first impressions do you make?

2. Practice your presentation skills by recording them if possible. Notice your mannerisms and bridging sounds.

3. Analyse your use of language and consider what needs to be changed.

4. Make an observation list for yourself that you can use in order to hone your observation skills.

5. Practice reflective listening.

6. Practice giving feedback to friends and colleagues.

7. Consider whether you can manage your defensive reactions when being given feedback by a group.

SECTION 3
FACILITATION PRACTICE

CHAPTER 9
Depth Facilitation in Detail

INTRODUCTION

This chapter considers depth facilitation in detail, looks at the situations in which depth facilitation is needed and considers the complications of this kind of facilitation.

Depth facilitation is a way of working with groups in organisations that resolves the deeper, often unspoken, conflicts that hinder organisational success. It also has the capacity to unleash the hidden creative potential of groups. It brings together the wisdom of more than a century of psychological thinking and the current knowledge in the disciplines of change management and organisational development.

Many leaders and practitioners sense a need to work at a deeper level with the individuals and teams in their organisations, but are without the benefit of a psychological framework that would ensure an effective and sustainable intervention. Depth facilitation is based in Depth Psychology, which offers of the psychological foundations necessary to ensure sound interventions in groups.

MAKING THE UNCONSCIOUS CONSCIOUS

Depth facilitation is concerned with working with the unconscious in the group; it is about making what is unconscious conscious. The unconscious in a group is that area of group functioning that is not openly discussed. It may be discussed in private sub-groups, but will not be talked about in the group as a whole. In addition, it may be a part of the group of which no one in the group is aware.

Depth processes are linked to the underlying duality in human nature. Most systems will have an underlying dilemma or conflict that will play itself out in the functioning of that system. A system can be one individual, a group, an organisation or even a country. Examples of such dilemmas include:

- Being personal versus being professional
- Being people-oriented versus being task-oriented
- Being creative versus being rigorously scientific
- Being risk averse versus being risk-taking
- Focusing on the individual versus focusing on the group.

A depth approach is therefore one of encouraging groups and teams to engage with both the depth as well as the surface processes. Also, it is taking the time initially to discuss the "can of worms" with the knowledge that time spent early on in a process often pays enormous rewards later. Having said this, it must be stressed that a facilitator does not embark on a depth process unless it is needed in order to ensure progress, or if the group specifically would like to work at a deeper level to resolve problems or enhance its creativity. Not every situation needs to have its depth process discussed.

APPROACHES TO DEPTH WORK IN ORGANISATIONS

Many different approaches to depth facilitation exist, some of which we have already referred to in this book. The main ones include:

- Arnold Mindell's Process Work or Process-oriented Psychology based on the work of Carl Jung and systems thinking
- The Tavistock approach originally based on the work of Wilfred Bion and Sigmund Freud
- Group Analysis based on the work of S.H. Foulkes.

The material in this book draws from as wide a variety of typologies and frameworks as possible. The approaches differ in terms of their basic philosophy, and in terms of their methodology. There is a broad split in Depth Psychology between work based on Sigmund Freud's thinking and that based on Carl Jung's, and this split has carried over to some extent into facilitation work.

Process Work is Jungian in nature while the Tavistock and Group Analytic Approaches are more broadly based on Freudian concepts. However, both Process Work and the Tavistock approach have embraced "systems thinking", the mindset discussed in Chapter 2 that developed in the natural sciences at end of the 20th century, which sees groups as organic, integrated systems, rather than an agglomeration of individuals.

This book offers does not favour one methodology over another. Rather, it hopes to expose the student to the strengths of a variety of methodologies, so that the student develops a broadly based toolkit.

WHEN IS DEPTH FACILITATION NEEDED?

Depth facilitation is needed when the usual team building interventions, training courses or other organisational development interventions, such as restructuring, fail to produce the required change, or when a group wants to work at a deeper level.

Examples of the symptoms that indicate the need for depth facilitation are:

- Recurrent conflict between individuals or groups
- Unexpected absenteeism, low morale or poor performance
- Repeated incidents that indicate an intolerance for diversity, manifesting as racism and sexism
- Recurring failure to meet deadlines, make or implement decisions
- Unexplained organisational problems of a chronic nature
- Continued failure of change processes and programmes
- Persistent "people" difficulties after mergers and acquisitions.

Increasingly, it has become clear that without the ability to work at a deeper psychological level with organisations, possibly even at the unconscious level, many of these problems will not be solved.

BENEFITS OF A DEPTH FACILITATION INTERVENTION

The potential benefits of a depth facilitation process for a group are outlined below:

- Individuals may know themselves better, are able to develop more of their potential, and may be more motivated and therefore more productive.
- Group members communicate more accurately and clearly, there are fewer misunderstandings, they feel more heard and as a result have better and more co-operative relationships.
- Conflict is handled more constructively, and is seen as an opportunity for growth and development. There is less displaced aggression, and less tension and stress.
- People are physically healthier, so there is less absenteeism and higher productivity.
- There is less destructive and dysfunctional behaviour, less politics and therefore better team functioning.
- All the above result in fewer disciplinary procedures, fewer dismissals, less industrial action, less sabotage and less unethical behaviour. Organisations are more effective and successful.

COSTS OF A DEPTH FACILITATION INTERVENTION

A depth facilitation intervention also has some costs attached to it. The possible costs are as follows:

- A change of thinking is required.
- Greater uncertainty often results in the short term.
- Established relationships may be disrupted and patterns of collusion may be exposed.
- Decision-making becomes complex and time-consuming in the short term.
- Long-buried emotions are unleashed and this can be disruptive and upsetting.
- Although results are beneficial, resources such as time and money are required.
- Commitment is needed because things may feel worse before they improve.
- It will change the culture of the organisation in sometimes strange and unpredictable ways.

IMPLICATIONS OF DEPTH FACILITATION FOR LEADERSHIP

The culture of an organisation is closely linked to the psychology of its leadership. Therefore to work with and change the culture of an organisation through depth intervention requires greater levels of consciousness from the leadership. It is often very difficult for leaders to become more psychologically aware, as they have a lot more at stake. Often, they also have too little support for the difficult job of increased self-awareness.

Nonetheless, for depth facilitation to be truly beneficial to an organisation it is imperative that the leadership is involved in the process. Leaders need to be open to receiving sometimes painful and difficult feedback during a depth intervention. The leader will often be in the spotlight during such an intervention, as the leader carries great psychological importance for the group. Leaders need to be prepared for that the fact that they may feel exposed during the process, and that any collusions they participate in, either psychologically or otherwise, cannot continue once the group becomes more conscious.

The following steps are important for a leader who wants to develop his or her capacity for depth work:

- The leader may need to work on his or her self-awareness and psychological self-management.
- The leader needs to ensure, if possible, leadership buy-in from the top of the organisation.
- The leader will need to commit resources to building awareness and skills.

IMPLICATIONS FOR BUSINESS PROCESSES

Depth facilitation has profound implications for business processes because it casts a different light on the ways in which we measure the success of a process. It demands a long-term, people-focused view of any situation. Business processes will feel more time-consuming in the short term, and will often feel as if they go against the approaches that seemed to work in the past. They require more involvement of people, and more introspection and reflection afterwards. Perspectives on issues will no longer be clearly right or wrong, and the real positive results will often only be seen later. Also, things will often feel worse before they get better. It will not be possible to design systems and execute tasks without the full involvement of people.

SITUATIONS WHERE DEPTH FACILITATION WILL NOT WORK

There are certain instances where depth facilitation will not work. A list of these possible situations is given below.

- Where the client is not willing to explore under-the-surface issues
- Where there is no leadership buy-in into the process
- Where there is a lack of ethics or some measure of dishonesty in the system, which cannot be challenged
- Where the system is corrupt, in other words, the people in power are using the system for personal gain in an unethical way
- Where participants in a group have not volunteered to participate in a depth process
- Where the facilitator is told that there are "undiscussable" topics
- Where the facilitator has been given a brief that serves the agenda of the leader or a powerful group in the system, and may not be in the interests of the whole system.

In the contracting phase, it is important that the facilitator clarifies as far as possible that the above instances do not exist. Where possible the facilitator should ask directly about these situations. Where it is not possible, the facilitator needs to watch for any signs indicating that one of the above situations could exist.

CAUTION REQUIRED

At this stage it should be clear that depth facilitation requires working in unchartered waters for a group. As a result, it is important to take the precautions you would take when entering any unknown territory. Firstly, no one should enter a depth process without permission. This is discussed in more detail later. Secondly, a facilitator must be prepared and equipped with the right skills in order to manage a process with the appropriate amount of care. In a sense, depth facilitation requires moving behind people's walls, or more technically, behind their defences, which means working in an area where there will be anxiety. A facilitator who is intent on reaching a result at all costs will not be sufficiently cautious when moving with a group into a depth process. Remember that if the group wanted to or knew how to deal with the depth process, it would have done so already. Depth processes are sometimes equivalent to radioactive material in the psyche, whether individual or group, and should be handled with extreme care, and above all, with the permission of the group that will have to go through it.

Facilitators who have not done their own depth work, tend to be the most cavalier when taking a group into a depth arena and so often do the most harm. It is important for you as a depth facilitator to have tapped into and explored your own hidden self, so that you know exactly how disconcerting and dangerous this kind of work is. Exploring your own unconscious or hidden self is a humbling experience because it means becoming vulnerable and being aware of exactly how defenceless and dependent you can be, even as a functional and apparently in-control adult. You must have experienced feeling your own anxiety when confronting your inner world.

Ideally a facilitator should subscribe to the equivalent of the Hippocratic Oath for medical practitioners, which is that, above all else, you should do no harm. The following things may well do harm:

- Moving into a depth process without the explicit permission of the group
- Moving too quickly into a depth process
- Pushing a group to explore when the members do not want to
- Not checking that everyone in the group is on board
- Deciding for the group what it needs to explore or deciding what insights are necessary.

THE IMPORTANCE OF CONTRACTING FOR DEPTH WORK

The above comments about caution suggest that it is critical to get the group's permission to work with under-the-surface material. Here we will discuss the important process of explicitly contracting for depth work.

The process of contracting starts with the first contact with the client. The leader of a group may initiate this contact, or sometimes a member of the group who is not in a leadership position may initiate it. If it is not the leader who is involved in the initiation of contact then it is imperative that the leader is engaged very soon after. Sometimes a group member consults a facilitator in the hope that the facilitator can convince the leader that the work is needed, or even "trick" the leader into accepting a depth intervention. A facilitator should avoid situations like this because without explicit leadership buy-in, the process is destined to fail.

In the contracting process, the following needs to be made explicit and agreed to by everyone involved:

1. The objective of the intervention
2. The agreed time allocation and scheduling for the work
3. The people who will be invited and the list of members who have to attend for the process to be able to go ahead
4. Fee arrangements (if any)
5. The limits of responsibility of the facilitator (Depth processes are potentially volatile and unpredictable. A facilitator cannot be held responsible for every outcome – especially if he or she has not been given all the information – but a facilitator needs to practise reasonable caution and skill when embarking on this work)
6. The nature of the work – that under-the-surface processes will be explored if necessary
7. The potential implications of the work – that matters which may not have been discussable previously will possibly be brought into the open and that there may be confrontations in the group. The leader, particularly, needs to be aware that he or she may receive difficult feedback.

In the pre-session contracting process, everyone involved may not be present. Therefore, once the group is all together, members should be informed of the factors above and asked for their explicit agreement.

THE IMPORTANCE OF DEPTH PSYCHOLOGY EDUCATION

Because of the complex and tricky nature of this kind of work, it is recommended that the group be prepared as far as possible for its potential experiences. One of the ways of preparing the group for depth work is to provide some education about depth processes. Knowledge about the dynamics of the psyche is not common. The notion of an unconscious is still a mysterious idea for many and is not widely accepted as a given. Many people conceive of themselves as only rational and conscious beings that can operate independently within a group and are in full control of their behaviour.

In order for group members to be better prepared for the unpredictability and unexpected vulnerability that depth work may entail, it is important that they learn the following important things:

- That there are processes, thoughts and feelings inside them that they do not know about and may not be able to anticipate
- That they may experience feelings of anxiety and discomfort throughout the process
- That when they are functioning in a group, they lose at least some of their autonomy over their own responses as they become subject to the group psyche.

The extent of Depth Psychology education varies depending on the group and will be subject to factors such as the scope of the work, time and money availability and the willingness of the group to engage with such education. Even if no separate education process is agreed upon, the facilitator can include explanations of what may be happening during the process if it may be helpful.

HELPFUL PSYCHOLOGICAL MECHANISMS

Fortunately, despite the caution and costs associated with depth work, there are two inherent human mechanisms that, if they can be encouraged, greatly assist the facilitator to help the group. These two mechanisms or tendencies are described below.

PHASE ENTRAINMENT

Phase entrainment, or phase locking, is the technical term for the tendency of systems to couple into larger wholes. In ordinary language, this means that there is a tendency for individuals to start functioning synchronistically, or in harmony with one another, if they spend enough time together and they are in the right atmosphere. If you hang two cuckoo clocks together, the swing of their pendulums will eventually become synchronised. Similarly, individuals in a group can become synchronised mentally, emotionally and psychologically. Once that happens, the individuals will feel themselves to be part of the whole without being constrained by it. This can be a hugely pleasurable experience that leads to great task success. As a depth facilitator you cannot make phase locking happen, but you can encourage an atmosphere in which individuals become open enough to one another that phase locking can happen by itself.

The transcendent function in groups

The "transcendent function" – a term coined by Carl Jung – refers to an inherent psychological predisposition for the psyche to move instinctively towards the transcendence of polarities, to a more integrated position. Jung suggested that the psyche does not ultimately like to side with one polarity rather than another, and if possible will always move towards a more integrated and balanced position. This inherent tendency ensures that a group will have an impulse to do depth work successfully, given the opportunity and a conducive environment.

CONCLUSION

This chapter outlines the important considerations when embarking on depth facilitation and emphasises the caution required in this work. Depth facilitation can be truly transformative for groups in that it can dismantle destructive patterns and develop latent potential, but only if it is managed with the appropriate care and skill. Specific facilitation practices according to the four facilitation tasks will be outlined in the remaining chapters.

PERSONAL EXERCISES

1. Consider what you know about depth work with groups. Write down your assumptions about this kind of work. In other words, what do you believe to be true about working at the depth level with groups?

2. Consider your experience with depth facilitation. How much work have you done yourself and what have been the results? How did you experience working with your own depth material? Was it difficult or easy? Did you work with someone else, such as a therapist or coach? Did you regard the other person as being good in the work? What skills and competencies did you see them use that you admired?

3. Consider why you would like to use depth facilitation in group situations.

CHAPTER 10
MANAGING STRUCTURE

MANAGING STRUCTURE OVERVIEW

This chapter considers each of the tasks of managing structure in detail. An overview of the role, tasks and skills are provided first as a reminder.

FACILITATOR'S ROLE

To design and implement the structure of a group interaction, which means managing the form and boundaries of a facilitated intervention. To maintain a strong structure within which a group can work.

FACILITATOR'S TASKS AND RELATED SKILLS

TASKS	SKILLS/KNOWLEDGE

1. Analysing client requirements
2. Contracting with the client
3. Designing a group session
4. Organising a session
5. Clarifying session objectives and structure
6. Clarifying session roles
7. Gaining group agreement for objectives, structure and roles
8. Providing information and education about depth facilitation, if needed
9. Ensuring task completion
10. Setting and maintaining boundaries and limits, including those of time and space
11. Ensuring that group agreements are adhered to
12. Managing housekeeping
	1. General psychology knowledge
	2. Depth Psychology knowledge
	3. Systems thinking
	4. Metaskills
	5. Self-management skills
	6. Communication skills
	   ▪ Presentation skills
	   ▪ Awareness and observation skills
	   ▪ Listening skills
	   ▪ Verbal skills
	   ▪ Feedback skills
	   ▪ Stimulation skills
	   ▪ Support skills
	   ▪ Control skills
	7. Process design skills
	8. Planning and organising skills
	9. Exercising authority
	10. Managing boundaries

FACILITATOR'S GUIDELINES, TOOLS AND TECHNIQUES

1. ANALYSING CLIENT REQUIREMENTS

In order to analyse the requirements of a group that requires facilitation, the facilitator needs to conduct different kinds of research. The first part of the research is a meeting with the client. The word "client" is used to refer both to an external client, if the facilitator works as an independent person, or to refer to an internal client, if the facilitator works in one organisation and performs the task of facilitation internally. The facilitator can ask the following questions as a starting point:

- What is the request or need from the client? (this applies whether it is an internal or external client)
- What outcomes are required?
- What are the issues that the client is concerned about?
- What may be other different points of view of the issues?
- What are the possible difficulties that may occur in a facilitated session?
- What concerns or other agendas may be important to the client or other stakeholders?
- Is the client aware of the nature of depth work?
- Is the client interested in exploring under-the-surface material if it appears to be important to the achievement of objectives?
- Would the client be interested in exploring depth material as a route to transforming the group dynamics?
- If depth work is required, would some depth education be a good idea first?
- What time is available and is there enough time available?
- What evaluation is possible and required?

After meeting with the client, the facilitator can then consider meeting with other stakeholders, including the prospective participants in a session. The discussions with these parties should be treated as confidential. Depending on the scope of the intervention, the facilitator should speak to as many people as possible. At these meetings, the facilitator should outline the brief from the client and thank the stakeholder for making time available. Stakeholders need to be assured of the confidentiality of the meeting and that nothing they say will be brought up by the facilitator in front of the group at the meeting. Any subsequent stakeholders can be asked some of the following additional questions:

- Who are you and what role do you play in the system?
- What do you think is needed as the next step for the particular group?

- What are the issues as you see them?
- Do you have any particular preference for the processes that need to be followed?
- Do you have any prior experience of group interventions that may be of importance?
- Do you have any concerns that the facilitator should know about?

The facilitator should also do desk research about the nature of the organisation (or the department if you are an internal facilitator). This could include visiting websites and reading relevant reports.

It is usually helpful to establish whether the group has had previous experience of facilitation and whether that was a good experience or not, particularly checking whether they have had experience of depth facilitation.

2. Contracting with the client

It is important to contract clearly with a client (or clients), whether you are an internal member of the group or an outside facilitator. Contracting means clarifying and preferably documenting the exact nature of the intervention required between the facilitator and the facilitated group. The guidelines for contracting for a depth process were discussed in Chapter 9.

The following items should be dealt with in a contract or contracting process, whether for surface or depth facilitation:

i. The objective(s) of an intervention
ii. The outcomes that the client hopes to achieve
iii. The scope of work and the exact time scale of the intervention
iv. The client's expectations of the facilitator's activities, competencies, deliverables
v. The facilitator's methodology(ies)
vi. Whether or not depth processes will be explored, and if so, the agreement of the group to explore such material.
vii. The clarification of the other roles that will be fulfilled in the process in terms of leadership, documentation, co-facilitation and any others that may be relevant
viii. Cancellation policies from both sides
ix. Clarity regarding accountability and responsibilities for outcome
x. Any contingency measures that need to be put in place
xi. Costs and responsibilities for cost, including payment terms.

A written contract should contain information about each of the following areas:

- The time, date and venue
- The size and composition of the group
- The agreed outcomes and performance measures
- The list of services to be provided, such as facilitation and documentation
- The nature of the process to be followed
- The fees, costs and terms of the agreement
- The nature of the evaluation process.

3. Designing a group session

The design of a group session needs to consider each of the following variables:

- The number of sessions and time scale for each session
- The number of participants and choice of participants
- The venue and room layout
- The number of facilitators
- Other roles and responsibilities needed (such as that of a scribe)
- Information needed by the participants to be fully prepared
- Information contributions required during the session, such as outside presenters
- Information needed by facilitator and others, such as scribe, to be fully prepared
- The process to be followed
- The interventions to be used.

A session design will have many components, including the contracting components listed above.

Matching process to outcome

Each session needs to have a process that will ensure the outcome. If the initial research indicates that there are important depth processes that need to be explored, then sufficient time needs to be set aside to do so. A depth process usually requires more than one session, and sessions should not be shorter than two hours if any depth material is to be discussed. It is difficult to give an exact time estimate for depth material, as the time it will take to unearth, resolve and integrate the depth process depends on many factors. Important variables include: the length of time that the group has struggled with unspoken depth processes; the psychological knowledge of the group; the degree of anxiety about the depth issues; the size of the group; and the level of commitment the group has to staying together and resolving difficult issues. Sessions should have breaks at least every 60 to 90 minutes.

Group sizes and design

A group of less than 15 can be considered a small group. A small group can be kept together for the duration of a process because it is small enough to ensure full participation. A session for a group of this size can be more loosely structured than larger groups because it is easier to contain.

A group with between 15 and 25 members is considered a medium-sized group. This group should be divided into sub-groups for some of the work because it is too big to ensure full participation. The facilitator should consider having a co-facilitator and definitely a scribe. The session process should be carefully structured.

A large group is one with more than 25 members. These groups are difficult to work with because the combined energy of such a group is usually more than one facilitator can manage. A group of this size should be seated in smaller groups, if possible, where participants are kept with their natural work groups. Ideally a team of facilitators should be used, with the process very carefully structured and tightly managed.

Further process design information is given in Chapter 13.

4. Organising a session

Planning and organising a group session involves:

- Inviting all the participants well ahead of time
- Informing them of the logistical information
- Providing information so that they can prepare for the session
- Booking the venue, the layout of the venue, and any audio-visual equipment needed
- Booking any other people to fulfil other formal roles, such as a scribe or a presenter of important information.

5. Clarifying session objectives and structure

When starting a group session, it is important for the facilitator to open the session clearly. A format for an introduction is given below.

1. Introduce yourself as the facilitator and give relevant information about your credentials as a facilitator for this session.
2. Discuss the brief for the session with the group and check for their agreement with the brief. This includes outlining the objective of the session, the process to be followed and the time frames involved. If a depth process is envisaged, ensure that the group understands this and agrees to it.

3. Outline the role of the facilitator and other formal roles (see the section below for more detail).
4. At this point, or before step 2, invite participants to introduce themselves. In a larger group, this introduction should be in the sub-groups. Ideally, an introduction should include as much relevant information as possible, but at the minimum it should include the participant's name and the role or capacity that he or she is in for this meeting.
5. If a group contract is to be used, it should be agreed upon at this time. Participants are invited to list things they would like from one another and the facilitator. Issues of confidentiality should be discussed here.
6. As a last part of the introduction, outline any housekeeping issues, such as timing of breaks, location of toilets, switching off of cell phones. Use this time to ask whether any participants have any special needs or time constraints.

6. Clarifying session roles

During the introduction (step 3 above), the facilitator should outline the nature of the formal roles to be taken in the session. It is usually a good idea to remind participants what a facilitator does, highlighting the idea of neutrality and the focus on process rather than content. If there is a scribe, or a co-facilitator, this person's role should be outlined too. If there is a leader in the room, it is helpful to mention the difference between the leader's role and the facilitator's role. This should be checked with the person concerned before the session, to ensure that he or she is comfortable with this.

7. Gaining group agreement for objectives, structure and roles

As we saw in point 2 of the section on clarifying session objectives above, the group agreement for the objectives, structure and roles has to be gained. It is important for agreement to be explicit and involve everyone in the group. As facilitator, you need to outline the objectives, session structure and roles as discussed, and then to check with the group as a whole that they understand all the elements and agree with them. It is worth taking the time to gain agreement and providing the opportunity for individual members to disagree if they would like to. Do not assume that there is agreement if there is no explicit response from the group. Spend time making eye contact with individual participants and checking for their understanding and agreement. If there is disagreement, a deep democracy process may need to be followed whereby you check for the wisdom behind the disagreement and modify the objectives, structure and roles accordingly.

Sometimes group members may disagree because there is an underlying conflict in the group. If the disagreement is not material, but rather seems to be a competition for leadership within the group, or possibly even with the facilitator, then you may need to exercise your authority and ask the group members whether they are prepared to go along with the planned process for the time being, if you note their concerns and keep them mind. As facilitator, you have authority over the process, but not the content. If some group members do not agree to continue, then the underlying depth process must be tackled before the overall objectives can be pursued. If the group does not agree to do this, then the session has to be called off, and further work must be done before re-embarking on a group process. You may need to re-contract with the client, given the new information.

8. Providing information and education about depth facilitation

If it is clear that a depth process is needed, or that the group is slipping into a depth process, the facilitator needs to interrupt the group and indicate that the agreed process is no longer being followed. The group has to explicitly decide whether to consciously change the agenda temporarily in order to pursue the depth process and resolve it. At this stage, it is useful to provide the group with some education about the nature of depth processes and what will be required to address such a process.

9. Ensuring task completion

It is the facilitator's job to ensure that the group moves towards task completion. It is helpful to comment on progress from time to time, and to remind the group of the time available and the steps still to be completed. This does not mean rushing the group; it is simply keeping them informed so that they can work responsibly towards their objective. It is important that the facilitator does not assume full responsibility for the task completion, but rather for reminding the group to take responsibility. If the group decides to take a detour, then the facilitator needs to follow this decision, as long as the decision is made by the whole group.

10. Setting and maintaining boundaries and limits, including those of time and space

The facilitator is responsible for managing the boundaries and limits of a session and setting those boundaries at the beginning of a session. Boundaries include time and space boundaries, and any other group agreements such as the turning off of cell phones, and the agreement for the group to listen to individual member contributions without interrupting each other.

Managing time
The facilitator is responsible for managing time during a group session. The time boundaries should be checked with the group. Once group members are in agreement, the facilitator needs to act as timekeeper. This includes helping the group to pace itself and reminding them of the time they have left.

At no point should the facilitator communicate a sense of urgency to the group. It is the group's responsibility to indicate urgency should they feel it. The facilitator can periodically check whether the group is comfortable with the pace or not. Participants can be brought back from detours by a gentle reminder of the time constraints. This should never be done with a critical tone of voice.

Managing space
The facilitator is responsible for managing the space in which the group session occurs. Some guidelines are given below.

- It is important that the group should feel physically contained, but not trapped, and comfortable in the environment. Ideally, they should be in a space that can be private, with a door that closes. They should be able to move freely in and out of the room.
- The seating should be arranged so that participants are evenly spaced throughout the room, and, as far as possible, can see one another and the facilitator.
- It is helpful if the facilitator is at the front of the room, or in some way a little separated from the group. A U-shape or circle tends to work best.
- It is important to ensure that the room is well lit and well ventilated, and warm or cool enough. This is often difficult because participants may have different requirements. If there is an air-conditioner in the venue, setting it at a temperature of between 20 and 22 degrees Celsius seems to work well.
- Ideally, there should not be a desk or a podium between the facilitator and the group, even if the group participants are seated behind tables or desks.

11. Ensuring that group agreements are adhered to

If group agreements are broken, you as the facilitator need to feed this back to the group in a non-critical way in the form of a gentle reminder. If your authority is not respected, then you can also feed that back to the group, and inform the group that you cannot successfully fulfil the facilitation role if boundary maintenance requests are not respected. If you have been clear from the start and the contracting process was well managed, then usually the group will respect your requests. If you struggle with exercising your authority, it may be important to do inner work on this area.

12. Managing housekeeping

A facilitator is not always explicitly responsible for housekeeping during a meeting or a group session, but a good facilitator will keep an eye on housekeeping issues anyway, ensuring that participants are as comfortable as possible.

The checklist below will help with housekeeping:

1. If you are using an outside venue, make contact with the venue manager before the session. Introduce yourself and ask that you be kept informed of venue details.

2. If possible, visit the venue before the meeting to check that it is suitable for the meeting.

3. Ensure that venue details are discussed and checked, including the following:
   - The room layout
   - The availability and use of audio-visual equipment
   - The timing of breaks
   - The nature of refreshments offered
   - Possible disturbances
   - The availability of breakaway rooms
   - The availability of heating and cooling mechanisms
   - The location of toilets
   - The location of a smoking area
   - The servicing of the room, including the supply of fresh water and other refreshments in the room itself
   - The privacy of the venue.

4. During the session, the facilitator needs to check that:
   - The temperature in the room is comfortable
   - Fresh water is available at all times
   - Participants are informed where the toilets are
   - The room is protected from unnecessary disturbances (ideally the door should be closed)
   - Cell phones are turned off
   - Valuables are locked away or protected during breaks
   - Rubbish and used crockery is cleared away during breaks
   - Refreshments are brought timeously and there are sufficient refreshments

5. After the session, the facilitator needs to check that:
- No one has left anything behind
- All documentation has been collected or removed in order to ensure confidentiality
- Equipment is safely packed if necessary
- The room has been left in a tidy state

CONCLUSION

This section considered how a facilitator should manage structure. Many detailed guidelines were offered to assist with this, but it is impossible to consider all variables and the variety of different situations that a facilitator might encounter. It is important to remember that adhering to clear limits is important to create emotional safety. The more comfortable a group is with one another, the more flexible you can be, and the more structure issues can be left to the group themselves. However, during conflict or other emotive processes, the facilitator's management of structure becomes very important. It is important to communicate that although there is a structure, it is always open for negotiation if it is not working for the group.

PERSONAL EXERCISES

1. Consider your relationship with issues of structure and then answer the following questions:

2. Do you prefer more or less structure?

3. Does structure make you feel contained or trapped? How do you manage your frustration when confronted with too much or too little structure?

4. How do you manage time constraints? Are you a punctual person?

5. Are you assertive enough to manage boundaries if needed?

CHAPTER 11
MANAGING PEOPLE

MANAGING PEOPLE OVERVIEW

This chapter considers each of the tasks of managing people in detail. An overview of the role, tasks and skills is provided first as a reminder.

Facilitator's role

To ensure that people dynamics enhance rather than detract from the achievement of objectives and to help a group to manage its dynamics by supporting and appropriately challenging all the members within the group as a whole.

Facilitator's tasks and related skills

Tasks	Skills/knowledge

1. Establishing session climate
2. Building containment.
3. Building rapport with group members and group as a whole
4. Providing support to participants
5. Ensuring full participation
6. Monitoring and managing group energy levels
7. Intervening to manage personal, interpersonal and group dynamics
8. Ensuring good group practices
9. Managing transference and counter-transference
	1. General psychology knowledge
	2. Depth Psychology knowledge
	3. Systems thinking
	4. Metaskills
	5. Self-management skills
	6. Communication skills
	   • Presentation skills
	   • Awareness and observation skills
	   • Listening skills
	   • Verbal skills
	   • Feedback skills
	   • Stimulation skills
	   • Support skills
	   • Control skills
	7. Containment skills
	8. Exercising authority
	9. Relationship skills
	10. Group intervention skills

FACILITATOR'S GUIDELINES, TOOLS AND TECHNIQUES

1. Establishing session climate

The climate is an intangible variable that is nevertheless very important to a group's functioning. It refers to the general mood and atmosphere of the group and is determined by many things. Some of the more important activities that a facilitator can do to ensure a positive and functional climate are listed below.

The facilitator needs to:

- Help the group to develop a group contract
- Build a sound container (considered in detail in the next task)
- Do inner work to manage your own mood as a facilitator
- Implement good group practices
- Remain aware of the climate and ask for "weather" reports
- Build rapport with the group
- Make sure that participants are as physically comfortable as possible

The facilitator's style and mood is influential in creating a productive and constructive climate for the group. Your use of metaskills will have a significant effect on the group's atmosphere. If you are calm, respectful, focused, but unhurried, then the group will usually follow suit. Of course, the climate in a group will be greatly affected by unresolved depth processes, and if you sense that the climate is tension-laden, it is important to keep an eye on depth signals.

2. Building containment

Containment of anxiety is an essential component of the facilitator's task when working with groups. As indicated by Malan's triangle (see below), and as understood by individual psychotherapists everywhere, it is only when you contain the individual's anxiety about expressing frightening or undesirable thoughts and/or feelings that those important underlying or unconscious elements can be expressed. Containment is the process whereby the facilitator employs a range of metaskills to create an atmosphere of relative safety, so that defences diminish and the important issues are discussed. It is vital to remember that as a facilitator, you are not truly creating safety if your presence is required in order to prevent a backlash from the organisation. The process of containment is essentially intuitive and subconscious. It requires the facilitator to initiate a process of step-by-step exploration, all the time watching for feedback.

Containment provides form and structure (boundaries, limits, direction, clarity, documentation, routine and information) and safety (listening, relationships, trust and empathy). The diagram below indicates the different types of containment that you as facilitator can offer a group, distinguishing between internal or "soft" containment and external or "hard" containment. Some of the hard containment activities, such as setting clear policies and procedures, may not be in your control, but it is important that the aspects that you can control are implemented throughout facilitation work. You can provide feedback about group activities that are causing a lack of containment in the group and encourage the group to change these activities to ones that provide greater containment.

INTERNAL AND EXTERNAL CONTAINMENT

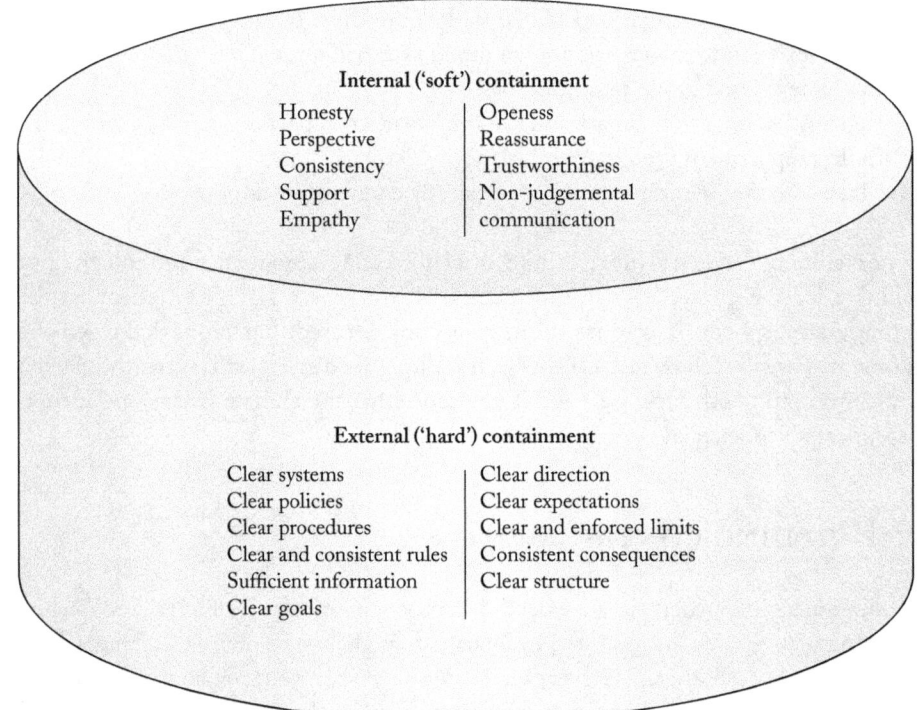

David Malan's triangle

In his book Individual Psychotherapy and the Science of Psychodynamics, David Malan suggested that when we express our true feelings we may feel anxious and that if our anxiety is not contained we quickly get defensive, reducing our expression of our real thoughts and feelings. The triangle indicates the dynamic relationship between potentially dangerous thoughts and feelings, anxiety and defence mechanisms. As a facilitator you can only work to reduce the group's anxiety in order to reverse this dynamic. If the group becomes less anxious because they feel contained, their defence mechanisms will drop and they will become more able to express potentially problematic feelings and thoughts.

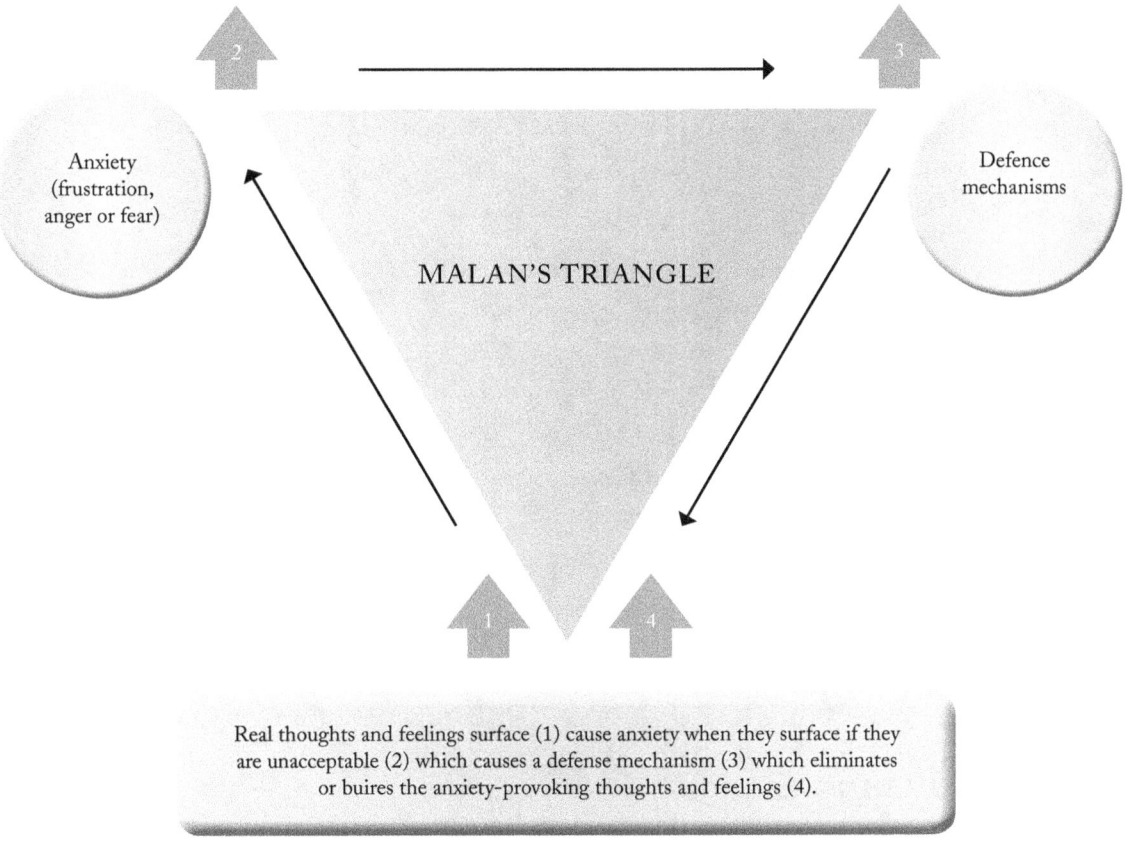

Real thoughts and feelings surface (1) cause anxiety when they surface if they are unacceptable (2) which causes a defense mechanism (3) which eliminates or buires the anxiety-provoking thoughts and feelings (4).

Containment during group sessions

If group members feel that others are trying to understand their points of view rather than criticise, they are much more likely to consider the points being made by others. They will try to weigh the ideas and experience of others as objectively as possible. They may even begin to reconsider their own viewpoints. If they feel they are being attacked, however, their emotional defences will quickly come up and cut off all further exchange of ideas. This may take the form of resentful withdrawal from the discussion, and one member may suddenly become silent. Alternatively, it may provoke a strong counter-attack on the person who criticised them, and two adults may begin squabbling like children. Either way, the effectiveness of the discussion will be damaged as soon as a threatening atmosphere replaces a co-operative atmosphere. To maintain a conducive atmosphere, the facilitator needs to use a combination of the containment techniques listed below.

1. Listen non-judgementally
2. Practise reflective listening
3. Empathise
4. Reassure
5. Give recognition
6. Avoid polarising (do not take a non-neutral role)
7. Self-disclose if needed
8. Provide space if needed
9. Admit mistakes
10. Take responsibility when needed
11. Set clear goals and objectives
12. Set and stick to clear time limits
13. Avoid distractions and interruptions
14. Pay full attention
15. Comply with agreements
16. Comply with procedures
17. Provide information
18. Follow through

3. Building rapport

Building rapport means establishing a level of comfort between you, as the facilitator, and the participants, so that the participants feel that they have a relationship with you and that they can trust you.

The word "rapport" refers to concepts such as "relationship", "affinity", "understanding", "bond" and "link". In order to build rapport, you can do some of the following things:

- Match the group's pace
- Match the group's style
- Make eye contact
- Use people's names and check the pronunciation and their preferences regarding their names
- Dress similarly in terms of formality and style (without relinquishing your identity)
- Use appropriate language
- Smile, be welcoming
- Remember who said what, and refer back to it
- Remember any promises made and keep them

4. Providing support to participants

In Chapter 8 we discussed some of the ways in which a facilitator can support participants. The facilitator needs to provide additional support if the group is involved in a depth process in which participants discuss issues that are likely to provoke anxiety. It is necessary to acknowledge that participants may be crossing edges and that it takes courage to do so. In order to support participants during edge crossing the following hints are helpful.

- Acknowledge that you are aware that they may be crossing edges.
- Maintain eye contact with and gently encourage an individual who seems to be crossing an edge.
- Ensure that the participant can do so at his or her own pace.
- If a participant seems unsure, suggest waiting until he or she is ready.
- Thank participants for their contributions, without indicating that you feel certain contributions are more important than others.
- Give all participants equal support.
- Use reflective listening if needed.
- Try to imagine yourself in the participant's position in order to activate your empathy, but remain neutral about the content of contributions.

5. Ensuring full participation

Many factors influence participation in a group. The main ones are given below.

- The individual comfort level with speaking in front of a group. Many people are not comfortable speaking in front of a group.
- The power dynamics in a room. People with less power will tend to speak less or become disruptive.
- Individual style. Some participants prefer to speak only when absolutely necessary.
- Level of comfort with the content. Some participants may not feel comfortable with the content discussed because they may not have the necessary knowledge.
- A lack of facilitation skill or neutrality. If the participants sense that the facilitator is not neutral, they will resist the process overtly or covertly.
- An underlying unaddressed issue will affect participation, especially if there is a lack of buy-in into the process.

Some general guidelines for managing participation are given below.

- Refer to situations relevant to the group.
- Be participant-centred – in other words, remain focused on the participants.
- Make eye contact with the whole group, without remaining with one person too long.
- Ask open questions in the form of invitations to participate.
- Refer to comments made by the group.
- Use participant names.
- Invite differing points of view.
- Without seeming critical, ask dominant participants to desist for a while by asking if anyone who has not yet had an opportunity to contribute would like to do so.
- Do not put one participant into the spotlight, rather provide an open invitation to anyone who has not spoken.

Managing silence

Sometimes it is important for the group to be silent. They may need to process or absorb something that has occurred, or they may need to think about something. It is useful to build some structured silent times into every process. It is important as a facilitator to develop a comfort with silence and not feel compelled to fill every silence. It is also important to remember that participants may be uncomfortable with silence, finding it easier if it is explicitly invited. This can be done by suggesting that the group takes some time to think before further contributions are made.

6. Monitoring and managing group energy levels

In order to manage the energy levels of the group, it is important first to monitor them. The group can be asked directly how energetic they are feeling. They can also be asked what restores their energy and what drains it. The atmosphere in a group will often be the best indication of the energy level.

As a facilitator you need to be aware that you are not responsible for energising a group; rather, you need to help remove any energy blockages. A leader may choose to energise or inspire a group, but it is not your task as the facilitator to do so. Energy levels are affected by many things, but low energy levels are sometimes an indicator of an unaddressed depth process. Sometimes individuals feel unheard, or feel that a process is a waste of time, and this will cause a drop in energy.

A list of factors that affect energy levels is given below:

- Poor ventilation and air quality
- A room that is too hot or cold
- Too few breaks
- Certain times of the day, such as straight after lunch
- Too many people in a group, and not enough time in smaller groups
- An inappropriate pace
- Tired or stressed participants
- A lack of interest and/or buy-in
- A dominant individual or group
- Unaddressed under-the-surface processes

The facilitator always needs to check with the group when addressing an energy issue. It is important not to make assumptions about the root cause. If it proves impossible to shift the energy levels if they are very low, then it may be necessary (with the agreement of the group) to negotiate the postponement of the session.

7. Intervening to manage personal, interpersonal and group dynamics

In order to intervene meaningfully during a group process, the facilitator has to apply a range of skills, including reflective listening and particular verbal techniques. These were discussed in Chapter 8.

Some general intervention guidelines for facilitators are given below.

- Practise self-disclosure of your own dynamics that could possibly influence the group unnecessarily
- Remember to focus on the group as a whole, rather than the needs of any one individual or sub-group
- Create an atmosphere of acceptance and a lack of judgement about the quality of participation
- Accept all participants equally and do not discriminate negatively in any way; communicate your acceptance through your body language and tone of voice.
- Ensure that any comments you make regarding personal, interpersonal or group dynamics are non-partisan and focused on the achievement of the group's objectives.
- If people dynamics are interrupting the achievement of objectives, gently bring this to the group's attention. Ask the group to decide whether they wish to discuss the dynamics, or proceed with the task.

EXAMPLES OF GROUP SITUATIONS AND FACILITATOR INTERVENTIONS

Examples of specific group situations and how to handle them are given in the table below:

POSSIBLE GROUP SITUATIONS	FACILITATOR INTERVENTIONS
A positive, motivated group	Do very little. Leave the energy with the group.
A quiet person or sub-group	Be aware of non-participation and try to involve quiet individuals by inviting participation generally from those who have not yet had or taken the opportunity to participate. Indicate that it is acceptable for people to be quiet if they feel that they have nothing to contribute at the time.

Possible group situations	Facilitator interventions
A dominant person or sub-group	Interrupt the dominant person, thank him or her for the contribution and suggest that it may be important to hear other points of view.
A disrupting person or sub-group	Try to establish the need behind the disruption by using reflective listening. Check whether anyone else feels the same way. Sometimes the contribution needs to be rephrased to sound more constructive or less vehement before others will join in with their opinion. For example, if one man says that he is bored, ask the group if anyone feels that it is time to move on or increase the pace. By softening the contribution, others may find it easier to add their voice. The disruptive element may be a symptom of an underlying issue, and this technique helps it to come to the surface.
A participant refers to or attacks another participant	Always give the participant on the receiving end an opportunity to comment or respond.
Non-participant	Try to identify the reason for non-participation. Do not force participation.
Conflict	Let all the different perspectives be fully heard. Set ground rules. Implement a conflict resolution process. This is discussed in detail in Chapter 13.

Possible group situations	Facilitator interventions
Negativity in the group	Allow the negativity to be expressed. If a group or an individual is allowed to express negative thoughts and feelings, they are usually able to move to a different point of view.
High-powered group	Meet them on their own terms. Establish authority and credibility. Do not allow the group to use its rank to dominate you or each other. Point out that rank differences may be inhibiting task achievement.
Mixes status group	In a mixed status group, support participants of different levels. Give people of lower rank an opportunity to speak and be supported until they are heard. Take care to simultaneously support the high-ranking group. Sometimes it may be helpful to make the high-ranking group aware of its rank and impact on others.
Strong sponsor versus group	It is important to establish agreement with the objective or task of the session. Ideally, this agreement needs to be given before the session. The facilitator needs to support the group and not become the agent of the sponsor. If the sponsor insists, remove yourself from the job.

8. Ensuring good group practices

Many good group practices have been discussed in the techniques covered thus far. Good group practices refer to ways of interacting that ensure constructive participation. If possible, try to ensure that the group includes the following aspects in their interactions:

- A clear purpose and vision
- Openly discussed, clear values and principles that are respected by everyone
- Clearly divided roles, and commitments to those roles
- Well-defined projects and goals for those projects
- Well-defined and understood identity
- Regular and comprehensive open communication, and communicating even when it is hard
- Regular expressions of acknowledgement and appreciation for each others' efforts
- Acts of celebration when goals are achieved
- Continuous relationship maintenance and feedback activities
- Apology and repair activities when needed.

As a facilitator, it is helpful to encourage these practices in the groups that you work with. If they are in place, groups tend to avoid difficulties.

If the group is engaged in counter-productive practices, the following guidelines may help you deal with these at a surface level if a depth process is not agreed to or possible.

Managing counter-productive practices

Firstly, you can manage counter-productive group practices by avoiding them as much as possible through good planning, preparation and preventative action. Some strategies for avoiding difficulties are given below.

- Gather information as early as possible
- Ensure that you have managed the structure of a session well
- Do your homework before a session
- Anticipate stereotypical responses and pre-empt them. For example, if you are a female facilitator in an all-male group, indicate your awareness of this fact and invite suggestions to stop it from being a problem.

When dealing with a challenge or difficulty that has arisen during a session, the following guidelines may be helpful.

- Acknowledge to the group that there appears to be a problem or difficulty
- Do not assume that you understand the roots of the difficulty or the roots of the behaviour
- Ask questions and practise reflective listening in order to gain an understanding of the nature of the difficulty
- Indicate to the group that you recognise that challenges and difficulties are part of a facilitator's job and that you will deal with them
- Ask the group for suggestions to resolve the problem if that seems appropriate.
- Remain neutral and supportive of everyone in the group.

When dealing with "difficult" people, it is sometimes possible to reframe what they are doing by not viewing their behaviour as difficult, but rather thinking of it as behaviour that is not understood. If you can establish the morally neutral need behind the difficult behaviour, it is often possible to solve the difficulty quickly.

DEALING WITH ANGRY FEELINGS

If there is conflict in a meeting it invariably produces heightened emotions. Also, if one side becomes emotional it often leads to an emotional response. The following guidelines will help you in such an emotional situation.

- First recognise and understand the emotions of both parties. Also consider your own feelings.
- Help participants to make their emotions explicit and acknowledge them as legitimate.
- Allow both sides to let off steam without becoming abusive to one another; help them to release their feelings.
- Do not over-react to emotional outbursts, but acknowledge that the participant has strong feelings about an issue.
- Encourage the use of symbolic gestures, e.g. a statement of regret, shaking hands, or an apology.

9. MANAGING TRANSFERENCE AND COUNTER-TRANSFERENCE

As a facilitator it is important to manage the transference and counter-transference phenomena. This was discussed in detail in Chapter 5. As a reminder, notice when you start feeling "compelled" to engage in a particular way with the group or an individual group member. This feeling of compulsion usually indicates that your own unconscious material has been activated. Do the necessary inner work to return to neutrality.

CONCLUSION

This chapter considered how a facilitator can manage people in a session. The techniques focused mainly on surface process facilitation situations. In Chapter 13, we will consider the depth process techniques in detail. The most important aspect of managing people, however, is managing yourself.

PERSONAL EXERCISES

1. Consider your own dynamics in a group. What situations do you find difficult?

2. Consider you feelings about difficult participants. To what do you ascribe their behaviour?

3. What makes you feel contained in a group situation?

4. Consider the judgements you make about the behaviour of others. Try to develop compassion for those behaviours by understanding the need behind them. Establish the unmet needs that may be motivating your own difficult or problematic behaviours.

5. Choose one case study that you have encountered in the past in which the people dynamics were difficult. How could you handle it differently now?

CHAPTER 12
MANAGING CONTENT

MANAGING CONTENT OVERVIEW

This chapter considers each of the tasks of managing content in detail. An overview of the role, tasks and skills are provided first as a reminder.

FACILITATOR'S ROLE

To keep track of content while holding a substantively neutral position. If needed, to maintain this neutral position while interpreting and exploring the deeper meaning of content during a depth process.

FACILITATOR'S TASKS AND RELATED SKILLS

TASKS	SKILLS/KNOWLEDGE

1. Maintaining neutrality
2. Managing agenda setting
3. Tracking content
4. Organising content
5. Clarifying content
6. Summarising content
7. Documenting content
8. Identifying depth content
9. Elucidating symbols
10. Interpreting from a depth perspective
11. Linking symbolism with concrete content
12. Maintaining multilevel perspectives
	1. General psychology knowledge
	2. Depth Psychology knowledge
	3. Systems thinking
	4. Metaskills
	5. Self-management skills
	6. Communication skills
	   • Presentation skills
	   • Awareness and observation skills
	   • Listening skills
	   • Verbal skills
	   • Feedback skills
	   • Stimulation skills
	   • Support skills
	   • Control skills.
	7. Group intervention skills
	8. Detachment and neutrality
	9. Conceptual skills
	10. Data classification and organisation skills
	11. Content documentation skills
	12. Depth analysis skills

FACILITATOR'S GUIDELINES, TOOLS AND TECHNIQUES

1. Maintaining neutrality

You can only truly facilitate group processes if one part of you as facilitator remains neutral and you maintain enough awareness to follow the process as it unfolds without any bias. A facilitator who does not hold a position of neutrality will influence the group negatively in the long run. Practising neutrality does not mean always feeling completely neutral; in fact, it may mean feeling intensely biased for a short time, in order to then relinquish a rigid adherence to a particular point of view. Moving quickly back towards neutrality is an advanced skill that only develops through practice.

Relationships are by nature conflictual. Often conflicts are characterised by a variety of different positions and viewpoints that eventually (with facilitation) polarise into two opposing voices. By sitting in the eye of the storm or sitting in the fire and remaining neutral, the facilitator helps the process of conflict resolution, as all sides feel supported during the process. To a large extent this prevents destructive behaviours.

In order to maintain neutrality, the facilitator can follow some of the following guidelines.

- Remember that what you see in the overt behaviour of the group is only part of the total field and that there are always other points of view.
- Remember that a point of view is dependent on where you are standing.
- Remember that behind every point of view lies an experience.
- Remember that behind every point of view there is a legitimate human need, although it may be disguised or distorted.
- Practise moving between points of view by finding the part in yourself that would agree with a point of view if you were in the same situation.

Sometimes it becomes necessary to break the neutrality rule. Facilitators can make contributions under the following conditions:

- As facilitator you can supply additional information if the group agrees, but you should only do this if you are the only one who has the information and it is critical to the group's functioning.
- If you really feel a need to get involved, you can ask to join the group and get another facilitator.

Avoiding polarities

In order to maintain neutrality, it is useful to consider the relationship between different polarities and the essence behind these polarities. Some examples of possible behaviours and their polar positions are given in the table below.

BEHAVIOUR	NEGATIVE VIEW OF FIRST POLARITY	POSITIVE VIEW OF FIRST POLARITY	POSITIVE VIEW OF OTHER POLARITY	NEGATIVE VIEW OF OTHER POLARITY	INTEGRATED POSITION
Degree of group cooperation/ compliance	Disloyal	Independent mindset	Loyal	Yes-man, conformer	Independent membership
Degree of task focus	Task-master	Driven	Relaxed	Lazy, slack	Optimal use of energy
Degree of playfulness or seriousness	Stern, boring, miser	Serious, frugal	Playful abundance	Childish gluttony	Sustainable pleasure
Degree of self-confidence	Timid, passive	Humble	Confident	Arrogant	Self-assured awareness
Degree of sociability	Antisocial, shy	Self-contained	Extrovert, gregarious, sociable	Loud, in your face	Self-contained and sociable
Degree of flexibility	No backbone, pushover	Easy-going, flexible	Determined	Inflexible	Focused adaptability

To remain neutral, especially when the group is trying to engage the facilitator's opinion, the following techniques may be useful:

- Restate the content that has been discussed so far.
- Summarise both sides neutrally if two sides have been offered, distilling the positive essence from each side.
- Hand back strong opinions to the group, in other words, ask the group how they feel about a strong opinion that has been expressed.
- Resist expressing an opinion and tell the group that it would not be helpful to do so because you are not part of the group after the session.

2. Managing agenda setting

Different meetings or sessions will require different types of agendas. All meetings have an agenda, but this agenda is not necessarily overt or documented. There are two ends of a spectrum where agendas are concerned. The first is a meeting that is very carefully structured according to a pre-prepared and clearly documented agenda that lists all the topics to be discussed and specifies the order in which they will be discussed. The second, at the other end of a spectrum, is an open and unstructured meeting in which the agenda emerges as the meeting unfolds.

Structured meetings

In the normal organisational situation meetings are often held on the spur of the moment and a quick agenda is drawn up at the meeting. If you as facilitator wish to have more success at a meeting, it makes sense to decide on an agenda before a meeting, to give the attendees time for preparation. For a formal meeting of a registered constitutional body of people, such as a welfare society, a sports club, Rotary, etc, the agenda should be sent out to members at least a month before the meeting.

The contents of an agenda for structured meetings

The agenda is a plan for a facilitated session. It documents the issues to be discussed and the process to be followed in a session. Formal agendas will contain the following items:

- The type of meeting to be held (such as an annual meeting, progress meeting, budget planning meeting, etc)
- The names of the participants
- The name of the facilitator
- The venue where the meeting will take place

- The date
- Arrival, starting and closing times for the meeting
- The times of tea and lunch breaks
- The objective of the meeting
- The topics to be discussed
- The processes to be followed
- Allocated blocks of time for each topic and/or process.

As facilitator of the meeting you need to do careful planning when compiling the list of items because you need to allocate blocks of time for the discussion of each item and to indicate these next to each item on the agenda. Liaise with people who need to prepare documentation for the meeting and indicate their responsibility on the agenda.

UNSTRUCTURED MEETINGS

Some meetings have an open process or structure in which the agenda is not specified before the meeting. Team-building sessions are sometimes unstructured in this way. The overall objective for the meeting will have been clarified, but the detail of topics and processes is expected to emerge during the session itself.

CREATING AN AGENDA IN UNSTRUCTURED MEETINGS

The creation of an agenda during an unstructured meeting can be thought of as "sorting the field". With this technique (originally developed by Arnold Mindell and adapted here), the facilitator opens a session by asking participants to list the topics that they would like to discuss. All topics are written down, whether everyone agrees or not. This kind of session is open, and therefore everyone is entitled to suggest topics. After everyone has had an opportunity to list their topics, the facilitator can group similar topics together. If the group is able to reach consensus on the priorities of the topics, then the list can be reorganised to reflect those priorities. If they cannot agree on priorities, then the list is worked through from the beginning. In each case, the topic is discussed until it is resolved, or until the group loses interest in that topic. As facilitator you need to check that the group is happy to move on.

3. TRACKING CONTENT

Although you as facilitator should not comment subjectively on content, it is your responsibility to keep track of the content of a session. Sometimes this means keeping track mentally, especially in a depth process, but often it means keeping track by publicly documenting the content. This will be discussed later in this chapter.

It takes concentration and practice to keep track of content, and initially it may be useful to make some notes. It is important to gain the group's agreement for note taking and to ensure that your main attention stays with the group. It is helpful if you tell the group that your note taking is for the purposes of keeping track and that your notes will not be shown to anyone.

4. Organising content

All content or information can be managed at different levels of abstraction. This means that all data can be grouped into some format that makes it more manageable. For the purposes of facilitation it is sometimes helpful to order or organise the content into a logical order. You should never do this without the permission of the group. If the group starts disagreeing about the order, then it is often an indication of other underlying disagreements. Do not try to resolve the disagreement, but rather suggest an interim structure that everyone can live with.

Some suggestions for logical ordering are given below.

Logical groupings	Description	Type of order	Example
Deductive logic	Reasoning deductively – if this is true and that is true, then a conclusion can be drawn	Argument order	Major premise, minor premise, conclusion. For example: "If the organisation increases the marketing effort, then it will have an impact on sales volumes, and therefore it will be necessary to increase production."

Logical groupings	Description	Type of order	Example
Chronology	Working out the flow of issues in terms of the time in which they occur or the order in which they should be addressed	Time order	First, second, third. For example: 1. Advertisement of new positions 2. Receipt of job applications 3. Interviews 4. Shortlisting 5. Final selection
Structure	Dividing a whole into its parts Analysing	Order of the structure	Organisational structure, for example: Head office The regions The districts The branches
Comparison	Comparison and contrast	Grouping according to similarities and/or differences	Projects on budget versus those over budget
Classification	Placing into categories	Order of size or importance	Leadership issues, team issues, communication issues
Priority	Ordering something in terms of importance or priority	Order of importance	First most important, second most important, etc

Often a group will have decided on the content structure that they want to follow. It is useful if you do not impose a structure on the group, but rather follow the preferences of the group.

5. Clarifying content

It is not always necessary for you as facilitator to understand every detail of the content. It is, however, important for you to check that all the participants understand the content. You need to observe the group carefully to check for signs of misunderstanding and confusion. It is also helpful to check explicitly from time to time whether everyone is clear.

Often you may work with groups where you are not an expert on the content of the discussion. For example, you may be working with a group of nurses who are discussing the shift roster. It is not important for you to know everything about organising a shift roster, but it is important for you to check that all the participants understand what is being spoken about. Sometimes you may be shy to check whether everyone understands, because you are afraid that it may reveal your own lack of expertise. It is better to self-disclose that you do not understand the detail, because it is not necessary as a facilitator to have content expertise about all the subjects discussed by your groups. In fact, sometimes too much knowledge may interfere with your neutrality. It is appropriate for you to ask for a content explanation if it seems necessary to gain clarity in order to manage the process better. Most groups are very willing to help the facilitator understand their worlds better.

6. Summarising content

Occasionally in a session, particularly before and after breaks, the facilitator should provide a summary of the content covered until that point. These summaries should do justice to the varying viewpoints expressed, and should always present a neutral, non-judgemental version of what was said. If you are unclear about the actual content, you can always ask the group to help with a summary. It is important to remember minority viewpoints in this process.

7. Documenting content

If a facilitated session is designed to have a particular outcome that will be acted on by the group members, it is useful to have discussion points and decisions publicly documented. If there is to be a great deal of documentation, or accurate records are needed for legal purposes, then it is useful to have a scribe for the session. However, it is important that facilitator and scribe have a good working relationship, and that the facilitator trusts the scribe's competence and neutrality. A scribe has power, and if the scribe does not have the same ethos as the facilitator or has a vested interest in the content, then the scribe can compromise the accuracy and neutrality of the documentation process.

General guidelines for successful documentation are given below:

- The documentation style should be dictated by the purpose of the documentation.
- Ensure that the venue is set up correctly so that documentation processes are clearly visible if needed.
- Let the group define the symbols or types of notation to be used.
- The group must participate and concentrate on the documentation process. If they are not interested, then documentation in that form is probably not appropriate.
- Use people's own words or existing phrases, or change them only with agreement.
- Clarify for understanding when taking down notes.
- If you as facilitator are not taking notes, ensure that someone else is if necessary.
- Ensure that all contributions are documented.
- Always check that the group agrees with the documentation.
- Ensure that information is presented concisely and neatly and clarify relationships between points, or the stages in a process.

Content can be captured on a variety of media such as a flipchart, a computer with a data projector, a whiteboard, or a smartboard. If verbatim minutes need to be kept then there should be a scribe who is qualified and competent to capture on a laptop everything that is said. These notes can then be distributed to the participants for checking after the session. If short notes need to be kept, then the facilitator can use a flipchart, white board or a smartboard to make notes.

The following guidelines should be followed for the writing of such notes.

1. If using a flipchart, check the stand for stability.
2. Write clearly with letters at least 5 centimetres high.
3. Leave about 5 centimetres between lines.
4. Do not stand in front of flip chart or whiteboard.
5. After you have finished writing, allow participants to read what you have written.
6. Allow participants to take notes.
7. Remove material that is no longer relevant.
8. Always ensure that you are using an erasable whiteboard marker on a whiteboard.
9. Use a consistent format for all documentation.

Some guidelines for presenting information

If you as the facilitator have to present some information, such as an agenda or process instructions, keep your visual aids simple and only use them when absolutely necessary. If a group is focusing on the visual aid, you will be losing contact with them as a group. It is useful to have the agenda clearly documented and to tick off items as they are completed. On the one hand, visual aids can be very effective in reminding a group of where they are in the process because they provide a form of containment. On the other hand, visual aids are almost always cumbersome because they slow the pace of the process far below what is required for complete participant involvement. As a rule of thumb, a facilitator should use visual aids sparingly because they can disrupt the rapport with the group.

Distribution of minutes

If minutes are to be distributed to a group, then this should ideally happen within 48 hours of the meeting if possible. A time limit should be set for participant feedback on the accuracy of the minutes, after which time you can integrate the changes and distribute the final minutes to the group members. It is important to ensure that all group members receive the documentation individually.

8. Identifying depth content

The tasks concerned with managing content up until this point apply to both surface and depth facilitation. However, managing content from a depth perspective includes an additional set of skills. In order to identify depth content, the facilitator needs an understanding of the nature of the content of depth processes. This section discusses that nature in detail.

Working in the concrete and mythological worlds

Human life embraces a fascinating combination of perspectives and levels of functioning. We have our concrete, visible and obviously physical world in which we all have to function. We also have the invisible world within our minds that is neither concrete nor tangible, but nevertheless undeniably real. At the other extreme of the concrete physical world, we have the mythological world, in which all the human stories through the ages are captured in symbolic form. We have the potential world with its archetypes and instincts that are the lifeblood of human behaviour.

In depth work, we move between the different worlds. We move from the concrete, practical and physical world into the mythical realm of the collective unconscious with its archetypes and instincts that drive individual and group behaviour, and back to the concrete world again. A depth facilitator needs to be comfortable with these different worlds, and to be able to translate meaning from one to the other.

So, whether we are aware of it or not, all individuals and groups operate on all these several levels at once. These include the following internal and external levels:

Internal levels

- physical
- practical
- cognitive
- emotional
- psychological
- imaginative
- ancestral
- spiritual

External levels

- immediate group
- family group
- community group
- cultural group
- religious group
- ethnic group
- national group
- species

There are always both concrete and mythological systems at work in a group's functioning. The group has an inner psychological world, just as an individual does. The psyche of the group and the individual is an inner world filled with archetypal and instinctual impulses. In order for the psyche to metabolise the concrete experience, it has to make symbolic sense of it. In other words, the psyche has to translate the concrete experience into its own language in order to integrate it conceptually. The language of the psyche is the language of symbols. In some ways, this language is universal and, in other ways, it is deeply personal. In order to help a group understand its depth processes, the facilitator has to help the group understand the symbolic nature of unconscious communication. The skills required for this are described in the following section.

9. Elucidating symbols

In order for depth processes to be transformative for a group, the group needs to derive meaning from it. However, understanding and being able to articulate the meaning of a depth process requires a conceptual and communication ability that transcends the use of ordinary language. It requires a language that can capture the full diversity and complexity of human experience, and yet be accessible to all who use it. The psyche uses the language of symbols in order to achieve this.

What are symbols?

Chambers Dictionary defines a symbol as "an emblem: that which by custom or convention represents something else". A symbol is different from a sign in that a sign stands for something or points to something in a literal way. A symbol carries the meaning of joining things together so that the whole becomes more than the sum of the parts.

Symbolism is a richly textured "language" in which an object, a picture, a sound, or any other coherent concept that can be perceived is used to represent an aspect of our life experience. Multiple meanings can be derived from one symbol, and associated meanings derived from one symbol will differ between individuals and groups.

The symbol in itself does not have complex meaning. A "tree" is a tree until we start using it as a symbol. The "cross", for example, has been used throughout history, in a variety of contexts, to denote many different ideas, all of them rich and complex. There is general agreement that it is an evocative and meaningful symbol, whether or not you subscribe to the doctrines in which is used. The meaning of the symbol is derived from the set of associations that have developed over time – associations that arise from all the varieties of human experience.

The psyche uses symbols to express complex experiential states, which can never be described as succinctly and as fully in ordinary language. A symbol is multifaceted in a way that a word is not. The psyche uses the symbolic world to communicate how it makes meaning out of depth processes. As a facilitator you must recognise that a symbol can contain all of the following meanings and possibilities at once:

- A literal meaning
- A practical meaning
- An emotional meaning
- A spiritual meaning
- An intellectual meaning
- A suggestion for proposed action
- A historical meaning
- A transformative capacity
- A transcendent meaning

Importantly, psychically useful symbols cannot be contrived through rational, logical processes. Rather, they seem to need to emerge through a creative process or dialogue between the conscious and unconscious mind, or simply be a product of the unconscious mind, as we see in dreams.

Recognising the group's "myth" or story

Usually symbols do not appear in isolation in a group's depth process. It will usually be part of a "myth" or story that is playing itself out in a group. When working with a depth process it is useful to try to identify the story or a myth that approximately describes the experience the group is having. Often the story or the myth will already be present in the way participants speak about the group, and you simply have to attend to the kind of words being used or the kind of metaphors and analogies used to describe the group. By using a story or a myth that captures important elements of the group's experience, the group can make sense of, or make meaning of, its experience in a way that enables change and transformation.

It may be useful to draw on any myths or stories that a group can relate to, if this story is not already present in the group conversation. Useful source material includes fairy tales, ancient myths such as tales about the Greek gods, tales from the ancestors, films and books, stories from the various religious documents, stories from the oral tradition and culture, or any story that spontaneously appears in the mind of the facilitator. The mythical story should be offered as a tentative possibility that may capture important elements of the group story. By being tentative, you allow the group to modify or alter the myth or story or generate one that is more appropriate to the group's experience.

Once a myth or a story that is useful to the group has been identified, the group can use it as a point of reference, as well as symbolically to better understand the situation and the attendant choices it offers. The group also now has the freedom to decide how the story will unfold from that point onwards, and so transformation becomes possible.

10. Interpreting from a depth perspective

As a facilitator you need to help the group decide what a symbol or a collection of symbols in a story means for them. Symbols become meaningful when we investigate the associations that surround them. Human beings create webs of meaning in their minds. Our minds are not neatly organised like filing cabinets in a legal firm. Rather, they are organic data storage networks where the main logic is determined by proximity in terms of time and space, and emotional similarity plays a large role.

If we accept the tenets of Carl Jung stating that there is a collective unconscious that we all have access to and that it forms the foundation for our own individual minds, then we can imagine each individual mind as having similar strata of potential concepts and associations. Each individual web of meaning may then start with similar bedrock, but how that develops in order to furnish the individual mind depends on the particular experiences and idiosyncrasies of the individual.

Meaning is created when a person experiences a particular state and has a feeling response to it. In other words, it is the feeling that provides the meaning. The word "feeling" here does not denote a sentiment but rather the placing of a personal value on a given experience. Individuals are always asking the question: how is this important to me? Or how does this affect my life or my development? Or my quality of life? If we can answer those questions in satisfying ways then we are attaching meaning to our experiences.

When exploring the meaning of symbolism in groups remember to investigate associations from multiple perspectives. Do not assume that your associations are appropriate for the group. Encourage the group members to offer associations from a variety of perspectives, including:

- Their individual, personal perspectives
- The group perspective
- The organisational perspective
- Relevant cultural perspectives
- Historical perspectives
- Any other relevant perspectives.

The group can then derive meaning from a synthesis of all the different points of view. You should not impose meaning on the group, but rather facilitate a discussion in which meaning emerges. Once this happens, it is likely that more symbols will shortly follow, spontaneously arising from the group. These symbols can become very powerful for guiding the group into the future.

For example, one of the groups that I facilitated was unhappy with the group leader. The leader was an autocratic and critical man, who often humiliated and belittled staff members. His style led to an added difficulty in that the individual employees were no longer able to be supportive of one another, because the leader attacked any of them who were. One member of the group mentioned that he felt as if he was living in an orphanage run by a cruel housemaster. This "myth" or story became very useful in understanding the group dynamic that was operating. The group started exploring what it meant to be orphans who were victimised when they tried to protect or support one another. They came to understand that they were not only suffering at the hands of the autocratic leader, but that they were also abandoning one another for fear of victimisation. They realised that by supporting one another, they could stop behaving like helpless "children" with no recourse, and could start taking action that would protect them. The leader was unable to do the inner work that would result in a different dynamic between himself and the rest of the group, and ultimately he left the organisation. However, the group's new awareness meant that they could prevent the perpetuation of the negative dynamic among them.

11. Linking symbolism with concrete content

Once the group has completed a depth process, it is important to move back to the current experience of the group and help to translate the myth or story into its meaning for the group as it goes forward. This means discussing in practical terms what the symbolism means for the group's decisions and interactions into the future. It is helpful to identify how relationships need to change and help the group to spell it out and document it in the form of specific actions.

12. Maintaining multilevel perspectives

Finally, from a content point of view, it is important for you to be able to maintain multilevel perspectives throughout facilitation work when thinking about the content of a group's discussions. The group may be discussing the intricacies of a difficult client relationship, but it is necessary for you to be thinking about the possible parallels between the client relationship and the internal relationships between members of the organisation. It is also important to remember all aspects of the group context, as discussed in Chapter 4, because these may be playing themselves out in the themes with which the group is pre-occupied. It means listening with a metaphorical ear, as well as a practical one, at all times. It is not necessary to feed back all the perspectives to the group every time, but occasionally, it may be helpful to remind the group of the different perspectives.

CONCLUSION

Managing content requires a great deal of skill in terms of neutrality. The other aspects of managing content are not as taxing, but require clarity of thought and organisation skills. There are some proprietary products available for documenting group processes and these can be investigated for their usefulness. Getting clarity and agreement are very important when managing content.

Managing content from a depth perspective requires an added set of skills. We considered the world of symbolism as the language of the unconscious and its relevance to depth facilitation. The basic ideas behind working with the content of depth processes were discussed, but it is necessary to note that it is a vast and complex field. In some ways, a text of this nature can only scratch the surface of all the theory associated with depth processes. However, it is a field with great opportunity, and one that depth facilitators should explore as fully as possible.

PERSONAL EXERCISES

1. Consider three areas in which you are not neutral, but rather have some strong feelings and opinions. Work to find the validity of the opposing opinion. Spend time convincing someone else of the opposing view to the one you really hold. Check if you are genuinely able to see the validity of both sides.

2. Consider areas in which you are unable to be neutral. Decide how you will handle situations in which they arise.

3. Think of three symbols that are important to you. Describe them and their meaning. Trace the origins of that symbol for you. Ask two other people what the symbols means for them. Compare your view with the view of others.

4. Think of a story or a myth that describes important elements of your life. Decide how you would like the story to end.

5. Consider your relationship with your inner world. Spend time getting to know which symbols are important to you and embark on a process of analysing your dreams for a while. If necessary, enlist the help of a professional. Actively develop a familiarity with the symbolic world.

CHAPTER 13
MANAGING PROCESS

MANAGING PROCESS OVERVIEW

This chapter considers each of the tasks of managing process in detail. An overview of the role, tasks and skills are provided first as a reminder.

Facilitator's role

To initiate and manage group processes whereby the group reaches their objective(s) and, if needed, to facilitate the emergence of group depth processes, supporting and ensuring completion of those processes.

Facilitator's tasks and related skills

Tasks	Skills/knowledge
1. Initiating and explaining group surface process 2. Facilitating surface process 3. Closing surface process 4. Tracking the group development process and intervening appropriately 5. Identifying depth processes 6. Surfacing depth processes 7. Completing depth processes 8. Integrating depth processes with surface process.	1. General psychology knowledge 2. Depth Psychology knowledge 3. Systems thinking 4. Metaskills 5. Self-management skills 6. Communication skills 　• Presentation skills 　• Awareness and observation skills 　• Listening skills 　• Verbal skills 　• Feedback skills 　• Stimulation skills 　• Support skills 　• Control skills. 7. Group intervention skills 8. Exercising authority 9. Process design skills 10. Process management skills 11. Group intervention skills.

FACILITATOR'S GUIDELINES, TOOLS AND TECHNIQUES

A DEFINITION OF PROCESS

Often in the notes here and in the work of a facilitator we refer to the term "processing" or the phrase "to process" something. These terms are used to denote a set of activities that lead the individual or group towards a planned or emerging goal.

The term "process" comes from the Latin word "processus", meaning a "going forward", according to the Penguin Dictionary of Psychology. The Oxford Dictionary of Psychology defines the term processing in the following way: "to advance – a sequence of events leading to some change or alteration in the state of a dynamic system."

In depth facilitation terms, "processing" something in a group means helping to unfold emerging events or trends in the most constructive way possible. In this chapter, we consider the facilitation tasks required for managing both surface and depth processes. We begin by considering basic surface process tasks.

1. INITIATING AND EXPLAINING GROUP SURFACE PROCESS

During this task, you as facilitator need to explain the choice of process and the rationale behind that choice, especially if you are the one who has made that choice. Explain why the particular process has been chosen and how it will contribute to the effective achievement of the objective. The group needs to be given an idea of the time required to complete the process, as well as the demands the process will make on them. The group has to be in agreement that they want to try the process before you embark on it.

Explain in detail the steps required to complete the process, and outline the use of visual or other aids. It is important to keep an eye on group members to check for understanding. Often adults are reluctant to admit that they do not understand a particular instruction, especially if everyone in the rest of the group seems to understand. It is helpful to write instructions down if they are complex so that group members can refer to them if necessary. Check if the group has any suggestions for modifications to the process that may be suitable for this particular group.

Types of surface processes

There are many group processes and they can be arranged along a continuum of largely task-oriented processes versus largely relationship-oriented processes. An idea of this continuum is given below.

↑ Task
- Generating ideas
- Problem-solving
- Decision-making
- Planning
- Completing tasks
- Learning
- Evaluating
- Relationship building
- Resolving conflict
- Ending

↓ Relationship

There are many different methodologies available for the more surface or task-orientated processes. It is beyond the scope of this book to consider the various methodologies in detail. As a facilitator you need to develop a toolkit of methodologies for these processes if you want to concentrate on surface facilitation. Methodologies available include the following:

- Creativity or ideas generation such as brainstorming
- Problem-solving steps, which vary from more mechanistically based processes to those based on systems thinking
- Decision-making processes
- Planning methodologies, including a variety for strategic planning and change management
- Learning or skills acquisition methodologies
- Evaluation processes that measure the success of tasks or projects
- Relationship or team-building methodologies ranging from physical outdoor activities to more psychologically based group interactions
- Conflict resolution methodologies based on a variety of frameworks
- Ending processes which help a group gain closure.

Each of the methodologies listed above could operate only on the surface level, or it could include a depth component. In this book, we consider the essential principles and practices of depth facilitation and these could be integrated with any of the methodologies that a group or a facilitator uses, including the ones listed above.

Most groups will have several processes running at once. The facilitator should always start by focusing on the process closest to the surface. Detours should only occur if they cannot be avoided because underlying issues continuously hijack the surface process. Be very clear with the group about your choices as a facilitator. If you start sliding into a different process from the one that the group agreed to, make the group aware of it and ask them to choose what they would like to do. Ideally, you should practise deep democracy during this decision. If the group explicitly requests a depth process that investigates the underlying group dynamics, then in effect, this becomes tantamount to being the "surface" process.

2. Facilitating surface process

Facilitating a surface process involves breaking it down into manageable steps and explaining each step as it is needed. As the facilitator, you need continually to observe the group and monitor the group climate to check if the group is functioning well. If it is necessary to document the results of various steps, the facilitator should do it, or take responsibility for appointing a scribe. You can invite feedback throughout the process to monitor the group's experience and progress. All the techniques for managing people need to be applied on a continuous basis.

Sound surface processes

Sound surface processes will have certain characteristics. We consider some of those characteristics here to help the facilitator choose appropriate processes.

A good surface process will not be characterised by the phenomenon known as "groupthink". The symptoms of groupthink are:

- When a very cohesive group exerts pressures on others to conform to the consensus view, or
- When there is an illusion of unanimity and correctness (and a subsequent lack of any creative search for other opinions) and
- When there is negative stereotyping of out-groups.

The following steps will help the group to avoid groupthink:

- Encourage the expression of the minority points of view.
- Do not leave it to just one individual to carry a dissenting voice. Spread the role if possible.
- Encourage maximum participation by all group members, which leads to improved problem-solving.

If it becomes clear during a surface process that the process is not working, it is important to take the following steps:

- Verbalise the fact that the process is not working.
- Ask the group whether they have ideas about what is most needed.
- Stay calm if the group becomes disruptive, and manage time and space boundaries.
- Be firm about the need for the group to make a joint decision about the new direction.
- Do not relinquish your authority, but consult with the group.

If it becomes clear that the surface process is not proceeding because of an underlying depth process, then you need to move into the depth process. The tools and techniques for this are described later in this chapter.

3. Closing surface process

It is important that the facilitator sees the surface process through to its conclusion, unless it becomes clear that it is not suiting the purpose of the group. Often a group will get distracted or sidetracked. This should not be allowed to happen without comment. Reflect back to the group that they are moving away from the process, and check whether they want to actively take the detour or return to the initial plan. An important rule of thumb is to "decide rather than slide". In most instances the reminder that the group has gone off track will be sufficient to return the group to the process. In closing the process, you can ask the group to evaluate the process and to check whether anything else is needed.

4. Tracking the group development process and intervening appropriately

In Chapter 4, we discussed the group developmental processes that a facilitator will encounter. In this section, we investigate the facilitator's intervention for these processes. Relationship building processes run concurrently with all other surface and depth processes too, so you as the facilitator have to keep this level of the process in mind all the time. However, it is important to have the explicit permission of the group to intervene in the relationship building process, and so you need to ensure that an appropriate contract is in place for this work before it is embarked upon.

Each group that you work with will be at a different stage. The guidelines below are offered to help with relationship building processes.

- Determine at what stage the group is.
- Ensure that the steps are followed methodically.
- Design an intervention appropriate for that stage of the relationship development.
- Ensure good surface process facilitation to ensure that steps are comprehensively implemented, such as ensuring a comprehensive "getting to know each other" right at the start.
- Make sure everyone has had an opportunity for each step.
- Avoid sub-groups dominating.
- Ensure that the whole group is part of the relationship building process.
- Notice group collusions and look for signals to indicate that those collusions are a problem.
- Remember the group task and keep it in mind in all interventions.
- Tap into the visions and the dreams that the group members have for the group.

The table on the next page uses the model described in Chapter 4 in order to outline the facilitation interventions required at each stage.

Stage of Group Develop-ment	Purpose of the Stage	Healthy Characteristics	Symptoms of problems/ inability to move on/ inappropriate behaviour	Interventions
Courting	Making initial contact Establishing commonality Exploring the possibility of relationship Group formation	Politeness Friendliness Courtesy Gathering information Openness Receptivity Everyone makes an effort Shyness	Suppressing feelings of disagreement so that it becomes uncomfortable Groupthink develops Difference is not tolerated	Opportunities to share information and get to know each other Joint activities that build a sense of group Socialising together Discussing and establishing shared values The allocation of roles and responsibilities The development of a shared vision

Stage of group develop-ment	Purpose of the stage	Healthy characteristics	Symptoms of problems/ inability to move on/ inappropriate behaviour	Interventions
Asserting	Establishing individual differences Testing the group acceptance of differences Testing the values Exploring conflict	Disagreement Healthy debate Challenging Listening Tolerance Openness	Disagreement becomes entrenched and the group polarises Sub-groups form and remain Scapegoating develops Individuals try to leave the group Individuals feel unheard and excluded	Developing and agreeing on a container A structured conflict resolution process Reconsidering values, roles and responsibilities Allowing differences to emerge
Revealing	Moving beyond the defences to the expression of real feelings Establishing trust Establishing shared feeling Establishing the possibility for group cohesion	Vulnerability Compassion Openness Respect	Group therapy Attempts to make it better Rescuing individuals Excusing individuals from responsibility	Ensuring a container Respectful listening to individual feelings Allowing opportunities for repair work Agreeing on ground rules

Stage of group develop-ment	Purpose of the stage	Healthy characteristics	Symptoms of problems/ inability to move on/ inappropriate behaviour	Interventions
Fully functioning	Development of group cohesion that is robust Use of the full intelligence of the system Ability to rotate roles as needed by task completion Supportive environment	Healthy debate Task completion Promises kept Cooperation Teamwork Mutual support and affection Openness to newcomers		Goal-setting Continued feedback and monitoring Recognition

In terms of depth facilitation, the facilitator has to be aware of how well the members know one another, and what the stage of development is in terms of interpersonal relationships. A more detailed breakdown of the important stages and the required facilitation interventions is given in the table below.

STAGE OF RELATIONSHIP	CHARACTERISTICS OF THE STAGE	FACILITATION INTERVENTIONS
1. Getting to know one another in terms of personal details	Individuals encounter one another as strangers and get to know demographic and biographic details about one another. They unconsciously get to know and assume psychological information about one another.	It is helpful to engage the group in a storytelling process, whereby individual members provide information about themselves in whatever way they want to. This helps to break down inaccurate stereotyping and dispel wrong assumptions about one another. Participants should not interrupt one another during this process.
2. Activation of projections	They develop their assumptions into opinions of one another and inevitably start projecting onto one another. Projective identification begins.	It is helpful to encourage the group to get to know one another even better. More individual information should be given to avoid projection if possible. Sometimes, the unconscious processes are too strong for this to be successful and a conflict resolution process may be needed.

Stage of relationship	Characteristics of the stage	Facilitation interventions
3. Managing differences	The group develops interpersonal relationships based on the information they have of one another and their projections. They find ways of managing the differences, usually initially by avoiding them. They may agree to disagree, or less powerful sub-groups may choose to become subservient to the more powerful sub-groups.	The facilitator needs to observe these processes in action and consider moving the group into a depth process.
4. Confronting differences	At this stage, it may no longer be possible for the group to manage differences and pretend that they are not problematic, in which case they may find some way of confronting them. They may choose to have open conflict, or they may try to involve third parties to help them address the conflict.	Often a facilitator is called in at this stage of the group's life and then it is necessary to move into a depth and usually a conflict resolution process. It may even be necessary to move into a reconciliation process if the group members have harmed one another through their projections and resulting actions.

Stage of relationship	Characteristics of the stage	Facilitation interventions
5. Splitting or transformation (consolidating or withdrawing projections)	In this stage, the group either resolves the differences and a process of transformation happens, or it chooses not to, or is unable to, resolve the differences and some form of splitting occurs.	A sound depth process will ensure that transformation rather than splitting occurs.
6. Task achievement	Group members are able to accept one another and value differences. They are able to work at the tasks they agree to and are able to use their diversity in order to enhance the task.	At this stage, the facilitator can usually move back into surface facilitation to ensure task achievement.

Stage of relationship	Characteristics of the stage	Facilitation interventions
7. Ending	At this stage, the group life ends either through circumstance or as the choice of the group members, or both. The group stops existing as an identifiable group in the here and now.	It is necessary for the facilitator to help the group confront the ending process. The group may resist this, but without an ending process in which the group is forced to accept the ending – and use it to honour their experiences with one another – they may end up feeling incomplete. Often the facilitator has to be quite firm and containing in order to avoid the defences caused by the anxiety of impending loss. Here the group needs to move into a cathartic process.

COMPLICATIONS IN RELATIONSHIP BUILDING PROCESSES

A complication to the development of interpersonal relationships in groups is that different sub-groups will be at different levels. This process needs to be addressed until all group members are functioning well from an interpersonal perspective.

A further complication is that as people change over time, so the depth and the nature of interpersonal relationships needs to change too. This means that the process described above is continually evolving.

5. Identifying depth processes

Once you as the facilitator have done the preparatory work of contracting comprehensively with the client and preparing yourself for neutrality, you can work with a depth process. In the meetings with a client before any group sessions take place, the client may specifically ask you to address a particular depth process when working with a group. You cannot assume, however, that the whole group is ready to do so. The group process can only be pursued if the whole group explicitly agrees that it is ready to investigate a certain area – something that we will look at in more detail later.

In order to create an environment where depth processes can be worked with as they occur, it is important to contract with the group explicitly that such depth work will be pursued if necessary. As the facilitator, you need to explain in general terms what this will mean, as well as to reassure the group that nothing will be pursued without its permission. Once this is agreed upon, you can open a session.

Creating an agenda for a depth process

If the group has difficulties, members will not necessarily openly discuss what the nature of those difficulties is. Psychological difficulties are hard to speak about for anyone, and sometimes they need to be brought to the attention of someone else before they can be tackled. Sometimes the problem we tell people about is not necessarily the same as the problem we need to solve. The technical term for this is the "presenting problem", which is the socially acceptable problem that we can talk about. It is important for a depth facilitator to recognise that there will be a presenting problem when working with a group and that this presenting problem may be linked to, but be different from, the real problem. Therefore, the facilitator needs to do some detective work to determine what the real problem in a group may be, making it impossible to set an agenda for a depth process. The agenda will often be set for the presenting problem.

All the guidelines for creating an agenda that were covered in Chapter 10 also need to be followed when doing depth work. Sometimes, when embarking on a session where depth work may be needed, the facilitator has an open agenda because the group wants to explore whatever may emerge. In this case, you may use the approach that Arnold Mindell calls "sorting the field". As we saw in Chapter 10, this involves asking the group members to list randomly list any issues that they would like to address in this group session. You allow the group to decide together which of the topics will take precedence. If a topic emerges that no one in the group wants to work on, other than the individual who listed it, this may be an indication that there is a depth process at work.

Ultimately, in depth work, the agenda is set by the group psyche itself. You as facilitator simply follow what is happening in the group and use the techniques outlined in this section in order to address important issues.

Once the group has agreed that it will pursue depth processes if necessary, you can start your facilitation work. The first step is to identify that there is a depth process that may need work, remembering that the group may not know what it is. Once the depth process has been identified, careful work is needed to bring it to the surface. Sometimes the identification and surfacing happen simultaneously. Either way, patience and delicacy is required.

BECOMING ATTENTIVE TO DEPTH PROCESSES

Most of us will pay attention to what is on the surface in a group situation. Obvious events and interactions capture our attention and there is often little room to notice the more subtle events and interactions that occur in a group. Arnold Mindell distinguishes between what he calls our "first attention" and our "second attention". Earlier we referred to a "surface" attention and a "depth" attention. The first attention is the awareness needed to accomplish goals, to do our daily work, and to manage our daily interactions with others. The second attention focuses on things we would normally neglect, such as external and internal subjective, irrational experiences. The second attention is the key to gaining access to unconscious or under-the-surface processes, and it means noticing and attending to, among other things, the accidents and slips of the tongue that happen every day. Below is a list of examples of the kinds of things to be aware of in order to develop a second attention.

- Body movements while someone is talking
- The way someone makes eye contact
- Interaction and eye contact patterns between individuals
- Thoughts and feelings that pop unbidden into your mind
- Internal voices (or thoughts) that tell you what to do
- Momentary or chronic physical sensations
- "Flirts" (a term coined by Arnold Mindell) – events from other systems that catch your attention, such as the light falling on water, or a bird moving almost invisibly in a tree, or any of the myriad other things that catch your attention for a moment
- Sudden awareness of certain sounds such as a clock ticking
- The appearance of a song inside your head
- The sudden awareness of an object or an image that was present all the time, but was not noticed before.

Learning to pay attention to these and other examples of signals from the depth takes practice. Asking the following questions in any given situation can actively develop this practice:

- What am I noticing?
- What else is also happening?
- What keeps catching my attention?

NOTICING THE POSSIBILITY OF A DEPTH PROCESS

Remember that a depth process should only be worked with if the surface process is being jeopardised in some way or if the group particularly wishes to explore the depth process even if the surface process is going well. The first thing to notice, then, is if the surface process is in some way not proceeding as effectively as it can. Look for signs that the process is getting stuck or taking longer than it should. For example:

- The group is unable to take the next step in a process.
- An activity is repeated.
- There is a lack of energy in the group that cannot be ascribed to other factors, such as it being directly after lunch.
- Only a few group members are participating.
- There is criticism of the process.
- There is a continual changing of direction.
- Process steps are interrupted regularly.
- Agreements are not kept.

Once you have noticed that the surface process is getting stuck, then you start looking for the depth process more specifically. In order to look for a depth process, it is important to understand where and how to look.

PATHWAYS FROM THE DEPTH TO THE SURFACE

Information from a depth process will invariably find its way to the surface over time. It is useful to understand the ways in which information from the less conscious parts of a system travel to the surface.

The possible pathways will consist of any methods that human beings use to experience the world or express themselves. A range of possibilities is listed below.

- We experience the world through our senses so there are pathways relating to touch, hearing, taste, sight and smell.
- We experience the world through physical sensations such as feeling hot or cold, pain or pleasure.

- We can experience the world through our intuition in which we "know" things in a way that has by-passed the physical senses.
- We can express ourselves through physical movement, through words and sounds.
- We can express ourselves through imagery in our minds, including dreams and visions that include all the senses.
- We can express ourselves through art, through our actions, including the ways in which we relate to people and things.

All these means of expression and experience can be pathways for information about depth processes. Individuals and groups will use different pathways, depending on their unique talents and preferences and the medium of communication that is appropriate to their given cultural and social environments.

Importantly, the information from a depth process usually will not use the dominant experiential or expression pathway in that system. If the group is communicating through talking, the depth information may travel via the touch or movement pathway.

Arnold Mindell refers to these pathways as channels, and defines the possible channels as follows:

1. The proprioceptive channel: refers to physical sensations
2. The auditory channel: refers to external and internal voices and sounds, including music (voices in your head, jingles/tunes that appear spontaneously in your mind)
3. The kinaesthetic channel: refers to physical movement
4. The visual channel: refers to external and internal imagery
5. The relationship channel: refers to the way people relate to and interact with one another
6. The world channel: refers to events and trends in the systems surrounding a group.

The following list provides some guidelines for using pathways of information in order to identify a depth process.

- Notice the pathway that the group is using for its ordinary communication.
- Notice any other pathways that may be carrying information.
- Tune into the subtle pathways that the group may be using and pay attention to any signals that occur in this pathway.
- Notice if the group switches pathways. This may be an indication of a depth process.
- Ask the group to comment on any unusual thoughts, feelings or experiences they may be noticing.
- Once the overt and subtle pathways that a group uses have been identified, the facilitator needs to notice and make sense of the signals that come through them.

SIGNALS FROM THE DEEP

A signal is essentially any piece of information that the psyche uses to communicate the nature of a depth process. A signal is a message from under the surface. The signal will be noticeable, because it communicates information that is different from everything else that is being communicated.

A signal should be taken seriously once it has occurred more than two or three times. Until then, it is difficult to know what information the signal is carrying. Also, it is important to understand that the signal is not being given consciously, and should therefore be treated with kid gloves. Guidelines on how to handle signals are given in the rest of this section.

USING SIGNALS TO IDENTIFY DEPTH PROCESSES

It is important to know what to look for in order to identify whether a signal indicates a depth process. Signals that indicate depth processes fall into the following categories: signs of anxiety, signs of defence mechanisms, signs of incongruence, and signs of conflict. In Chapter 3 we discussed these signals as being "edge" symptoms. More information is provided below about each of these areas.

Signs of anxiety

An unaddressed depth process will cause anxiety in the group and its members. It is therefore important to look for any signals that indicate anxiety. Anxiety produces adrenaline in the body, which has the following effects, some of which are directly related to the effects of adrenaline.

- Nervous silence
- Nervous laughter
- Confusion
- Fidgeting
- Losing focus or "going blank"
- Mental interference – inability to hear or follow current experience
- Dry mouth
- Increased blood pressure
- Sweating
- A loss of energy

Signs of individual and group defence mechanisms

If you observe an intensification of a particular defence mechanism, or the arrival of the new defence mechanism, it may be a sign of a depth process. Any other defence mechanisms mentioned in Chapters 3 and 4 may be a sign of the depth process.

Some of the more common individual defence mechanisms, as well as some general group ones, are listed below.

- Withdrawal – lack of eye contact, or physical withdrawal
- Aggression
- Searching for an escape
- Chaos – everyone talking all at once
- Discussion of unrepresented third parties
- Sleepiness or boredom
- Continual references to the past or future and an inability to stay in the here and now
- Incomplete acts
- Unfinished sentences
- Switching pathways

Signs of incongruence
Any signs of a lack of congruence in an individual or a group or a process may indicate the presence of a depth process. The most common example of incongruence is what Arnold Mindell refers to as a "double signal". People communicate simultaneously in many different ways. Double signals occur when more than one message is sent out and the messages that are sent are not congruent. They are the result of unconscious processes that contradict the surface one.

For example, while talking, the tone and tempo of someone's voice may be incongruent with the content of what is being said. Another example is where members of a group may send out a message verbally that they are saying yes to a particular request, but through movement or actions they may be "shaking their heads" to indicate that they are saying no. Those hearing these messages are unconsciously aware of the "no" message and are often confused by it. They unconsciously realise that regardless of how they respond they will invariably negate one of the two messages and, effectively, one part of the message.

Other signs of incongruence are:

- **Lack of follow-through** – decisions are not implemented
- **Gossip** – communication is not congruent in different settings
- **Cycling** – a group approaches a process, but never quite completes it

Signs of conflict
Many depth processes are partially or completely about conflict. It is therefore useful to look for signs that there is a conflict, such as:

- Brief or prolonged verbal disagreements between group members
- A lack of overt communication or participants remaining separated from one another in some way
- Individuals or sub-groups talking about others who are not present
- Individuals or sub-groups being suspicious or mistrustful of the motivations of others.

Anything indicating that all is not what it seems may be a signal of the presence of a depth process that needs to be tackled. In ordinary language, it is useful for a depth facilitator to look for three general signs when identifying potential depth processes:

- Anything out of the ordinary in the behaviour of an individual member or the group as a whole
- Processes that cannot be completed
- Mixed messages of any kind.

6. Surfacing depth processes

Once the facilitator has identified the existence of a depth process, the decision has to be made about how to bring it to the surface. This task is considered in detail in the following section. However, since the most important part of bringing a depth process to the surface is to gain the permission of the group to do so, this is discussed first.

Gaining permission for the depth process

Once you as facilitator have identified a depth process, it is important to gain the permission of the group to pursue it. This permission can be gained in general at the beginning of the session, but it is also important to gain permission specifically for the particular process that you are about to pursue. You gain permission by alerting the group to the fact that you are about to explore a deeper issue and asking for its agreement to go ahead.

It is useful to practise the process called "deep democracy" (introduced in Chapter 2), in which consensus is sought before the facilitator goes ahead. The consensus is achieved by making modifications based on the concerns and underlying wisdom of all the opinions of the group. The group needs to be given permission to say no and any individual who exercises this choice needs to be supported and asked what he or she would need to be able to proceed. As the facilitator you may need to go through several iterations of this process before the whole group is comfortable to proceed.

If you go ahead without gaining everybody's permission, it is not only potentially very damaging to individuals and the group, but you are also unlikely to get sufficient cooperation from the group in order to resolve the depth process successfully.

Containment during depth processes

Before surfacing any depth processes it is important to remember that helping a group to deal with depth processes requires containment – providing a safe enough space for the group to explore tricky territory. Containment was discussed in detail in Chapter 11, but a summary of the most important aspects for depth processes are given here. Containment has two broad elements:

- The provision of structural safety in terms of setting and maintaining boundaries related to issues such as time and space, as well as offering a clear structure for the process to be followed. This includes managing the physical environment and ensuring that ethical considerations are in place.
- The provision of an emotional container that holds and soothes the group in order to counteract anxiety. The facilitator provides an atmosphere of care, compassion and respect.

Specifically, containment during a depth process needs to have the following elements:

- Firm management of time and space boundaries
- Clear and detailed information provided about what a depth process may involve
- Careful maintenance of a neutral attitude
- The provision of education and information about psychological processes when necessary
- Active application of the metaskill of compassion, which is non-judgemental about ways of being human
- Firm implementation of professional boundaries
- The continual practice of deep democracy.

Surfacing depth processes by naming them

There are different ways to bring depth processes to the surface. They can be brought to the surface by naming them, or by helping them unfold. Ideally, a mixture of these two approaches should be used. Each approach has its roots in a particular methodology, as is explained in the discussions that follow.

Facilitators who use the Tavistock-based methodology (or any other similar approach) may use the intervention of naming or interpretation as a way of bringing a depth process to the surface. By providing a depth interpretation about the dynamics that the facilitator witnesses in the group, the group members can become aware of their own dynamics and how they are being affected by them. Therefore, in a group that is concerned primarily with the competition between the group members, mentioning your observation of such competition may be sufficient to make group members aware and eliminate the destructive element of competition. The difficulty of making an interpretation is that, as facilitator, you are in the role of the observer, and could be seen as a critical observer or even as a judge. A judgemental comment will almost always produce a response of feeling judged and may result in greater defensiveness on the part of the group members.

Interpretations need to be selectively given and phrased very carefully. The attitude behind an interpretation is almost more important than interpretation itself. The most important metaskill when giving an interpretation is that of compassion. This means valuing and respecting the human needs that lie behind any particular behaviour. If the group is caught in a dynamic of competition, you need to see the requirement to be valued that lies behind competitive behaviour. It is also very important that interpretations are not made as absolute statements, but rather as tentative suggestions. It is useful if you indicate that you have a hunch rather than that you are certain about something.

Some examples of appropriate and inappropriate interpretive statements are given below. Remember that tone of voice is almost more telling than the actual words used, and unfortunately these cannot be captured in examples.

Inappropriate interpretation	Appropriate interpretation
This group is only interested in competition.	The urge to prove your own value seems to be very important in this group.
The women are being marginalised in this group.	It seems that men's voices carry more weight in this room than the women's voices.
By interrupting each other you avoid getting any group work done.	It seems hard for this group to allow individuals to take centre stage, even temporarily, and this seems to be preventing completion of any task.

SURFACING DEPTH PROCESSES THROUGH UNFOLDING

Other methodologies, such as Process Work, are less interested in naming the process than helping it to unfold. By not naming or identifying the underlying dynamic in a group, as mentioned in the previous section, the facilitator avoids being seen as a judge. However, there are other problems associated with not making explicit what you can see. If you start using a technique such as amplification (which is described below) without explaining to the group what you are doing and why, group members may become confused and lose concentration. However, by not interpreting, you do not prejudice the process with a label that may be inaccurate.

Amplification

Amplification is a technique that helps to bring the depth process to the surface. Information regarding a depth process often first appears in the form of subtle signs that need to be made more explicit. Amplification is the process of exaggerating or "turning up the volume" of a signal. This technique needs to be done with neutrality, without judgement or ridicule. As facilitator, you may need to reassure individuals that the amplification is not done to embarrass or mock them. Amplification is different from interpretation. As facilitator, you add nothing but volume to the behaviour and should therefore check continually for feedback from the participant that you are in fact following the behaviour correctly. Amplification works best when it is done respectfully, but playfully. Some examples of verbal amplification are given below.

ORIGINAL STATEMENT	EXAMPLE OF AMPLIFICATION
The engineers in this company are so irritating, because they just know everything.	When I am in the company of engineers from this organisation, I find it hard to feel that my contribution is also legitimate. That makes me feel unsure and unheard.
I am not so sure that our new strategy is a correct one.	We need to do more work to ensure that our strategy is in fact correct.
There is no point in discussing this further.	The way we are communicating is not productive.

Original statement	Example of amplification
Um, OK, if that is what you want.	I don't really feel like doing it but I will go along with you because I do not believe that my opinion will make a difference.

The group member can also be asked to amplify a particular signal without the assistance of the facilitator. A way of doing this is to ask the group member to tell the group more or to give some more information about what he or she is saying or doing.

General guidelines for amplification
Here are some general guidelines to follow when using amplification as a technique.

- When amplifying, make sure that the person is agreeing with what you are doing. Watch for feedback.
- If the person disagrees with your amplification, ask him/her to help you.
- When you notice a signal in a particular pathway, it is useful to amplify that signal in its chosen pathway.
- When working with double signals, amplify both signals from a position of neutrality.
- In conflict situations where the opposing parties are attempting a conflict resolution process, amplify the feeling and experiential aspects of the communication and turn down the volume on blaming and accusations if possible.

STOPPING

In order to surface a depth process, you can also use the technique of "stopping". This is a technique by which the unfolding process is prevented from happening. Paradoxically, this feeds more energy into it. If you stop something the person (or sub-group) is trying to do, the person (or sub-group) may well become aware of the importance of what s/he has been stopped from doing; this often makes the person more able to do it. As with amplification, the facilitator needs to be cautious of maintaining neutrality.

Meta-communication

One technique for bringing depth processes to the surface that is similar to interpretation, but does not ascribe meaning to the group process, is that of meta-communication, a term from Process Work methodology. Meta-communication is when you as facilitator comment about what you are noticing in the group as a whole, without suggesting what it means. Rather, it offers an opportunity for the group to investigate it further and decide what it means. One version of meta-communication to is to give "weather" or "climate" reports.

A climate report is when a facilitator, or person adopting the facilitator role, reports on what is happening in the room. The report will neutrally comment on both the surface and depth processes that are taking place. The facilitator would normally give a climate report when there is a need for clarity and particularly when the group is cycling. The climate report enables the group to gain greater awareness. An example would be to say: "It feels like there is a less energy in the room this afternoon. Is that so, what do you think?" Note that the report is not an interpretation, but rather an observation about what is happening in the room. The facilitator gives no direction. Once you have given a climate report, you can watch for the response.

Disturbing a group

Sometimes a group is unable to allow the process to surface because the anxiety is too high and the defence mechanisms too strong. In both cases the group may need more containment or more time before the depth process can be handled. Sometimes a group is unable to allow the process to surface because they are caught in a habitual pattern of behaviour. Then it may be necessary to facilitate disturbance in a group, so that the group can move through its defensive structures. Most groups will provide the disturbance from inside their ranks. Occasionally the facilitator may need to help the group to activate a disturbance if the surface process is not flowing, but nothing else productive is possible either. It is important to remember that anyone who disturbs the group is taking a leadership position, and stops being a pure facilitator. This may open the facilitator up to difficult projections and transference.

If you decide that some disturbance is needed because the group is really stuck and further containment is needed, the following guidelines may be helpful.

- Switch to a different pathway – for example, if the group has been mainly engaged in talking, suggesting an activity that requires movement may be useful
- Change the environment
- Introduce an activity that reorganises the rank distribution
- Work with counter-transference by self-disclosing to the group

- Give the group feedback about your experience without being judgemental
- Give a break
- Describe the status quo
- Ask members of the group to share their visions and dreams with one another.

7. COMPLETING DEPTH PROCESSES

This section considers the facilitator's activities while completing a depth process in a group. There are certain general interventions that are required no matter what the process is, and there are some specific interventions designed for the particular processes.

These notes are divided into the different categories of process, but in most real-life situations processes do not unfold in neat categories. Rather, each group process is a unique blend of the different categories. Each facilitation situation therefore requires a blend of the interventions, tools and techniques listed in this section.

MAINTAINING CONTAINMENT

The importance of containment has been mentioned several times throughout this book. It is critical to maintain a strong container while completing depth processes. The following aspects of containment are specifically important while completing depth processes.

- Ensure that the boundaries of time and space are used so that group members stay together in order to complete the process. Often the process will become very difficult and group members attempt to leave in order to avoid the difficulty. However, it will be more destructive for the group if individuals leave in the middle of a process, than to manage the stress of staying until completion.
- Attend to individual anxiety levels to ensure that the group members are able to manage the process, by going slowly and providing emotional support along the way.
- Carefully outline and explain any processes to be followed so that group members know what to expect next.
- Give the group feedback about the progress that has been made.
- Allow some time for reflection if necessary.

ATTENDING TO MULTIPLE LEVELS

As a facilitator you have a delicate task when you are completing a group process. You are working both with the group psyche, a collective entity, and with a collection of individuals, as well as a set of sub-groups. Also, collective processes beyond the group will play themselves out in the group, ranging from the archetypal at the broadest level, to processes from all the systems in the group field. Neglecting any of these psychic levels can cause mischief in groups. You need to pay attention to the collective process and be able to view individuals as members of the collective process. However, each individual will be experiencing a process of his or her own, often feeling quite bewildered at the power of the group process and the loss of feelings of autonomy.

Your task is to provide containment for the whole group, and to prevent one member of the group from dominating the entire process. Simultaneously, individuals and their personal experiences need to be attended to.

Some guidelines for attending to these multiple levels are given below.

- Regularly move between levels, reminding the group of the collective and personal aspects of the process.
- People cannot process a depth dynamic on an abstract level. Most groups will begin dealing with an issue from an abstract level. Depth work requires moving beyond abstract debate into interpersonal territory. After all, we can only integrate, understand and meaningfully use the archetypes once we have personalised them (made fingerprints from blueprints).
- Once the group has raised an issue at the abstract level, encourage the members to make it more personal and discuss how it has a bearing on the issues and relationships in the group.
- This may take the group into a conflict resolution, cathartic or reconciliation process, in which it will be required to work at the personal level.
- Once resolution has been reached at the personal level, it is important to move through the levels, eventually getting back to the more general, archetypal level, and then to show how these interactions are part of being human. This serves to normalise and legitimise the difficulties experienced, and it also involves other group members in the process. A personal interaction between two group members may well be representative of the larger group process.
- It is also important to keep the context in mind and remind the group of the larger forces at work in order to balance the role of the individual with the role of the collective.

Role management

In depth processes, there is an ongoing risk that an individual will over-identify with a particular role and potentially be the target of scapegoating. To avoid this, continually take action to prevent over-identification with roles, both on the part of the individual and of the group. Intervention guidelines for preventing role over-identification are given on the following page.

- Remember that individual expression in a group is always an expression of the group psyche too. The individual is greater than the role and the role is greater than the individual.
- Continually distinguish roles from individuals, and remind the group of the universal nature of the roles or archetypes being played out. After a role is identified and acted out, remind the group that the person may be speaking on behalf of others in the group.
- Support all roles that appear in the group, finding and emphasising the wisdom in each one. There is generally some wisdom behind a role, no matter how apparently unacceptable it might be.
- Continually try to spread a given role in a group. This can be done by distilling the essential useful quality of that role, and checking whether anybody else in the group identifies with it.
- Assist an individual group member who is caught in a role to move into a different role, by giving the member feedback about what he or she is doing, and alerting him or her to the danger.
- Remember that a new, unusual or unexpected role is usually a response to one-sidedness in the group.
- Whatever role is being expressed, remember that the opposing role is also a possibility, and may well be needed by the group psyche.
- Where possible, ensure that roles are shared.
- Try to encourage conversations between roles.
- When a role is spoken of as being "out there", in other words occupied by a person or a group not present in the room, ask the group to consider how that role may in fact be present in the room.
- Avoid being caught in a role yourself.

Facilitator role detachment

As a facilitator, the most important part of managing collective behaviour is to ensure that you do not start expressing the group psyche unconsciously. Obviously, this is very difficult to do, and from certain perspectives may in fact be impossible, but it is important to practise role detachment all the time. Role detachment does not mean not experiencing aspects of the group life. Rather, it means being able to experience what is happening in the group, but not identifying with it. As a facilitator you need to be very fluid, and avoid getting caught or stuck in any particular role. The best way not to get stuck is to be able to experience an impulse as fully as possible, so that it can move on and make space for the next experience. Here are some guidelines to help with role detachment.

- If you notice yourself repeating a comment or an intervention, it may be an indication that you are being caught in a role.
- If you notice yourself judging the group, or feeling partial to a particular individual, you may be getting caught.

- If you start feeling passionate or very strongly about something, you may be in a role.
- Articulate any of your current life dilemmas clearly to yourself, and make a note of the roles you are struggling with. This will help you to be alert to areas of vulnerability in terms of role identification.
- If possible, work with a co-facilitator in large groups or particularly adversarial groups.
- Work on your metaskills, particularly the metaskill of compassion.

The "soft shoe shuffle"
In Chapter 4 we discussed the basics of roles. In this section we will investigate in more detail how to work with those roles in depth processes.

The "soft shoe shuffle" is a Process Work approach to working with roles during a depth process. It is an intervention that uses physical movement to indicate the essential fluidity of roles. It is a conversation on one's feet. Individuals are asked to use their physical presence to indicate agreement with a particular point of view expressed by going to stand next to the person who made the comment. Group members vote with their feet, through clustering or grouping. They are encouraged to move every time someone speaks, even if the next comment comes from an opposing position to the one that they have just supported. Group members are also encouraged to add their own views to anything with which they have agreed.

This technique allows group members to take up opposing views and disagree with what they may have originally expressed. It helps to prevent over-identification with a particular role, and helps individuals to see the plurality of the psyche in action. The technique also helps to remove hierarchical levels, allowing people to participate in a non-threatening manner. It frees people to make statements but not necessarily to remain attached to the view. Difficult issues can be presented without people being scapegoated for them. The technique encourages low-ranking issues to be voiced and heard.

As facilitator it is important that you can encourage all sides. It is particularly important to support the side of a minority or low-ranking view, which may be very unpopular and possibly expressed by only one person. It is important to show that the role is greater than the person by standing next to him or her.

This technique should only be used if it has been clearly explained to the group members and some psycho-education has been offered to explain the distinction between the individual and the role.

Managing specific roles

There are some specific roles that appear during depth facilitation processes that may require special management. These roles are described in the table on the following pages, and some guidelines are offered for how to manage them.

Role description	Facilitation guidelines
The ghost role A ghost role (a term coined by Arnold Mindell) is an absent role that the group is talking about; it is not present or not being owned in the room. In the case of employees talking about management, the ghost role of "management" is clear. Often the role is not clear; for example, when people are talking about being criticised but are not acknowledging who the critic is, the critic is the ghost role. Another example is when people are talking from the victim position and no one is prepared to step into the role of the abuser or perpetrator (understandably so); the abuser is the ghost role.	Role theory indicates that all roles are in fact psychologically present in the room, but they are not consciously being recognised. The task of the facilitator is to actively bring the ghost role into the room, if not in reality, at least symbolically, so that the dynamic with that ghost role can be addressed. Ideally, you as facilitator should encourage the group members to see if they can take the position of the ghost and so bring it into the conversation more directly. If that is not possible, you can introduce the ghost role by taking up the role and speaking from it. It is important that you are neutral in relation to the role before adopting it. If there is a lack of neutrality you will be attacked very quickly by the group. You can amplify the role of the ghost in order to make it more real for the group. The exaggeration of the role makes the ghost "visible and real". It "gives permission" for the people to disagree. In so doing they will actually begin to identify the true nature of the ghost role.

Role description	Facilitation guidelines
The ghost role *(continued)*	You can also encourage people to adopt the ghost role in a playful and non-threatening manner. The participants may move in and out of the ghost role as they wish. The ghost role is often representative of an unconscious or an unacknowledged part of the group; it is difficult to acknowledge. You need to practise strong containment during this process.
The silent role There are of course many reasons that people may be silent in a group. From a depth perspective, it is important to consider the following: People who are silent are often holding the visionary role. Their silence often signifies that they are "done" with the now and are already, metaphorically, in the future. People concerned with safety and abuse issues may also occupy the silent role. These people are more aware of what is going on and are often beyond the surface process.	A silent participant is treated differently in depth facilitation from how s/he is treated in on-the-surface facilitation. Unlike in the more rational modes of facilitation, the silent role is not perceived as a "shy" person who needs to be encouraged to talk. In relation to the silence being a role in the room, the facilitator will wait till the silence is more present and then address it. At this stage you can invite the silent people to comment. You can also show support for the silent person by moving into her/his space and adopting the role.

Role description	Facilitation guidelines
The disturber role The disturber role refers to the role that continually works against the prevailing process in the group. The disturber may be critical of group members, or the process, or even the facilitator. This role is disruptive through the process. In depth work, the facilitator is seen as the source of information about the underlying issues in a group. The disturber is often the messenger for the depth process.	A facilitator needs to help the disturber express his or her views in such a way that the other group members are able to hear them. It helps to search for the wisdom in the disturber's contribution, as it will invariably be designed to balance a one-sided surface process. The disturber needs to be helped not to over-identify with the role, as there is a very high chance that the group will scapegoat this individual.
The scapegoat role Often depth processes play themselves out in groups by targeting one individual or a sub-group as the "scapegoat" or the problem. The group believes that its problems will be solved if that individual or sub-group is no longer part of the group. In this case, it is likely that the group is projecting its unconscious roles onto the scapegoated individual or sub-group. The targeted individual or sub-group is often lower in rank and unconsciously volunteers for this position, and may entrench the group's view by becoming a disturber or disturbing element in the group. Alternatively, the targeted individual or sub-group becomes marginalised and may choose to actively or passively withdraw from the group.	As facilitator you need to help the group become aware of the "scapegoating" element of their interactions. Help the projecting group to consider how the projected quality may in fact be a shared, albeit unpopular role in the group, and may in fact need to be consciously integrated by the group as a whole in order to transform the group dynamics into a healthier pattern. For example, a very hardworking, driven group, may be projecting its need for rest onto the least hardworking member of the team. The group needs to understand how embracing the need to rest in a constructive way may be more sustainable for the group in the longer term. Often when the projection is withdrawn, the "scapegoated" individual or sub-group can become a productive participant in the group.

Role description	Facilitation guidelines
The "messiah" role The "messiah" role is an alternative to the scapegoat role; it uses the same mechanism but is the result of positive rather than negative projection. Often one individual or sub-group is seen as being the potential "saviour" of the group in some way. However, this is unrealistic as no one individual or sub-group can transform a group's difficulty without the involvement of the whole group. The problem with this mechanism is that it is seductive for the individual or sub-group to be given this role and they often willingly take on the role.	As facilitator you need to help the group in the same way as when scapegoating occurs, but particularly to help the targeted individual or sub-group to disidentify with the role. The group as a whole needs to understand that they all have to be involved with resolving their difficulties.

Rank management

As discussed in Chapter 4, rank differences are part of the depth dynamic found in almost all groups. Managing rank differences and minimising the impact that they have on the group is therefore an ongoing task for the facilitator. The guidelines below suggest how these rank differences can be handled during the completion of depth processes.

- Continually keep your eye on rank differences.
- Notice when they are interfering with the process – when minority opinions cannot be openly expressed.
- Offer psycho-education if necessary; in other words, teach the group about the dynamics of rank differences and how these affect relationships and interactions.
- Try to bring awareness to those with rank of the impact of their rank on other group members.
- Support minority voices to be expressed, but do not use your rank as a facilitator to give them undue power.
- Also support those with rank.
- Avoid what Arnold Mindell calls "the tyranny of the minority". The minority opinions are used to modify and improve the majority opinion, not to hold the majority hostage.

- Practise deep democracy whenever possible.
- Keep an eye on minority positions that use subtle pathways to express themselves.
- Always check for minority positions before moving on to a new process or step in the process.

GUIDELINES FOR THE FACILITATION OF SPECIFIC PROCESSES

In Chapter 4, we distinguished between four different types of group processes: relationship building processes, polarising processes, cathartic processes and reconciliation processes. Earlier in this chapter, we considered the facilitation of relationship building processes. Here we consider the facilitation of the other three depth processes in groups in detail.

POLARISING PROCESSES

Polarising processes essentially lead into conflict resolution because the group needs to move past the split caused by the polarities onto common ground. From a depth perspective, it is important to recognise that conflict is an inherent part of depth processes, as a result of the duality in the psyche. It is also important to remember that the psyche has the mechanisms available for transcending that duality given the right environment, and that what causes the splitting in the psyche is anxiety. Conflict is therefore resolved and change occurs not as the result of force, but as a result of gentle guidance that contains anxiety.

DIFFERENT APPROACHES TO CONFLICT RESOLUTION

There are many different approaches to conflict, and many methodologies for addressing it. It is useful to make the distinction between a legalistic approach to conflict resolution and a depth approach.

LEGALISTIC APPROACH TO CONFLICT AND CONFLICT RESOLUTION	DEPTH APPROACH TO CONFLICT AND CONFLICT RESOLUTION
- Conflict is caused by a division of resources - Compromise is regarded as the solution to the conflict	- Conflict is caused by a psychological dance/pattern stemming from an intra-psychic conflict being played out between two people

Legalistic approach to conflict and conflict resolution	Depth approach to conflict and conflict resolution
<ul><li>Attempt to implement fairness</li><li>Involves lawyer, third party, etc, who makes the decision</li><li>Resource division often leaves one party or both parties unhappy</li><li>Very rare that both parties feel it was a fair decision</li><li>Results in either a win/lose or lose/lose scenario</li><li>Usually ends in termination of relationship.</li></ul>	<ul><li>To resolve is not about division of resources or compromise, but about helping the transcendent third position to emerge</li><li>Results in a win/win scenario if it works – integration between different parts rather than division</li><li>Third party does not make decisions – s/he plays a facilitation or mediation role</li><li>Ends in a stronger sustainable relationship</li><li>Facilitator provides containment.</li></ul>

Root causes of conflict and appropriate conflict resolution mechanisms

Most conflict is the result of individuals or groups misunderstanding one another and can be quite easily solved through communication. Other causes of conflict are less easy to address. The most complicated kind of conflict between individuals is caused by an unresolved intra-psychic conflict in an individual that is played out personally with another individual. In groups, an intra-psychic conflict plays out between the members of the group, and a depth intervention will be needed to resolve it. In order to ensure that a depth intervention is really needed, first try the easier conflict resolution mechanisms, such as communication or attempting to find compromise. The various levels of root causes and proposed interventions are listed on the following page.

Root cause	Conflict resolution mechanism
Miscommunication/misunderstanding	Surface facilitation: helping group members to communicate and clear up misunderstandings
Misperception/stereotyping	Surface facilitation: helping group members to get to know one another better, possibly by using storytelling
Differing preferences/needs	Surface facilitation: helping group members to alternate in meeting their needs and to compromise
Scarce resources/unshared resources	Surface facilitation: helping group members to share resources, exercise fairness by holding a systemic view and emphasising interrelatedness
Power imbalance leading to communication breakdown and oppression	Depth facilitation: helping a group to develop consciousness about power and privilege differences, and facilitating conversations that activate empathy
Projection, present used to address historical conflict	Depth facilitation: helping group members to develop psychological self-awareness leading to the integration of the projection through becoming aware of history, accepting the losses of the past, and using the conflict resolution steps discussed in the sections that follow

The Process of Unmanaged Conflict[1]

Intra-psychic conflict that has not been managed tends to unfold in a predictable way. An example of how that might happen is given below.

1. A difference in content or expectations occurs. Individuals develop emotional responses to the disagreement. One party starts feeling anxious, but this is usually ignored.
2. Communication difficulties arise.
3. Projection and projective identification mechanisms are used and result in increasing rigidity in roles.
4. The group starts repeating actions and communication that entrench the division. Incongruities and double signals develop. The group starts cycling and is unable to move forward. These are signs that the system is trying to balance itself.
5. With each cycle the polarities increasingly define themselves in relation to each other.
6. At each cycle massive amounts of energy flow into the conflict. The sides begin to switch roles unconsciously.
7. The conflict eventually becomes contentless. Once the content is lost attention will focus on the past or the future, but not the present.
8. Rigidity in roles becomes complete and communications are severed. Direct communication is replaced solely with gossip and projection.
9. The system now either implodes or explodes and there is a complete breakdown in the relationships.
10. At the point of breakdown, there is an opportunity for growth. In many cases, breakdown is a necessary precursor to growth and a prerequisite to openness to the depth process and the healing power of conscious awareness.

Inflammatory behaviour

As a depth facilitator, it is useful to recognise which behaviours are inflammatory and escalate conflict. If you witness some of these behaviours during a conflict resolution process, it is useful either to amplify an aspect of the communication that is less inflammatory, or to help the speaker to re-frame the comment in a less inflammatory way. Many of the behaviours that escalate conflict are unconscious, and so sometimes it is helpful to make the speaker aware of the inflammatory nature of his or her contribution. A list of behaviours that escalate conflict and potential interventions are provided in the table on the next page.

---

[1] These conflict resolution notes have been adapted from course notes on Process Facilitation developed by Myrna Wajsman and her late husband Greg Lewis.

Inflammatory behaviour	Proposed facilitation intervention
Double signals or any examples of incongruence. For example, someone saying she is angry, but doing it with a smile on her face.	Make the speaker aware of both parts of the message by amplifying both sides of the double signal. Suggest that the speaker may be unsure or ambivalent or indecisive about the best approach.
Reference to third parties, conscious or unconscious coalitions, references to the past and the future, but all avoiding the here and now. These are all signals of anxiety. Examples are: "Mary said she also has trouble with your being late." "Two weeks ago, your secretary complained to the boss."	Assist speakers to express their own difficulty with the person that they are addressing, recognising that they feel their own opinions are insufficiently powerful. Spread the role if possible.
Denying accusations. An accusation is often a statement about an underlying process said in an aggressive way.	Assist the person on the receiving end to acknowledge whether any part of the accusation may be accurate. Encourage the person to pick up the 1% of the accusation that may be true.
Projection. There may be an unacknowledged unconscious part of an individual that the individual is having difficulty recognising or accepting, and hence projecting onto and only seeing in the other.	Encourage a conversation where each party can express what it feels like in his/her shoes. Amplify the feeling and experience component of the conversation. Play down the accusatory parts of the communication.

Inflammatory behaviour	Proposed facilitation intervention
Denying or ignoring abuse. Denying that abuse is occurring causes the conflict to escalate because it tells the abusing side that s/he is not being heard.	Slow the process down and allow the person being abused to react. If the person can express his or her real feelings of being abused, it may de-escalate conflict.
Ignoring de-escalation signals and feedback.	Amplify the de-escalation signals and alert the speaker to these signals.
Continuing the conflict or the attack, even after the other party has stopped attacking.	Bring to the speaker's attention that the other party has stopped attacking. Help the other party to articulate the new role that s/he is in.
Being condescending, patronising or indirectly hurtful. Those symptoms may indicate a part of the individual or group that does not want to be in relationship.	Alert the speaker to the fact that his/her comment was hurtful to the listener. Encourage the listener to express his/her experience of the comment.

STRATEGIES FOR DEALING WITH CONFLICT

Groups will use many strategies to deal with conflict, and some of the more common ones are described below. Ultimately from a depth perspective, resolution is the only option. Without it, conflict will reappear later.

Avoidance: There are many ways groups can avoid conflict, from running away, to ignoring it or denying that it exists. Quick apologies and breaking off contact also work to avoid exploring the conflict. But avoiding conflict is avoiding the opportunity for the creation of something new.

Acceptance: Knowledge and acceptance of conflict, without doing anything about, avoids the chance for resolution. "We shall have to agree to disagree" is one well-known way that conflicts are accepted and not dealt with. Acceptance can also be a form of resignation: "OK, so there is a conflict, but I don't want to argue." The effect of such resignation is damaging to all involved; no one is satisfied.

Elimination: The elimination of conflict can happen in two main ways. The first is flight, where one combatant leaves the battlefield to the victor. The second is to fight, where battle takes place and one party is defeated. The conflict has been eliminated, one side has triumphed over the other, but it leaves at least one party dissatisfied and probably resentful. This type of outcome will usually flare up again later.

Resolution: Resolution occurs when all the people involved have explored how the conflict has arisen; how it has affected the parties, what they want to happen, what is happening, and how everyone involved can achieve a satisfactory outcome. Resolution occurs when the polarities in a conflict are transcended and a transcendent "third" position emerges that all parties can identify with and feel comfortable with. From this point it is possible to start work together instead of in opposition to reach a new point of agreement. Of course this form of resolution is difficult to achieve. The facilitator, who knows how to work with the group in depth, may assist with the achievement of resolution.

SURFACING THE POLARITIES

Polarisation is a necessary process in a group in order to resolve conflict. The facilitator needs to help the polarities emerge. This is different from traditional conflict resolution where we seek compromises. From a Jungian perspective, it is understood that resolution will emerge if the two polarities are held long enough for both sides to see and hear each other clearly. Yet it is important continually to separate the person from the role, because the polarities will tend to constellate between two people in a group. Polarisation involves insisting that each party take its own side as fully as possible. This is often resisted because it feels dangerous, but it is a necessary step for the eventual wisdom that comes through resolution. All members of the group are encouraged to become involved in this process.

Polarities that remain under the surface are damaging to group functioning. It is important to channel the polarities into some form of expression, whether it is language, movement, or some form of art or sound. The vehicle of expression serves as a container for the energy behind the polarity. Also, the vehicle provides the opportunity for conversation, so the group can have what my daughter, Sophia, calls a "talk fight", rather than one of the more destructive alternatives.

Amplification of the polarities

Sometimes it is important to amplify the polarities in order to express the two positions more clearly. People may be reluctant to risk distinguishing themselves to that extent from others in the group, and so it is useful to explain the value of polarising to the group. Individual contributions can then be amplified in order to express all aspects of the position, particularly focusing on the experience and feeling components of the position. The transcendent function can only work its magic once the polar positions are very clearly defined.

Early compromise delays transcendence. Amplification needs to continue until the transcendent third emerges. The facilitator will know when this happens because the atmosphere in a group changes completely. There is a moment in which suddenly each party starts identifying with the polar opposite position. This will be palpably felt in the atmosphere, and it will be clear to everyone that a de-escalation of conflict is happening. In that moment the projections are withdrawn, and the tension is released.

Conflict resolution steps

The following steps provide guidelines for facilitating a conflict resolution process from a depth perspective that offers the opportunity for a transcendent third position to emerge.

1. Getting agreement to attempt a conflict resolution process
This step requires that all parties to the conflict agree to attempt a resolution. Parties need to agree to meet for at least an hour to discuss the conflict. They have to commit to the whole process and should not be allowed to leave half way through because this will cause worse conflict. A neutral time and place should be agreed on. If one or other or both of the parties do not agree to try to resolve the conflict, they can be worked with individually until they are ready to come together.

2. Opening and explaining the process
The process should be opened with each side being helped to state its goals and motivations for resolving a conflict. The process should be explained in simple terms. If the parties want to agree on ground rules they can, but it is unlikely that agreement will be reached on more than the most basic rules. Both parties need to agree to stick to the rules of the process described below.

3. Each party gives its own side
Each party gets a turn and is helped to express its side of the story in as much detail as possible without interruption. A coin can be flipped to decide who goes first. Parties need to be encouraged to take their own side as much as possible and not try for an early compromise.

4. Each party plays back the other side

Each party then is asked to play back what they heard, or take the side of the other party. Invariably they will not be able to do this for long, and will quickly revert to responding from their own side. At this point the facilitator needs to interrupt and ask the parties to repeat step 3. The process moves between step 3 and step 4 as many times as needed until the parties start to be able to see the point of view of the other. The more heard they feel, the more likely they will be able to hear and withdraw their projections.

5. Each party restates its original position with new awareness

If step 4 has been successful, parties will automatically move into this step. At this stage, each party needs to include in its side the acknowledgement of the truth of the other side. At this stage it may be appropriate for parties to apologise to one another, which they will do spontaneously or with a little assistance if necessary.

CATHARTIC PROCESSES

Cathartic processes require the facilitator to create an environment in which the group members feel safe enough to explore and express their feelings. As facilitator you may need to alert the group to the underlying feelings, by amplifying signals that indicate those feelings. The following set of guidelines will assist you when the depth process requires catharsis.

- Provide a strong container and ensure that the group will not be interrupted during this process.
- Prepare the group for the possible discomfort that may occur in such a session.
- Remember that group members are often ashamed of expressing emotion, and that it causes them great anxiety to do so.
- Create an atmosphere in the group that is accepting of the expression of emotion through appropriate self-disclosure and discussion of behaviours and ways of being that would be considered apt.
- Provide ample time for this kind of depth process because catharsis cannot happen under pressure.
- Once group members start expressing emotions or sharing their experiences hold off with new interventions and simply be quietly and patiently present.
- Do not intervene to make individuals or groups feel better; the expression of emotion will ensure that.
- Remember that catharsis is a process and the group may need to go through several different emotions before the process is complete. Sometimes anger is a precursor to grief, or hurt. Allow the process to unfold.

Reconciliation processes

Reconciliation processes are notoriously difficult. Both parties need to be available for the complex emotions that will arise in such a process. In a sense, a reconciliation process is a combination of a polarising process, conflict resolution and catharsis, and so all the guidelines mentioned above apply. It is important that all parties state their objectives about entering into such a process, and commit explicitly to the full duration of the session. As facilitator, keep the following guidelines in mind.

- Be aware that most perpetrators have been victims in the past, so resist over-identifying with the parties in the victim role.
- The perpetrator needs support because s/he is in the minority position, and does not hold rank morally.
- The perpetrator may be suffering from shame, which is one of the most debilitating emotions. Treating all parties concerned with equal respect and compassion can help to counteract this.
- Ensure that a new role division does not emerge in terms of moral righteousness.
- Ensure that the victim is fully heard for his or her experience.
- Encourage the use of symbolic gestures, e.g. a statement of regret, shaking hands or an apology. These symbolic gestures should not be prescribed, but rather chosen by the participants.

A reconciliation process has additional stages to polarising and cathartic processes and these are outlined below. The terms "victim" and "perpetrator" are used to discuss the steps. These terms do not refer to one specific individual in each case, but rather to the roles in such a situation, and more than one person may occupy these roles. Also, a person or sub-group may be both a perpetrator and a victim. In this case, there will be several iterations by different parties of the steps listed in the following table.

Stages in a reconciliation process	Characteristics of that stage
1. Gaining agreement to attempt reconciliation	Here both parties have to agree to enter into a reconciliation process. Often the party who has been aggrieved will refuse to enter into such a process because s/he does not believe that the damage can be repaired or at least forgiven. The party who is viewed as the perpetrator may also refuse to enter into a process, either not believing that s/he is a perpetrator or that reconciliation is possible.
2. Victim's expression of the experience of harm	At this stage, the individual perceives him/herself to be a victim and needs to express his or her experience of the hurt. The victim may not be fully aware of the levels of hurt, or may be unable to express it. Also, victims often need to express their outrage at the hurt that was caused to them before they can articulate the suffering. Victims need to articulate their experience as fully as possible for this stage to be successful. This may also be traumatic for the victim to do and therefore the facilitator needs to be as supportive as possible.

Stages in a reconciliation process	Characteristics of that stage
3. The perpetrator's acknowledgement of the harm that he or she caused	The perpetrator needs to be able to hear and absorb what the victim says s/he has experienced. This is an exceptionally painful and anxiety-provoking stage for the perpetrator, as it evokes guilt and requires the ability to integrate a negative view of her/himself. The perpetrator risks being annihilated psychologically and needs support for the healthy part of her/him in order to survive it. Once the perpetrator has heard the victim's experience, s/he now needs to be able to acknowledge the harm that has been done. The perpetrator will need a great deal of support and containment from the facilitator during this process.
4. Perpetrator's apology for harm done, and commitment to efforts to repair the damage	The perpetrator needs to apologise for the harm caused, and needs to take steps to repair the harm. The victim can help the perpetrator to identify suitable reparation activities.

Stages in a reconciliation process	Characteristics of that stage
5. If necessary, the victim's acknowledgement of his/her role in the situation	Very few situations are as one-sided as having a clear perpetrator and clear victim. Often the victim did not take enough steps to protect him/herself, or may have in fact provoked the perpetrator. It is important that the victim acknowledges his/her own role. In many aggressive interactions, the harm done is reciprocal, and unless this is acknowledged, it is likely to be repeated.
6. Forgiveness and reconciliation	Both parties have a better understanding of why the hurt occurred, and the victim is able to forgive the perpetrator. This effectively means that the victim pardons the perpetrator and no longer feels angry about the situation. This does not mean that the victim will forget, but will be able to resume a relationship with the perpetrator.

Reconciliation processes are difficult, and should only be attempted with full agreement of the parties. They are psychologically harrowing and the facilitator needs to build a very strong container, particularly ensuring that parties do not leave halfway through the process. However, although they are difficult, reconciliation processes can be enormously rewarding to facilitate and to witness.

Special cases and situations

Here we list a few special cases and situations, giving indications of how they should be addressed from a depth facilitation point of view.

Case or situation	Facilitation guidelines
Working with resistance Resistance in a group or an individual	This is a sign that there is an anxiety present. In other words, the individual or the group is using defence mechanisms to deal with anxiety. Either there is an unaddressed depth process that is interfering with the surface process, or someone is being taken into a depth process against her/his will, i.e. being asked to reveal something which s/he cannot or will not. In the case of an unaddressed depth process, it is important to gain the group's permission to work with the depth process or simply make it aware that there may be something that needs to be tackled. In the second case, it is important to slow down and hold the group at the edge. In this way, the edge can be negotiated until everyone is ready.

Case or situation	Facilitation guidelines
Working with explosive anger	If someone is very angry in a group, that person will almost certainly be in a role for the whole group. In this case, the person will probably be terrified by his/her rage. The facilitator needs to contain the strong feeling by showing calm acceptance, no judgement, and a willingness to hear. If possible, slow the process down, and allow the person to speak. Also, separate the person from the role as far as possible. Try to spread the role. Remember, though, to give other participants an opportunity to express their feelings at being the recipients of such strong feeling. They may need to express hurt if they felt abused.
Managing a saboteur	Sabotage happens in a situation where someone with less rank is trying to communicate with an individual or sub-group with more rank, but cannot do so directly. The person with less rank will attack the power and privilege of the individual or sub-group with rank in an attempt to force that individual or sub-group to become aware of his or her rank. The saboteur needs to be assisted to find support and to find other ways to communicate. The individual or group under attack needs to become aware of the power of his or her rank and be assisted to listen to the person with less rank. This is often a long, delicate and complicated process.

Case or situation	Facilitation guidelines
Working with large groups	Work with large groups with great care and only once you have a lot of experience. The power of the roles in large groups is equal to the combined power of all the individual psyches, as well the collective power of the whole group. In a situation where you are addressing depth process issues, always use more than one facilitator. Never attempt conflict resolution in a large group without at least two facilitators.

Additional guidelines for managing special cases

Here are some additional guidelines for managing special or difficult situations.

- Remember your brief.
- Remember your metaskills.
- Check whether you are hooked.
- Do inner work if necessary until you feel able to be neutral.
- Refrain from further intervention until you feel clearer.
- Take a break.
- Check in with the group.
- Work with a co-facilitator.
- If possible, work with your dreams (ask your unconscious to help).

Finally, remember that as long as you stick to your brief or contract with the client, you maintain ethical and personal boundaries and ensure that your metaskills are in place, you cannot do harm to the group. There are some groups that you cannot help, and it is important to accept such a situation with grace.

8. Integrating depth processes with surface process

In order to complete a depth process, it is always necessary to ensure that integration has occurred and that it is possible to return to the surface processes with enthusiasm. The depth process is only complete once the group has indicated a willingness to return to the surface process. It is useful for the group to have a discussion about how the depth process and its outcomes can be integrated back into future group interactions.

If the depth process was successful, there will be several signs that the facilitator can watch out for to confirm it. Some of these signs are listed below.

- The group atmosphere will feel calm, and the body language will indicate relief and a sense of ease.
- The group may articulate the presence of a transcendent third position, which unites the polarities previously explored. They will be in agreement about how to proceed. There will be both a feeling and concrete examples that common ground has been reached.
- The group may spontaneously start talking in symbolic language. They may use metaphors or images to describe the current psychological state. These symbols will resonate with everyone else in the group, and other group members may elaborate and build on the symbols used.
- The group will indicate the readiness to move back to the surface process or close the session.
- They may well be a feeling of exhaustion, but also have the energy to embark on a new process after appropriate rest.

Allowing the magic

Depth facilitation has been described as work requiring great caution, skill and attention. However, there is also magical aspect to the process. Groups doing depth work often encounter their archetypal roots that are embedded in the life force. Carl Jung spoke about the fact that when we come into contact with our archetypal roots we may have what he referred to as a "numinous" experience. The word "numinous" was first used by a theologian called Rudolf Otto to describe a sense of awe-inspiring wonder, which may feel like being in the presence of something "divine" (in whatever way one understands the notion of the "divine").

A numinous experience is most likely to occur when someone encounters an archetype that was lodged in the unconscious. When in a state of "numinosity", the individual experiences feelings that are similar to an altered state. The individual will feel as if she or he is in the grip of something bigger than her- or himself, and this can either be pleasant or unpleasant, but either way may feel overwhelming for the individual.

When you allow unconscious contents to emerge in a group and there is a successful integration into the conscious world, the connection between the two worlds produces great psychic energy and gives the individual or group a numinous experience. When in the grip of such an experience, the individual or group will feel a powerful sense of awe, as well as a sense of goodwill and belonging to the collective of which he or she is part.

Positive numinous experiences can result from depth processes where the unconscious encounters the conscious in a sufficiently constructive and creative way to achieve a new integrated state. In some ways, this is the ultimate work that a depth facilitator can aim for. It can be enormously rewarding for the facilitator and life-changing for everyone who participates in such a process. In all the depth processes discussed in this book – including relationship building, polarising, cathartic and reconciliation processes – numinous experiences are possible. However, encountering the numinous in an uncontrolled and uncontained way can be dangerous and too overwhelming for the psyche. It will be psychologically too burdensome if the individual is over-identified with the archetype. All the cautionary notes and injunctions about appropriate containment, role management and strong ethical boundaries are in part to ensure that numinous experiences are psychologically constructive.

Here are some guidelines for ensuring that depth interventions allow constructive encounters with the numinous.

- Be faithful to the pace of the group.
- Work hard to prevent role over-identification.
- Identify and work with transference, and prevent the group from attributing a role or archetype to you as the facilitator, or a member of the group.
- Remember that a numinous experience is a gift from the unconscious and cannot be manufactured by the facilitator.
- Remain connected to the concrete rational world and the primary group task.
- Avoid providing the group with spiritual guidance.
- Do not impose symbols on the group, but work with emerging symbols that arise spontaneously in the group.
- Remember that you are human and offer but one limited perspective.
- Practise the metaskills of reverence, compassion and humility.

CONCLUSION

Depth processes are complex and difficult to work with, and should only be approached by a facilitator who feels equipped to manage the difficulties they represent. However, if you work carefully, depth processes are truly transformative to groups. Fundamental problems are solved and great potential is unleashed. Working as a depth facilitator for the past fourteen years has enriched my life enormously, and while my work has enabled transformation for some groups (success is never guaranteed), it has also resulted in continuous learning and transformation for me as a person.

PERSONAL EXERCISES

1. Choose a group of which you are a member. Describe the processes that you have witnessed in the group that relate to the depth perspective. Which process needs attention? Is the group mainly concerned with defensive processes or developmental processes? What could you do to help the group?

2. Make a list of all the potentially difficult roles that you have encountered in groups. Decide how you, as facilitator, will manage these roles from a depth perspective.

3. Consider any experiences that you have had of depth processes. Remember how you felt after the process. Decide what helped you survive the process and what made it more difficult for you to complete the process.

4. Consider your experience of processes that have been successfully completed. What factors assisted with the successful completion, and what factors or interventions hampered the process? Identify critical success factors for completing depth processes.

5. Identify special cases and situations that you do not know how to deal with. Work with a partner to consider how to address them.

6. Start developing your own toolkit of depth facilitation interventions.

BIBLIOGRAPHY

Armstrong, D. (2005). *Organization in the Mind: Psychoanalysis, Group Relations, and Organizational Consultancy.* London: Karnac.

Becker, L. (Ed.)(2005). *Working with Groups.* South Africa: Oxford University Press.

Bentley, T (2000). *Facilitation.* England: The Space Between.

Berne, E. (1964). *Games People Play: The Psychology of Human Relationships.* England: Penguin Books.

Bion, W.R. (1961). *Experiences in Groups: and Other Papers.* New York: Brunner-Routledge.

Blackman, J.S. (2004). *101 Defences: How the Mind Shields Itself.* New York: Brunner-Routledge.

Brown, D. & Zinkin, L. (Eds.)(1994). *The Psyche and the Social World: Developments in Group-Analytic Theory.* London: Routledge.

Campbell, D. & Groenbaek, M. (2006) *Taking Positions in the Organization.* London & New York: Karnac Books Ltd.

Casement, A. & Tacey, D (Eds.) (2006) *The Idea of the Numinous: Contemporary Jungian and Psychoanalytic Perspectives.* London & New York: Routledge.

Chevalier, J. & Gheerbrant, A. (1982). *Dictionary of Symbols.* England: Penguin Books.

Cloke K. & Goldsmith J. (2000). *Resolving Personal and Organizational Conflict* San Francisco: Jossey-Bass.

Colman, A.D. & Bexton, W.H. (Eds.) (1975). *Group Relations Reader 1* USA: A.K Rice Institute.

Colman, A.D. & Geller, M.H. (Eds.) (1985). *Group Relations Reader 2* USA: A.K Rice Institute.

Colman, A.D. (1995). *Up from Scapegoating: Awakening consciousness in Groups*. Chiron Publications.

Corlett, J.G. & Pearson, C.S. (2003). *Mapping the Organizational Psyche: A Jungian Theory of Organizational Dynamics and Change*. USA: Center for Applications of Psychological Type, Inc.

Cytrynbaum, S. & Noumair, D.A. (Eds.) (2004). *Group Dynamics, Organizational Irrationality, and Social Complexity: Group Relations Reader 3*. USA: A.K Rice Institute for the Study of Social Systems.

Czander, W.M. (1993). *The Psychodynamics of Work and Organizations: Theory and Application*. New York & London: Guilford Press.

De Board, R. (1978). *The Psychoanalysis of Organizations: A Psychoanalytic Approach to Behaviour in Groups in Organizations*. New York: Routledge.

Foulkes, S.H. (1986). *Group Analytic Psychotherapy: Method and Principles*. London: Maresfield Library.

Gardner, H. (2004). *Changing Minds: The Art and Science of Changing our own and other People's Minds*. Boston, Massachusetts: Harvard Business School Press.

Grant, J. & Crawley, J. (2002). *Transference and Projection*. Maidenhead: Open University Press.

Ghais, S. (2005). *Extreme Facilitation: Guiding Groups through Controversy and Complexity*. USA: Jossey-Bass.

Gobodo-Madikizela, P. (2003). *A Human Being Died that Night: A Story of Forgiveness*. SA: David Philip.

Goleman, D. (2006). *Social Intelligence: A New Science of Human Relationships*. London: Hutchinson.

Gould, L. Stapley, L. F. Stein, M. (Eds.) (2006). *The Systems Psychodynamics of Organizations: Integrating the Group Relations Approach, Psychoanalytic, and Open Systems. Perspectives* London & New York: Karnac Books.

Houston, G. (1993). *Being and Belonging*. England: John Wiley & Sons Ltd.

Huffington, C et al (Eds.) (2004). *Working Below the Surface: The Emotional Life of Contemporary Organizations.* London: Karnac.

Hunter, D, Bailey, A. & Taylor, B. (1996). *The Facilitation of Groups.* England: Gower

Johnson, R.A. (1986). *Inner Work: Using Dreams & Active Imagination for Personal Growth.* San Francisco: Harper.

Johnson, R.A. (1971). *Owning your own Shadow: Understanding the Dark Side of the Psyche.* San Francisco: Harper.

Jung, C.G. (1966). *The Psychology of the Transference.* London: Routledge.

Malan, D. (1999). *Individual Psychotherapy and the Science of Psychodynamics* (2nd edn). Oxford: Butterworth-Heinemann.

Mindell, A. *(1990). Working on Yourself Alone: Inner Dreambody Work.* London: Arkana.

Mindell, A. (1995). *Sitting in the Fire: Large Group Transformation Using Conflict and Diversity.* Portland: Lao Tse Press.

Mindell, A. (2002). *The Deep Democracy of Open Forums: Practical Steps to Conflict Prevention and Resolution for the Family, Workplace and World.* USA: Hampton Roads Publishing Company, Inc.

Mindell, A. (2000). *Quantum Mind: The Edge Between Physics and Psychology.* Portland: Lao Tse Press.

Mindell, A. (1985). *Working with the Dreaming Body.* London: Arkana

Mindell, A. (1987). *The Dreambody in Relationships.* London: Arkana

Mindell, A. *(1993). The Shaman's Body: A New Shamanism for Transforming Health, Relationships, and the Community.* San Francisco: Harper Collins.

Mindell, Amy (1995). *Metaskills: The Spiritual Art of Therapy.* Arizona: New Falcon Publications Tempe.

Oakley, C. (Ed.) (1999). *What is a Group? A New look at Theory in Practice.* London: Rebuss Press.

Papadopoulos, R.K. (Ed.) (2006). *The Handbook of Jungian Psychology: Theory Practice and Applications.* London & New York: Routledge.

Peck, M.S. (1978). *The Road Less Travelled: A New Psychology of Love, Traditional Values and Spiritual Growth.* UK: Arrow Books.

Peck, M.S. (1983). *People of the Lie: The Hope for Healing Human Evil.* USA: Touchstone Simon & Schuster.

Peltier, B. (2001). *The Psychology of Executive Coaching: Theory and Application.* USA: Brunner- Routledge.

Samuels, A. (1993). *The Political Psyche.* USA & Canada: Routledge.

Solomon, H. M. (2007). *The Self in Transformation.* London: Karnac.

Stapley, L.F. (2006). *Individuals, Groups, and Organizations Beneath the Surface.* London & New York: Karnac Books Ltd.

Stein, M. & Hollwitz, J. (Eds.) (1995). *Psyche at Work: Workplace Applications of Jungian Analytical Psychology.* Wilmette, Illinois: Chiron Publications.

Surowiecki, J. (2004) *The Wisdom of Crowds: Why the Many are Smarter than the Few.* UK: Abacus.

Winnicott, D.W. (1964). *The Child, the Family and the Outside World.* UK: Penguin Books.

ABOUT THE AUTHOR

Hélène Smit was originally trained as an English and Mathematics teacher for high school pupils. After completion of an MBA in 1991, she started the consultancy now named Feather Associates (Pty) Ltd. For the past 20 years, Feather Associates has offered a variety of training courses, including psychological literacy, facilitation, leadership and business thinking skills training. Through Feather Associates, Hélène facilitates a variety of processes, including team building, strategic planning, stakeholder involvement and conflict resolution in a range of contexts and sectors.

Hélène has worked with NGO's, Local and Provincial and National Government, and many large and small business organisations. She is a trained Executive Coach and holds a Certificate in Executive Coaching from the Tavistock Institute.

In addition to running Feather and working as a facilitator and coach, she was a Visiting Senior Lecturer at the University of Cape Town Graduate School of Business in the areas of psychological literacy, systems thinking, people skills, change management, diversity management and facilitation for 15 years. She has lectured on the MBA, Executive MBA, and other executive programmes since 1996. Together with the South African College of Applied Psychology, she launched the (first of its kind) National Diploma in Facilitation and was the Programme Director for five years.

She recently established The Depth Leadership Trust, a non-profit organisation that aims to develop and promote understanding of depth psychology amongst leaders, organisations and civil society.

Hélène has published two other books: *Beneath – Exploring the Unconscious in Individuals* and *Depth Leadership*. She lives with her family in Prince Albert in the Karoo.

Hélène can be contacted at The Depth Leadership Trust
www.depthleadership.co.za
helene@feather.co.za

www.ingramcontent.com/pod-product-compliance
Lightning Source LLC
Chambersburg PA
CBHW080545230426
43663CB00015B/2718